White Rage

G000320791

White Rage examines the development of the modern American extreme right and American politics from the 1950s to the present day. It explores the full panoply of extreme right groups, from the remnants of the Ku Klux Klan to skinhead groups and from the militia groups to neo-nazis.

In developing its argument the book:

- discusses the American extreme right in the context of the Oklahoma City bombing, 9/11 and the Bush administration;
- explores the American extreme right's divisions and its pursuit of alliances;
- analyses the movement's hostilities to other racial groups.

Written in a moment of crisis for the leading extreme right groups, this original study challenges the frequent equation of the extreme right with other sections of the American right. It is a movement whose development and future will be of interest to anyone concerned with race relations and social conflict in modern America.

Martin Durham is Senior Lecturer in Politics at the University of Wolverhampton, UK. He has written extensively on right-wing politics in Europe and America. Among his publications are *Women and Fascism* (Routledge, 1998).

White Rage

The extreme right and American politics

Martin Durham

LONDON AND NEW YORK

First published 2007
by Routledge
2 Park Square, Milton Park, Abingdon, Oxon OX14 4RN

Simultaneously published in the USA and Canada
by Routledge
270 Madison Avenue, New York, NY 10016

Routledge is an imprint of the Taylor & Francis Group, an informa business

© 2007 Martin Durham

Typeset in Times New Roman by
Taylor & Francis Books
Printed and bound in Great Britain by
TJ International Ltd, Padstow, Cornwall

British Library Cataloguing in Publication Data
A catalogue record for this book is available from the British Library

Library of Congress Cataloging in Publication Data
Durham, Martin.
    White rage: the extreme right and American politics / Martin Durham.
        p. cm.
    Includes bibliographical references and index.
    1. Radicalism–United States–History–20th century. 2. Right and
left (Political science). 3. United States–Race relations–History–
20th century. I. Title.

HN90.R3D87 2007
305.809'073–dc22   2007006064

ISBN 978–0–415–36232–0 (hbk)
ISBN 978–0–415–36233–7 (pbk)
ISBN 978–0–203–01258–1 (ebk)

To Stephanie, Nicholas and Laura

Contents

Acknowledgements

This book has long been in gestation, during which time I have been helped by a number of people. I would like to express my thanks to Michael Barkun, Betty Dobratz, Laura Lee Downs, Richard Hawkins, John Hope, Jeff Kaplan, George Michael, Darren Mulloy, Nick Toczek, Aaron Winter and Nigel Woodcock. I would particularly like to thank Chip Berlet, Alan Schwartz, Brian Marcus and Laird Wilcox for generously facilitating my research at Political Research Associates, Somerville, Massachusetts; the Anti-Defamation League, New York; and the Wilcox Collection of Contemporary Political Movements at the University of Kansas. I am also grateful to the Learning Centre at the University of Wolverhampton and the University of Ulster, Jordanstown Library for arranging my access to the latter's holding of the wonderful University of Iowa Right-wing Collection. Finally, I would like to thank Gerry Gable for allowing me access to material from the American extreme right when I first started working in this area.

Introduction

Just over sixty years ago, the Supreme Court struck down segregation in America's schools. For the Civil Rights Movement, this represented a crucial moment in its struggle for racial justice. In the years that followed, American society became increasingly integrated, large numbers of blacks were registered to vote and affirmative action aided the growth of the African American presence in education and employment.

It was not a change that was universally welcomed. In the South, elected officials played a central role in the massive resistance that was unleashed against the Supreme Court's decision while nationally, the leading conservative periodical argued that the South was facing an onslaught against its way of life. Segregation was defeated and the conservatism that has become powerful in America no longer defends it. This study will make reference to conservatism. But it will not be our focus. Instead, we will be examining a movement which has continued to argue that the central issue is race. We will be looking at the American extreme right.

It is a movement strongly linked with violence, from the Ku Klux Klan's bombings of black churches in the 1950s to the shootings of racial minorities by lone assassins in the 1970s and the 1990s. But extreme rightists have been highly active in other ways, from seeking to gain electoral support to attempting to permeate movements that have emerged from elsewhere on the political spectrum. In using the image of white rage, there is a danger in exaggerating the unreasoning fury so often evident in extreme right actions. But, as its rhetoric often shows, we cannot understand the extreme right if we do not appreciate the centrality of its belief that the white race is under attack, and its only salvation is to fight against those who would destroy it. It is mobilized around deep anger, at the heart of which is race.

We should not mistake the extreme right's support for segregation or, to use the language it has more recently adopted, the defence of a white nation, with a single-minded focus on the position of whites and that of blacks. In recent decades, they have become increasingly concerned not with the most visible minority in America but with other groups. They have called not only for a reversal of the Supreme Court's 1954 decision but have become highly agitated over immigration, arguing that the influx of Mexican and other immigrants threatens to change America's racial character forever. Indeed, while most frequently using the term extreme right, we will also be using other terms – racist, racialist and white nationalist – to define the movement with which we are concerned.

To characterize the extreme right as racist does not only refer to its attitude towards blacks or Latinos. It refers to other groups, and in the context of this study it has a special importance as regards anti-Semitism. For many on the extreme right, Jews are the greatest enemy. Unemployment and the collapse of small businesses, immigration and the deaths of Americans in wars are all seen as the responsibility of a Jewish conspiracy. Furthermore, the depths of the extreme right's feelings over race are not only crucial to understanding what it believes. It is vital too to how we can distinguish it from other strands of the American right.

At points during our exploration, we will be considering the relationship between conservatism and race. But this will not be the main focus of our concern with different strands of the right. We will be particularly concerned to explore another problem. If many of the inhabitants of the farther shores of the American right believe in a life and death battle for a racially defined republic, they have not been its only inhabitants. At the end of the 1950s, the John Birch Society was set up to oppose a communist plot to take over America. At the beginning of the following decade, a paramilitary group, the Minutemen, began preparations to resist a communist invasion. In the early 1990s, armed militias sprang into existence, in part to fight a feared United Nations occupation. It is a central contention of this study that racism is not only crucial in understanding the extreme right. It is important too in demarcating it from another grouping that believes that America is threatened by a hidden enemy, but do not define it racially. The American right includes conservatives, extreme rightists and what we will describe as a radical right, and it is not always easy to draw distinctions between them. But it is important to do so if we are to understand the character of the extreme right.

If both conservatism and the radical right can be distinguished from the extreme right by the latter's racial framing of the threat to the nation, how can we distinguish within the extreme right? One way is by locating the primary reference point for its different strands. Some look to the experience of early twentieth-century Germany. This identification revolves around the belief that National Socialism fought both international finance and communism and was right in identifying the Jewish enemy as the force behind both. The same battle, its adherents claim, will have to be waged in America. Others on the extreme right are shaped by the experience of the vanquished Confederacy and the consequent and ultimately unsuccessful battle to sustain the South as a segregated society. If the most important form of extreme right identification with the embattled South is the Ku Klux Klan, there have been other examples. Support for National Socialism has also taken different forms, and not all of its admirers agree with the

Third Reich's policies towards the economy or other European countries or find it politic to declare that they do. Yet while identification with the nineteenth-century Ku Klux Klan or with National Socialism encapsulates much of the extreme right, a third strand is more amorphous. The Patriot movement sees itself as continuing the original Revolution of 1776. Importantly, however, only some Patriots hold that the battle they are waging is a racial one. It is a highly diffuse movement, and when discussing Patriots it is vital to retain our focus on race in distinguishing those who are accurately to be seen as extreme rightists and those who are not.

None of the groupings within the extreme right are completely sealed off from each other, and this is particularly due to the influence of National Socialism among some whose primary identification is with the South. The three-way division we have suggested is nonetheless a highly useful approach to understanding differences on the American extreme right. But it is not the only way. After a chapter on each of these three strands, we will examine how the extreme right takes different religious forms. For Christian Identity, God's chosen people is not the Jews but whites. But there are other strands, stretching from Odinism to occultism to doctrines that refuse the supernatural but sacralize the racial. In subsequent chapters, we cut into the extreme right in two further ways: first in terms of how different groupings understand the role of women, and, second, how they see the role of violence. In Chapter 8, we will examine how the extreme right relates to other sections of the American right, and trace its bitter rivalry with both conservatism and the radical right. Finally, we will draw the different threads together and reach some conclusions as to how the American extreme right has developed over some six decades. The Supreme Court's decision in the case of *Brown v. Board of Education* marked a key moment in the development not only of black civil rights but of white backlash. Ultimately, most whites came to terms with *Brown*. Not only has integration sunk deep roots in American soil, but only a small fraction of those who opposed it have been won to the extreme right's ranks. In the pages that follow, we will examine the extreme right's efforts to gain a white nation, the different organizational forms it has taken and the disputes which have divided it. But the extreme right was not born in the aftermath of *Brown*. Although almost none of the organizations we will be examining existed in 1954, many of the elements they could draw on did. The ideas of white superiority, of anti-Semitism, of bitter opposition to immigration, were all present. The Ku Klux Klan had already twice played an important role in American history, and remnants were still active. Finally, in the 1930s, the American extreme right had briefly been highly visible and, in the aftermath of Germany's defeat, a smaller movement still persisted. This study is concerned with the development of the American extreme right in the aftermath of *Brown*. First, however, we will consider its pre-history.

1 Before *Brown*

There is no one moment that the modern extreme right came into existence. But the Supreme Court's 1954 decision on *Brown v. Board of Education* is crucial. In deciding to rule that segregation in schools was unconstitutional, the Court not only struck a death-blow against the way in which the white South had organized relations between the races. It was crucial to the rise of the Civil Rights Movement. It was central to the future of both the Democratic and Republican parties. It was key too for the extreme right.

Defined by the centrality they gave to race, extreme rightists could not but react vitriolically to a Supreme Court decision that ruled that whites and blacks should no longer be educated separately. Within five years, not only had the oldest racist organization, the Ku Klux Klan, revived but new extreme right groupings had emerged. In the years that followed other groupings have sprung up, and in the following chapters we will be examining a wide range of organizations. We will be exploring the strategies they have forged and the issues they have taken up, and will argue that it is not only the organizational landscape of the extreme right that has changed since *Brown*. In important ways, how it sees the new order of the future and how it proposes to get there is new. But it is not wholly so. It has inherited much from the extreme right of earlier years. In this chapter, we will be particularly concerned with organizations and issues of the earlier decades of the twentieth century. But we also need to go back further, and it is to the original Ku Klux Klan that we should first turn.

The Klan first emerged in the aftermath of the American Civil War. Created in Pulaski, Tennessee, it was set up as a social club by a group of former Confederate soldiers. Named after the Greek for circle (*kyklos*) and the Scottish word, clan, the club initially dressed up in hoods and cloaks and carried out pranks. But politics soon intruded. The victorious Union had not only ended slavery but was now engaged in an attempt to remake Southern society. Just as with the *Brown* decision almost a century later, Reconstruction led to widespread white resistance, and the Klan rapidly became a vigilante body. Hooded night riders attacked 'impudent negroes and negro-loving whites', inflicting beatings and carrying out murders. In 1867 the Klan was organized into an 'Invisible Empire', in which each state was led by a Grand Dragon and the role of emperor was taken by a Grand Wizard. Its campaign of terror was not without dangers for the organization, and in 1869 the Grand Wizard, General Nathan Bedford Forrest, declared that in some localities the Klan was being 'perverted from its original honorable and patriotic purposes'. He decreed that 'the masks and robes of the Order' should be destroyed. Klan activity, however, continued. In 1871 Congress passed legislation forbidding 'two or more persons' from going in disguise to deprive others of their rights. Mass trials resulted in the conviction of many Klansmen, and the organization effectively ceased to exist. But Northern enthusiasm for Reconstruction also passed away, and by the end of the century Southern blacks were disenfranchised, while a rigid system of segregation ensured that in education, hotels, public transport and much else the two races were kept apart.[1]

The Klan declared that its 'fundamental objective' was 'the MAINTENANCE OF THE SUPREMACY OF THE WHITE RACE', and the segregation that came to define the South assumed that whites were a more advanced race.[2] In the North, a more informal segregation kept white and black apart. But here, other conflicts took on importance.

Before the Civil War, nativist organizations had emerged, declaring that the United States was a Protestant nation. Catholic immigrants were accused of taking jobs and adhering to a religion which was antagonistic to liberty. But nativism was not solely opposed to Catholics. It privileged 'Anglo-Saxons' over 'the dregs of foreign populations' it saw as threatening America, and was as capable of being turned on non-Catholic Europeans as it was on Chinese or Japanese. Having declined with the rise of the conflict between North and South, nativism revived in the 1880s, but by then hostility to 'Dago and Pole, Hun and Slav' was not only accompanied by hostility to Orientals, it was coming to be joined by yet another antagonism, anti-Semitism.[3]

As with opposition to Catholic immigration, opposition to the entry of Jews revolved in large part around rivalry for jobs and for housing. It had a religious element too, focused on the belief that the Jews were Christ-killers. But it had a distinctive economic component, centred on the belief that it was Jews that controlled the centres of finance, and it was this conviction that showed itself in a movement that appealed particularly to beleaguered farmers in the late nineteenth century, Populism.

This movement had a number of different faces, and historians have disputed the degree to which it was affected by anti-Semitism. What is clear, however, is that at least some of Populism's attacks on international finance were suffused with images of the Jew as exploiter. One writer, Ignatius Donnelly, was not only the author of much of the People's Party's 1892 platform but had shortly earlier written a novel vividly depicting Jewish oppression of American farmers. Other accounts of the depradations of Jewish bankers appeared from Populist publicists, and one account of the 1896 Populist convention commented that one of its most striking characteristics was 'the extraordinary hatred of the Jewish race'.[4] As we shall see, attacks on Jewish bankers would be crucial to the later extreme right. But so would other antagonisms. In the early twentieth century, opposition to immigration intensified. It was, however, going through important changes. In part, this was linked with the rise of eugenics, the claim that in a world in which nations were increasingly in conflict, the greatest danger was the failure to reproduce of the 'fit' and the multiplication of the 'unfit'. For some eugenicists, the most important conflict was between white nations and 'the rising tide of color'. But there was anxiety about divisions among white nations too, and for writers such as Madison Grant and Lothrop Stoddard, those of Nordic stock stood higher than other Europeans. Earlier immigration restrictionists had claimed that America was Anglo-Saxon and Protestant. The new restrictionism was racial, but exactly who would be counted as within the favoured race was still uncertain. Nor was race the only antagonism that we should consider.[5]

Already in the 1880s, opposition to labour militancy had been connected with opposition to immigration. Nativism and anti-socialism came together dramatically during the First World War. Ultra-patriotic groupings denounced socialists as disloyal. The attack was aimed at both German-Americans and Russian Jews, and in the immediate aftermath of the war, the attorney general declared that 90 per cent of extreme left activity was 'traceable to aliens'. The so-called Red Scare that resulted, in which large numbers of leftists were detained and some deported, was short-lived.[6] But anti-socialism had achieved a centrality in American politics, and for some this would give new impetus to anti-Semitism.

By then, however, the very danger that socialism seemed to pose had been transformed. In 1917, it achieved power in Russia. Communist parties sprang up across the Western world (and beyond) while in Russia itself a bitter civil war raged between revolutionaries and counter-revolutionaries. The counter-revolutionaries lost, but in fleeing to other countries, some of them brought with them a remarkable forgery, *The Protocols of the Learned Elders of Zion*. Apparently created by Tsarist police agents in France in the 1890s, the *Protocols* claimed to be the minutes of a meeting of the international Jewish conspiracy. The spread of Marxism, it claimed, had been deliberately encouraged by Jews. They controlled the press, and thanks to their control of gold, an economic crisis could be created which would throw vast numbers onto the streets. The resulting mobs would attack 'those whom, in the simplicity of their ignorance, they have envied from their cradles'. Just as with the French Revolution, the people would stumble around, seeking new leaders. Ultimately, in place of the different nation states, a world government would be created, at whose head would be the 'King-Despot of the blood of Zion, whom we are preparing for the world'.[7]

To those susceptible to its appeal, the *Protocols* appeared to explain not only the events of the nineteenth century but the twentieth, and among those it influenced was the leading car manufacturer, Henry Ford. In the early 1920s in a series of articles in his newspaper, the *Dearborn Independent*, the notion of a Jewish conspiracy was used to explain post-war developments. Suggestive popular music, decadent plays, 'the menace of the Movies', were all attributable to Jewish influence. American Jewish money had helped to bring about the Russian Revolution, just as Jews were involved in Bolshevik activity inside America. They were central too to the creation of the Federal Reserve, which instead of being government-owned had led to 'a banking aristocracy'. Many of these articles were brought together in a four-volume collection, *The International Jew*, and it was in this form that it passed onto later generations of anti-Semites.[8]

If Henry Ford's post-war pronouncements were one influence on the later extreme right, the First World War saw another crucial development. The original Ku Klux Klan had been a Southern insurgency against the spectre of black equality, and in 1915 it was revived. Once again, it arose in the South, and racism was central to its re-emergence. The occasion was the Atlanta premiere of an immensely popular early movie, *The Birth of a Nation*. The film glorified the Klan, portraying members as heroes for killing a black man whose pursuit of a white girl had caused her to leap to her death. Shortly before, the rape and murder of a 14-year-old factory employee, Mary Phagan, had resulted in the lynching of her Jewish employer, Leo Frank, by a masked group, the Knights of Mary Phagan. Some of its members were among the first members of the Klan. In crucial ways, the new group continued in the traditions of its forebear, declaring its belief in Christianity, 'White Supremacy' and the 'Protection of our Pure American Womanhood'. Other elements, however, were new. Shaped by wartime jingoism, it called for opposition to 'Foreign Labor Agitators'. It was anti-Semitic too. Bolshevism, the Klan declared, was 'a Jewish-controlled and Jewish-financed movement', and Jewish international bankers were seeking to dominate the governments of the world.[9]

The Klan had changed in other ways. The pope, it declared, was an alien despot, and his church hated America and sought to crush it. The Klan was fiercely opposed too to what it saw as a rising tide of immorality. The country, Klansmen claimed, had entered a 'corrupt and jazz-made age', and 'degrading' films and 'filthy fiction' were undermining America. Most strikingly, while the Klan was bitterly hostile to the integrationist demands of such organizations as the National Association for the Advancement of Colored People, it did find common ground with another black organization. Briefly large numbers of blacks followed the black nationalism of Marcus Garvey and in the early 1920s the Klan's Imperial Wizard met with Garvey and declared his admiration for a politics that vigorously opposed integration.[10]

Although emerging during the war, it was not until afterwards that the Klan massively grew, and its growth extended far beyond the South. In Colorado, it has been claimed, one Denver resident in seven was a member, while in its strongest state, Indiana, some 200,000 gathered in 1923 to hear addresses by the Imperial Wizard and the newly inaugurated Grand Dragon. The Klan revived the hooded terrorism that had been so important in the aftermath of the Civil War, but this time the Klan rooted itself in local communities, organizing widely-attended social events, sending deputations to donate money to churches and taking part in election campaigns. It met with opposition, and the organization itself experienced several splits. In Indiana in 1925 the former Grand Dragon (he had led one of the splits) was sentenced to life imprisonment for the death of a white woman state employee he had sexually assaulted. Support for the Klan fell not only in the state, but nationally. Severely diminished, the organization continued into the 1930s. (In 1931, for instance, members in Dallas, Texas, inflicted a whipping upon two communists who were organizing for racial equality. Later in the decade it was similarly violent towards left-wing union activists).[11] By then, however, the Great Depression had hit, and new organizations had emerged.

The collapse of the American economy in 1929 affected both the countryside and the cities. In rural areas, many farmers faced ruin while in the cities, spiralling unemployment devastated the workforce. In 1932, this crisis brought to power the Democratic presidential candidate, Franklin Delano Roosevelt. His promises of a New Deal were followed by the massive growth of government intervention. Roosevelt was re-elected to office in 1936 and again in 1940. But if the Depression led to a strengthening of the Democratic Party, it led too to an increase in both trade union militancy and support for the Communist Party. All of these would be crucial in the emergence of a new wave of extreme right organizations. Its anti-Semitism would be aimed at the Roosevelt administration and international finance, its anti-socialism at the spectre of a communist seizure of power. Its debt to Populism would be expressed not only through its hostility to bankers but through its championing of embattled farmers. But there was a new element. The Depression was not a solely American phenomenon. It hit Britain, France and other countries, leading to the growth of both communism and the extreme right. In 1933 in Germany, however, it resulted in the victory of national socialism. In the early 1920s, Mussolini's fascists had come to power and crushed the Italian left. Where this had had little effect on the American extreme right, Hitler's victory had a more far-reaching effect.

One was the creation of one of the key groups of the period, the Silver Shirts. Writing in 1934, its founder, William Dudley Pelley, recalled his reaction to a newspaper headline announcing Hitler had become the German chancellor. Some years earlier, he had received a psychic message that when a certain German house-painter came to power, then he should bring 'the work of the Christ Militia into the open'. Now that prophecy had come to pass, he had launched the Silver Shirts to challenge Jewry's plan to impose 'satanic protocolism' on America.[12] Having already gained a following in the late 1920s by his claims of special spiritual powers, the transition to political leader did not represent a break with occultism. Pelley linked the Silver Shirts to 'Biblical ... Prophecy', and part of his criticism of the American economy was that a better economic system had already existed in Atlantis. Other of his arguments, however, were less surprising. The Jews, he declared, controlled international banking. They controlled the Federal Reserve, and they had extended their power into other domains. Now, he declared, they controlled the press, the stage, the cinema and the radio. Pelley called for the establishment of a Christian Commonwealth, in which 'every native-born citizen of proper racial qualifications' would be entitled to a minimum income. Above that, the government would judge what every individual was contributing to the economy, and what remuneration they should receive.[13] In 1936, declaring his intention to 'disfranchise the Jews by Constitutional amendment', Pelley ran for president on his own National Christian Party ticket. The result fell far short of his expectations (he only appeared on the ballot in the state of Washington, where he gained less than 1,600 votes).[14]

If Pelley was an occultist, two other leading extreme rightists of the period came from very different backgrounds. In the late 1920s, Gerald Winrod was a prominent fundamentalist, battling to defend what he saw as Biblical Christianity against theological liberalism, evolution and immorality. This even involved arguing that Mussolini might be the long predicted Anti-Christ, but the coming to power of Roosevelt drew him towards the extreme right. The New Deal was seen as communist, and while Winrod drew on the *Protocols*, a more significant development was his championing of an older conspiracy theory. In the aftermath of the French Revolution, counter-revolutionaries had claimed that it had really been brought about by a sinister secret society, the Illuminati. This group had been uncovered by the Prussian authorities and reportedly disbanded before the Revolution. But in fact, counter-revolutionaries claimed, it had survived to overthrow the French monarchy. According to Winrod, Marx's *Communist Manifesto* embodied 'both the principles and the spirit of the Illuminati' and the real conspirators behind Illuminism and the Russian Revolution were Jewish.[15]

Yet another variant on the extreme right was to be found in the politics of a Catholic priest and radio broadcaster, Charles Coughlin. Initially a supporter of Roosevelt, in late 1934 he announced the formation of the National Union for Social Justice, which called for the abolition of the Federal Reserve, the payment of a living wage to everyone willing to work and a fair profit for farmers. A fervent opponent of international finance, Coughlin subsequently turned against Roosevelt who, he declared, was 'engaged in keeping America safe for the plutocrats'. In the 1936 presidential election, as we have seen, Pelley ran against Roosevelt. Coughlin, however, supported a different candidate.[16]

The Depression had brought a variety of movements into existence. One was the Share Our Wealth Society, which called for limits on wealth so that every family could be paid an annual income. Others supported the Townsend Recovery Plan, which argued that the payment of a monthly pension to senior citizens could bring about the injection of increased purchasing power into the economy. In 1936, Townsend and the former national organizer of the Share Our Wealth Society, Gerald L. K. Smith, joined with Coughlin to create the Union Party. As its presidential candidate it selected Republican congressman William Lemke, who had already sought to introduce legislation to protect farmers from the loss of their farms. Unless Roosevelt stopped flirting with communism, Coughlin announced, 'the red flag of communism will be raised in this country by 1940'. Despite the following Coughlin and the other components of the Union Party had built up, however, it gained less than 2 per cent of the vote.[17]

In 1938, Coughlin launched yet another organization, the Christian Front. Greedy capitalism, it claimed, was pushing 'mistreated workers' towards communism. The Christian Front would force industry to give labour a fairer share of America's wealth, would curb international finance and would not be afraid to be called fascist. Nor, it declared, would it be afraid to be called anti-Semitic, and subsequently it was accused of launching attacks on Jews in New York. Coughlin supported Franco's nationalists in the Spanish Civil War and in 1938, his paper, *Social Justice*, published the *Protocols*. Its accuracy, he declared, was demonstrated by the advance of communism, the control of international banking by 'some unseen force' and the campaign against Christianity being waged by 'the synagogue of Satan'.[18]

These were not the only forms the extreme right took in the 1930s. Its propaganda was circulated in individually produced newsletters such as the *X-Ray* and the *Broom*. It was produced too by a wide array of groupings. The American Nationalist Confederation, for instance, adopted as its symbol, 'the swastika, a real Christian Cross', declaring that just as it had brought Germany out of despair, it could do the same for America. Another grouping, the Christian Mobilizers, organized a 'BUY CHRISTIAN' campaign to build up Christian business and defeat 'the growing despotism' of 'the Internationalists'. What was needed, it declared, was 'another Franco' to fight for a Christian America.[19] Again as in the 1920s, there were attempts to forge links with black nationalists. The Christian Front, for instance, had links with the Ethiopian Pacific League, an African-American group formed in the mid-1930s which combined anti-Semitism with enthusiastic support for Japan.[20] Other groupings had emerged among different nationalities within the United States. In the early 1920s, the Fascist League of North America was established, and was succeeded at the beginning of the following decade by the Lictor Federation. A rich exile set up the All-Russian Fascist Party in Connecticut, while an extreme right existed in the Ukrainian community. Unsurprisingly, the most important groupings emerged among Germans. A New York cell of the NSDAP was set up as early as 1922, and another group, the Teutonia Association, was formed in 1924. In 1933 the Friends of the New Germany was set up. In 1936 it was succeeded by the group that would be best known for organizing

German-American supporters of the Third Reich, the German-American Bund. The Bund distributed a pamphlet calling upon readers to 'Read the Protocols of the Elders of Zion and Understand the New Deal'. But the Bund also denounced blacks, declaring in 1936 that 'a Roosevelt victory would mean that every black male would have a white woman', and in 1940 it achieved considerable publicity when it held a joint camp with the New Jersey Ku Klux Klan.[21]

This was denounced by others in the Klan, and Coughlin was also wary of links with the Bund. Other groupings, however, were more willing to cooperate with it, and the Nazi regime itself made considerable efforts both to distribute propaganda and forge alliances with the American extreme right. Two organizations that predated the Third Reich were particularly crucial here. One, the Deutscher Fichte-Bund, had been created in 1914, but after the emergence of Hitler's regime saw itself as having two purposes. One was was the protection of 'human culture and civilization by dis-seminating facts about world Bolshevism'. The other was serving 'the cause of peace and understanding by giving free information about the New Germany'. Where much of its activity involved the provision of leaflets to foreign sympathizers, another organization, World Service, had a different emphasis. Dating back to 1920, it had long distributed anti-Semitic litera-ture. As part of the Nazi propaganda machine, however, it not only dis-tributed its bulletin in the United States but invited American delegates to its 1937 international conference. (Immediately before, it submitted a report to Hitler on 'achieving collaboration of Germans with the National Men of America on behalf of both countries'.)[22] It was a connection that would come back to haunt the American extreme right once war broke out.

Opposition to American involvement against Germany drew support from several points on the political spectrum, and in 1940 anti-war cam-paigners formed the America First Committee. The Bund's paper, the *Free American*, called upon its readers to join the Committee and Coughlin too declared his support. Efforts were made to exclude the Bund but extreme rightists were active in many of the Committee's branches (*Social Justice* even published an announcement that Coughlin supporters were welcome in the organization) and in 1941 one of the Committee's leading figures, the aviator Charles Lindbergh, already much praised on the extreme right, brought on new controversy by claiming that war was being promoted by the British and the Jews.[23]

Japan's subsequent attack on Pearl Harbor dealt a fatal blow to the America First Committee. Extreme rightists continued to be active, how-ever. In Detroit, the newly formed National Workers League organized against the introduction of black workers into industry, while many of those who carried on the fight against the war were women. While the New York-based Molly Pitchers called for a boycott of 'the English Jew Controlled Radio', the Cincinnatti-based Mothers of Sons Forum complained that 'Our boys will die on the golden cross of international Jewry!' Most importantly, in 1942, a Chicago group, We the Mothers Mobilize for America, launched a journal that would last for the next twenty years, *Women's Voice*. The men who were fighting, it declared, were being used by 'international bankers' while some women were 'so drunk with war propaganda that they have helped the butchery of their sons'.[24] During the war, a number of extreme rightists were put on trial, charged with seditious conspiracy. Coughlin was not among their number (he had been instructed by his church superiors to withdraw from political activity). But Pelley and Winrod were among the accused. Another was a former Foreign Service officer whose book, *The Coming American Fascism*, had argued not only that what America needed was the coming to power of a 'fascist-minded' leader, but that the crisis of capitalism was making 'fascism inevitable'. Others among the accused included former leading members of the German-American Bund, the editors of several extreme right newsletters and the leaders of the Christian Mobilizers, the American Nationalist Confederation and the National Workers League. They were charged with attempting to undermine the American war effort, and links with the German propaganda machine were emphasized by the prosecutor. The trial was protracted, but the fatal heart attack suffered by the judge towards the end of 1944 also struck a fatal blow to the prosecution's chance of success.[25] Nonetheless, the extreme right itself was hit hard. The Bund had dissolved before the trial, while Pelley was convicted of sedition in a separate trial. The Klan, while declaring support for the war effort, had nonetheless continued to circulate *The International Jew*, and in 1944 the organization was suspended following its receipt of a bill for nearly $700,000 in taxes going back to the 1920s.[26] Several sedition trial defendants, however, remained active, while probably the most important extreme rightist to continue activity had not been among those indicted. Gerald L. K. Smith created his own America First Party in 1943 and ran for president the following year. His platform included the repatriation of blacks to Africa and an investigation of the role of Jews in communism and the New Deal.[27]

After the war ended, Smith replaced the America First Party by the Christian Nationalist Crusade. Among its leaflets was one which declared:

DANGER!
WARNING!
Pro-Stalin Politicians
And Alien-Minded Traitors
in Cooperation with
Blind Sentimentalists are
Attempting to Force
Negro Rule
Negro-White Intermarriage
Negro Invasion of White Schools

Under the aegis of the Christian Nationalist Party, he ran for president in 1948. Once again his platform accompanied anti-Semitism with a call for the repatriation of blacks. 'Shall the lovers of Jesus Christ or the enemies of Jesus Christ' it declared, 'determine the destiny of America?'[28] In the immediate post-war period, other groups emerged. In 1946, for instance, the Columbians was set up in Atlanta, Georgia. It called for the removal of blacks to Africa and Jews to Madagascar, leaving a 'nationalist state' to preside over a 'one race nation'. 'The JEWS and the newspapers are AFRAID of us', it declared, 'because we are organizing the white people of the South.' One of its founders, Emory Burke, had been active in the pre-war extreme right, and he would long be involved in the post-war movement. The Columbians, however, was short-lived. Its activists had tried by intimidation to prevent blacks from moving into white areas, and in 1947 its leaders were imprisoned and the group ceased to exist.[29]

Another group would exist for longer. In 1946, the Atlanta paper reported that a local Klan organizer, J. B. Stoner, had called for making being Jewish a capital offence. 'That may sound a little extreme but other countries have done it.' He was planning to launch a party based on a nucleus of Klansmen, he declared, and a subsequent report noted that while in the Klan, he had already circulated a petition calling on Congress to declare Jews as 'the children of the devil'. He had gone on to organize the Anti-Jewish Party, subsequently the Christian Anti-Jewish Party. Jews, it declared, were behind 'RACE MIXING', and communism was 'a Jew plot' to 'conquer the world'.[30]

As Stoner's 1946 interview indicated, despite its tax problems, the Klan too remained active. Soon after its suspension, an Association of Georgia Klans was launched, and for a period it spread to other states. A court case later in the 1940s, however, forbade the Georgia group's continued use of the suspended Klan's charter. Klan splinters, however, proliferated. In Georgia, for instance, the Original Southern Klans emerged; in Florida, the Southern Knights of the Ku Klux Klan; in Alabama, the Federated Klans.[31] Amidst the splintering, however, the Klan propensity to violence continued. In Alabama, Klansmen launched violent attacks on left-wing union organizers. In Florida, a series of bombings in 1951 culminated in the Christmas Day murder of the leader of the state National Association for the Advancement of Colored People and his wife.[32]

If extreme rightists were active in the South, they were active in the North too. In New York, Karl Mertig continued to organize the pre-war Citizens Protective League, while in Philadelphia W. Henry MacFarland formed the Nationalist Action League. In 1949, they were instrumental in the formation of the National Renaissance Party. Behind the scenes, however, much of the power in the party was concentrated in the hands of another veteran German-American activist, Frederick Charles Weiss. Weiss was in contact with extreme rightists in Germany including Erich Schmidt, an ex-stormtroop major, and Peter Wallraf, the former Nazi governor of the Ukraine, and National Socialism in turn was crucial to the NRP. Its programme called for the deportation of non-whites, the abolition of 'parliamentary government' and the creation of an economy whereby labour and management would 'serve the interests of the State'. Jews, it held, were the 'financial and intellectual force behind Communism' and had gained 'a tremendous hold' on American society. But they were 'an alien virus in our national blood stream' and needed to be 'purged from our cultural, economic and political life'.[33] In one early issue of its bulletin, it claimed to be carrying on the work of Coughlin, but this was not its only allusion to earlier forms of the extreme right. One issue of its bulletin included an article entitled 'Adolf Hitler: An Appreciation'. America, it claimed, had been led to war by Roosevelt and the 'Jewish International bankers' behind him. Eventually, however, the nation would realize that it was the German leader who had first called for Aryans to unite. Another issue declared: 'What Hitler accomplished in Europe, the National Renaissance Party shall yet accomplish in America'.[34]

Other groups existed elsewhere in the North. In Missouri, for instance, the Citizens Protective Association produced the monthly *White Sentinel*. Association literature invited those made unhappy by 'Negroes in White Swimming Pools ... Negroes Buying Homes Next Door to You' or 'Negroes Playing With Your White Children in School' to help the organization. In Chicago, the White Circle League denounced attempts to move into white neighbourhoods. It declared that 'federal bureaucrats' would not stop white men from fighting for God's plan for 'segregating beast and man', and called for 'North and South' to 'Unite to Preserve and Protect The White Race, Christianity and America.'[35] Once again, not only membership organizations but independent publications were crucial. In 1947, a weekly paper, *Common Sense*, was launched. It took on an anti-Semitic colouration, and in 1952, for instance, published a supposed speech by an Eastern European rabbi, in which the speaker declared that in the near future whites would be forbidden 'to mate with whites' and the white race, 'our most dangerous enemy will become only a memory'. A second publication, the monthly *Williams Intelligence Summary*, was produced by a former military intelligence officer, Robert Williams. Williams would be an early pioneer of Holocaust denial. At the end of 1952, his publication declared that 'the myth of the slaughter of six million Jews' was 'the most fabulous lie' ever imposed on 'the gullible West'. Such views appeared elsewhere on the extreme right. The same year the NRP reprinted a report from *Women's Voice*, which had called upon 'God in Heaven' to 'forgive the American people' for believing the 'lie' that Hitler had murdered six million Jews, while Gerald L. K. Smith had already claimed in 1948 that millions of Hitler's supposed victims were instead now living in the USA.[36]

If anti-Semitism was crucial to the extreme right, so too was anticommunism. Roosevelt had been succeeded by Harry Truman, and the outbreak of the Cold War between America and the Soviet Union led to furore over communist spy rings and a campaign to remove communists from Hollywood. In 1950, Senator Joseph McCarthy declared that communists had been allowed to infiltrate the State Department, and extreme rightists sought to take advantage of his new-found prominence. The National Renaissance Party declared that he was 'the national hero of patriots', while Gerald L. K. Smith described him as a 'fearless statesman'. In 1954, Smith would be among those who attended a meeting to support the senator, while among the platform speakers was General Pedro Del Valle, who would long continue to be active in the extreme right.[37]

In addition to their enthusiasm for McCarthy, extreme rightists declared their support for another prominent figure during the early 1950s. Truman's decision to recall General MacArthur from Korea following his confrontation with China made him a hero to many on the right, and the 1952 presidential election enabled them to argue that he, and not another general, should be America's president. Having achieved prominence in the Second World War, General Dwight Eisenhower would be selected as Republican presidential candidate in 1952 and be in office for the remainder of the decade. In the run-up to his nomination, however, *Williams Intelligence Summary* described Eisenhower as 'The Man Most Wanted by the Zionists to Head the Government', while the still active Gerald Winrod described him as the tool of 'Jewish plotters'. MacArthur, Smith declared, would be 'the miracle that would redeem America', and he nominated him as the presidential candidate for his Christian Nationalist Party. MacFarland and other extreme rightists made him the candidate for a rival grouping, the Constitution Party.[38]

Just as the extreme right was racist, it was hostile too to Marxism. Whether that hostility would extend to all forms of socialism is a more difficult question. National socialism had seen itself as a form of socialism, and the idea that extreme rightists could adopt a type of socialism would appear on American soil. But there was another complication. Extreme rightists frequently supported both McCarthy and MacArthur. But this did not necessarily mean that they always supported the Korean War or the larger confrontation of which it was part. Anti-Semitism might reinforce opposition to communism, or it could conflict with it. In 1951, *Women's Voice* published an article arguing that the Korean War had two secret purposes. One was to protect the investments of Jewish bankers. The other was the slaughter of hundreds of thousands of American soldiers to soften up America for a Russian invasion. In 1953, *Common Sense* even denounced what it saw as American plans to attack Russia. (The supposed rabbi's speech it published the previous year had claimed that bringing about a new world war was vital for the victory of the Jewish conspiracy.)[39] As we will discuss in the next chapter, this reluctance to embrace America's anti-communist crusade would be taken to even greater lengths by the National Renaissance Party, and not only by the NRP.

In the years before *Brown*, the extreme right had forged a politics that sought to restore America. At its core was a fierce racism. It defended segregation in the South and sought to fight integration in the North. In many cases, this was underpinned by an anti-Semitism which claimed that behind groups like the NAACP, and indeed behind all that it objected to in America, was the power of organized Jewry. This focused on international finance, attacked the power of the media and linked in turn with anti-socialism. Jews, it was claimed, had brought about the Russian Revolution as part of an ancient plot, and the threat that communism continued to pose was part of that same conspiracy.

At first sight, how such a movement would react to the *Brown* decision and the rise of the Civil Rights Movement would appear thoroughly predictable. Yet as the Klan's relationship with the Garvey movement should forewarn us, it might be rather more complex than we might expect. Nor would its anti-Semitism always sit comfortably with its racism. Already in the early 1950s, extreme rightists had set about forging links with Middle Eastern opponents of Israel. Robert Williams, for instance, discussed with a Syrian minister the possibility of producing an Arabic edition of his book on 'the Jewish problem', while Gerald L. K. Smith met with a representative of the Egyptian embassy.[40] As we will see, extreme right involvement in the politics of the Middle East would continue in later years.

If the extreme right might prove surprising in how its racial politics might play out, it could prove unpredictable in other areas too. As Pelley's Silver Shirts and Coughlin's National Union for Social Justice had demonstrated, its economic proposals could be highly critical of capitalism, arguing that the government of the future would deliver a more just order in which workers and farmers could prosper. (To give an even more surprising example, Berlet and Lyons have commented on the Klan of the 1920s taking part in strikes and even forging electoral alliances with the Socialist Party.)[41] Nor is economics the only area in which we should prepare for the unexpected. As we discuss in Chapter 6, the Klan of the 1920s reacted to the enfranchisement of women by claiming to support women's rights. Pelley too was at pains to argue that in the Christian Commonwealth of the future, the entitlement of all citizens to an independent income would bring about 'the true liberation for which women have been striving for centuries', and we would be wrong to assume that the extreme right is necessarily misogynist. We should also not assume it to be religiously monolithic. Pelley complained that Winrod refused to publicize his work because he disagreed with the Silver Shirts leader's 'esoteric researches'. Likewise, where Coughlin's denunciation of the private control of credit was based on papal teaching, the Klan continued to believe that Catholicism was incompatible with American values.[42]

In part, this latter tension linked with unresolved arguments from earlier in the century. Who did the extreme right seek to represent? Was it still affected by anti-Catholic nativism, or had a more recently forged racism taken nativism's place, and if the latter was now the case, was it still the case that it saw only some whites as truly American? But the extreme right was troubled by more recent quandaries. As its response to McCarthy presaged, it was going to have to come to grips with the rise of a new conservative movement in America. As the emergence of Holocaust denial graphically illustrated, it was also going to have to find an answer to the wartime defeat of national socialism in Germany. As we shall see, for some on the extreme right, their roots lay wholly in America. But for others, the German experience was crucial, and it is to those who tried to build a modern national socialist movement in America that we will first turn.

2   American Reich

The fall of the Third Reich was followed by the banning of any attempt to revive national socialism in Germany. Despite this prohibition, it re-emerged in the country which had given it birth. It re-emerged too in other countries, not least the United States. But it is not always clear whether particular post-war groupings are to be described as national socialist, and even when exactly national socialism re-emerged in America is a matter of argument. As we will see, there is good reason to define certain groups in terms that they themselves would not use. But to justify a characterization of national socialism as extending beyond those groups that expressly define themselves as such, we need to discuss what we might mean by national socialism.

Where socialism is customarily associated with notions of social equality, this is not what it meant for the founders of national socialism. Socialism has long had connotations of social solidarity, of collective interests coming before individual interests, and it is this which national socialists were alluding to when they separated socialism from both egalitarianism and internationalism and wedded it instead to a belief in a national resurrection and a racial destiny. Germany, they held, had not been defeated by superior force but by betrayal, and in order to rise again, the nation had to confront its internal enemies. This would mean fighting against Marxists, seen as committed to a bloody revolution that would destroy private property and nationhood alike. But it would also entail fighting against bankers, who were portrayed as manipulating the economy, bankrupting companies and creating unemployment. National socialism attacked international Marxism and international finance and linked both to its greatest enemy, international Jewry.

As the Second World War graphically demonstrated, national socialism was in crucial respects a German phenomenon. It was hostile not only to Jews or to blacks but to Poles and Slavs, while the alliances it sought to forge with fascist movements in Western Europe were severely tested by Nazi belief in German superiority. But while shaped by its birth as a German nationalism, its emphasis on the Aryan race reached beyond Germans to other Nordic groupings and at least potentially to whites more generally.

In the 1930s, national socialism was most clearly represented by the German-American Bund. Some more indigenous manifestations of 1930s American fascism could also be seen as national socialist. Indeed, as a neo-Nazi publication of the 1980s was later to suggest, Pelley's Silver Shirts and several lesser groupings can be understood in this light.[1] But if national socialism existed in America before the Second World War, what of the immediate post-war period?

As we have seen, in its early years the National Renaissance Party declared its support for national socialism. But it was not simply nostalgic. As we discuss in Chapter 5, it was later noteworthy for its attachment to occultism. But it was distinctive in other ways. It forged a link, for instance, with the Greenshirts, a New York-based Islamist group led by a white Muslim convert, John Hassan. The party was striking too for the radicalism of its foreign policy views. In part, this involved support for nationalist revolution in the Third World. It sold publications from both the Nasser regime in Egypt and the Baathist government in Iraq. It also supported the Sukarno government in Indonesia. The peoples of these countries, it declared, wanted 'to throw off the oppressive yoke of foreign colonialism just as our heroic American ancestors rebelled against the unjust taxation and repressive laws of the British Empire in 1776'.[2]

More strikingly, the NRP did not take the stance that we would expect of the extreme right, especially in the particular circumstances of Cold War America. In 1953, in the aftermath of an uprising in East Germany, it praised what it described as a working-class rebellion against communism. The previous year, however, it had published a very different view of communism. In 1952, eleven Jewish communists were executed in Prague. 'The Russian leadership is killing Jews for treason to Russia', the NRP declared, and the 'European fascist elite' should 'note this fact and act accordingly'. By threatening the leaders of American Jewry with 'the Russian bogey', it was suggested, Europe could be liberated from 'American bayonets'. The author of these words was one of the most intriguing figures of the post-war extreme right, Francis Parker Yockey.[3]

Arrested after the discovery of a suitcase full of false identity documents, Yockey committed suicide in a San Francisco jail in 1960. He had been active in the extreme right in the 1930s. At the end of the Second World War, however, he was somewhat surprisingly employed as a lawyer at the Nuremberg war crimes trials before taking on a murky role within the international extreme right.[4] Most importantly for his future influence, in 1948 he published a book, *Imperium*. Jews, it claimed, were strangers to 'the soul of the West', but were seeking to direct it away from 'its true Life-path'. American victory at the end of the Second World War was the work of the Jew, an alien 'Culture-Distorter', standing atop 'a mountain of Western dead', and while a Russian occupation of Europe would engender resistance, American occupation would be far worse. When the new American Revolution took shape, 'its inspiration will come from the same ultimate source as the European Revolution of 1933'. For now, however, and into the future, America was in the service of the West's 'total enemy'.[5]

Both Yockey and the NRP would be accused by others on the extreme right of being tools of international communism, and one of his associates has described Yockey as once taking payment to act as a courier for Czech intelligence.[6] But whatever the truth of such entanglements, both Yockey and the NRP were extreme rightists. Their arguments owed much to national socialism, but in supporting Third World revolutions (including Castro's seizure of power in Cuba)[7] and treating the Soviet Union as a lesser threat than the United States, they were reacting to new conditions in ways that separated them from pre-war national socialism and much of the post-war extreme right. In particular, they would diverge from the group that first declared itself to be reviving national socialism in America.

It was in late 1958 that American national socialism emerged in a full-fledged form. Its founder, George Lincoln Rockwell, had already been involved in a National Committee to Free America from Jewish Domination. He also took part in the founding meeting of a Southern-based organization, the United White Party. Most importantly, Rockwell had met DeWest Hooker, a Hitler admirer who had already recruited New York street youth to his Nationalist Youth League. Convinced that only an open revival of national socialism could save white America, Rockwell decided to launch the American Nazi Party. Nor were his ambitions limited to America, and he initiated too an international grouping, the World Union of National Socialists.[8]

Rockwell held that the open espousal of national socialism would generate publicity and attract 'the kind of daring, bold, devil-may care fighting YOUNG men we need'.[9] He believed too in organizing events that would generate publicity. Thus one ANP activist picketed a protest against the Vietnam war, carrying a placard offering 'FREE GASOLINE AND MATCHES FOR PEACE CREEPS'. But if Rockwell was determined to oppose the left, he was above all concerned with waging a racial struggle. In a pamphlet published in 1960, he declared that he was prepared to lead white men in battle against 'the unspeakable menace of the colored population of the earth rising to slaughter and rapine'. Hitherto, those few who had seen the dreadful urgency of the situation had fought in small groups gathered behind different national flags. But the Jews were sending 'their black armies' to attack every white nation. 'Under the Swastika banner of Adolf Hitler, White men around the world will master the planet to save civilization'.[10] But he sought to win the battle between the races in America itself where, he declared, the great danger came from the rising Civil Rights Movement.

In 1961, in response to the 'Freedom Rides', whereby groups of northern civil rights activists travelled by bus into the South to challenge segregation, the ANP sent a van full of uniformed stormtroopers. This, it declared, was 'Lincoln Rockwell's Hate Bus'. Party members sought to disrupt civil rights activities. At one NAACP event, for instance, a stormtrooper with a blacked-up face rushed in, declaring 'Ah's your Uncle Remus and Ah's come to take you niggers back to Africa.' Two other activists infiltrated a civil rights march, wearing gorilla costumes and carrying a placard reading 'Join Our March for Civil Rights'.[11] In doing this, they were not only attempting to gain publicity. They were graphically illustrating their claim that the civil rights movement was a tool of Jewish communism. But they were also alluding to another core belief – that whites were superior.

The 'Negro', ANP publications declared, was 'a less advanced branch' of the species; whites were 'the Master Race'. Such a view lent itself easily to the most perjorative language and in one article Rockwell declared that the 'LOWEST forms of humanity (the colored races)' were threatening to overwhelm the white race. 'The children of today, I predict, will be forced to exterminate swarms of niggers until all of them are fully corraled in Africa.'[12] But while American Nazis bitterly opposed the Civil Rights Movement and believed the white race superior, this did not mean that they were hostile to black political organizations as such. The ANP advocated that blacks be sent to Africa, and in this found affinity with the leading force in black nationalism, the Nation of Islam. Its leader, Elijah Muhammed, Rockwell declared, knew that the mixing of races was 'a Jewish fraud', and he was certain that 'a workable plan for separation of the races could be effected'. In 1961, Rockwell attended a Nation of Islam rally. The following year, he spoke at the national convention of the Nation. Muhammed, he declared, was the 'Adolf Hitler of the black man'.[13]

While believing that blacks would willingly leave America, Rockwell took a very different view of the group he saw as manipulating them. What the ANP would do when it came to power, Rockwell declared, was gas 'Jew-traitors'. (He told one interviewer that it was likely that 80 per cent of adult American Jews were traitors.) When Israeli commandos kidnapped Adolf Eichmann for trial for his role in the Holocaust, the ANP demonstrated outside the White House, calling on Eisenhower to help free him. 'Eichmann Did Not Kill ANY Innocent Jews', one placard read. In a subsequent interview, however, he signalled his conversion to what would soon become a central belief of much of the extreme right, that gas chambers had not existed in Nazi Germany and that the Holocaust had never happened.[14]

In arguing that the extreme right needed to be explicitly national socialist, Rockwell was rejecting other alternatives. Groups that focused on the defence of Southern segregation, he argued, were incapable of appealing to 'the victims of the Jews' in the North. Furthermore, the Klan alienated potential supporters with its 'anti-Catholic overtones' while the group that had emerged from the United White Party, the National States Rights Party, was accused of refusing to admit its true 'Nazi character'.[15] Nor did Rockwell only criticize Southern-based groupings. The NRP was attacked for its belief in 'the monstrous fraud of Soviet "anti-Semitism"'. Weiss was accused of being an agent of the leading Jewish anti-fascist group, the Anti-Defamation League. As for *Imperium*, Rockwell's deputy declared, it was a dangerous book. It emphasized authoritarianism, racial exclusiveness 'and other tenets of Nazism'. But it did not understand the danger from the Soviet Union. 'Yockeyism', he held, represented an attempt to divert potential recruits from true national socialism.[16]

In part, the heat generated in these conflicts was linked with disputes over membership and finances as different groups sought to poach each other's members. One of Rockwell's lieutenants, James Warner, defected to the NSRP before in turn abandoning it, each time allegedly taking with him the organization's mailing list. Another key figure, Matt Koehl, had belonged to the NRP and to the NSRP before joining the ANP. More complexly, another figure, Dan Burros, produced his own paper, the *Free American*, which attacked Rockwell for advocating a war with the Soviet Union, and defended both Yockey and Weiss against Rockwell's criticisms. At the same time, he urged support for the American Nazi Party.[17] But while Rockwell insisted that only open national socialism was the answer, this did not mean that he was unable to modify his strategy. In 1965, using the name American Majority Party, he ran for governor of Virginia. He used the Confederate flag as a symbol of his campaign, and while a segregationist candidate gained considerably more support, attracted nearly 6,000 votes. Subsequently, in response to the spread of demands for Black Power, Rockwell came up with a call for White Power, and in 1966 the party played a leading role in white opposition to a civil rights march in Chicago. Opposition to this march had come from Poles and Italians, and where some in the ANP argued that Nazism was only for Nordic Americans, Rockwell insisted that White Power should encompass Southern and Eastern Europeans too. In 1967, the party changed its name to the National Socialist White People's Party. It was time, Rockwell declared, to change the party's image and become an American white people's movement. A monthly paper, *White Power*, was launched and, in a parallel development, Rockwell attempted to win back a breakaway group, the White Party, which called for 'White Men' to rally against 'the raging flood of "civil rights"' without describing itself as national socialist.[18]

Whether this would have led to further changes remains uncertain. The White Party had not been the only splinter from the ANP, and in 1961 another group, the American National Party, had broken away. What was needed, it declared, was an immediate declaration of war against the Soviet Union. In 1963, however, its leader, John Patler, declared in its magazine, *Kill!*, that he no longer rejected Rockwell's leadership. He rejoined the ANP, only to be expelled in early 1967. In August he ambushed Rockwell and shot him dead. Some on the extreme right, including within the NSWPP itself, believed that the death of Rockwell had been engineered by leading figures in the party.[19] This only intensified the tendencies to schism that were already very evident.

In the period that followed Rockwell's assassination, different groups of national socialists attempted to revive his movement. (Even Warner himself was involved in one such foray.)[20] The NSWPP continued under Koehl. In

1971, for instance, it denounced leftists for taking up the issue of environmentalism when, it claimed, they were really 'hirelings of high finance' and it was Jewish capitalism that was responsible for high pollution and a level of economic activity that was endangering the planet. The advance of the Civil Rights Movement had led to the introduction of affirmative action, whereby blacks gained increased chances of employment and education, and conflict broke out over both this and busing, where white children were transported to preponderantly black schools to ensure integration. The party took up both issues, and also turned its attention to the flow of immigration over the Mexican border.[21] During the 1970s it undertook a number of election campaigns, while at the beginning of the decade it attempted to recruit for a White Student Alliance which, it declared, would be open to racialists who did not adhere to national socialism. (The leader of the student group was a young David Duke, a figure we will encounter again when we discuss his later role as a prominent figure first in the Klan, then in later organizations.)[22] But this willingness to ally with non-national socialists did not mean that Koehl's party had abandoned its beliefs. In early 1975, one cover article in *White Power* declared 'WE NEED A HITLER! No Mickey Mouse Politician Can Do the Job.' A few months later, on the first day of its party congress, it laid a wreath at a war memorial for 'those Aryan servicemen who died in Jewish wars.' The Congress's theme, its paper reported, was 'Build National Socialist Power'.[23]

The NSWPP remained devoted to what it understood as Rockwell's legacy, and having never forgotten Warner's defection, it sent a young member, Don Black, to infiltrate the NSRP and attempt to obtain a copy of its mailing list. As he was later to recall, he 'ended up nearly bleeding to death' after being shot by a NSRP member.[24] While the attempt to poach large numbers of NSRP members failed, national socialism continued to splinter. In 1974, for instance, the National Socialist Liberation Front emerged in California, calling for the creation of a 'Revolutionary Army'. It initiated a short-lived campaign of political terror, in which explosive devices devastated left-wing bookstores and a gas-grenade was set off in a left-wing meeting. (The following year, its founder, Joe Tomassi, was killed by a member of Koehl's party during a fracas outside the NSWPP's California headquarters.)[25] In 1974, another California group, the National Socialist League, was set up as a specifically gay Nazi organization. Where homosexuality had been denounced by both Hitler and Rockwell, the League declared that it was a tragedy that white men could argue while 'our racial enemies advance on all sides'. When sexual preference was accepted as a matter of choice, the League would cease to exist. Until then, it would fight separately.[26] Yet another grouping, the National Socialist White Workers Party, also emerged in California while national socialist groups came into existence elsewhere. Most importantly, an earlier split had resulted in the creation of the National Socialist Party of America under the leadership of the former NSWPP Midwest coordinator, Frank Collin. For a while,

Collin's group appeared the most dynamic. In 1977, it claimed that a black march to an all-white district of Chicago had been 'smashed by the bricks and fists' of local residents 'under the aegis' of the NSPA. In the same period it achieved considerable publicity over its announcement of plans to march through Skokie, a largely Jewish town near Chicago, and its subsequent victory in a court case against its elected officials. The two parties were bitter rivals. In early 1978, for instance, one of the NSPA's leading figures, Harold Covington, declared that Koehl was not only incompetent as a leader but 'more concerned with ideological trivia ... than with White Victory'. There would always be a 'hard-core of Koehlites' wasting their time 'pursuing lines of arcane irrelevance. As we of the new party march ... towards the White House ... we'll give them a friendly wave'. The NSWPP responded to the threat of a rival party by denouncing Collin, declaring that he was really the son of a Jewish refugee from Nazi Germany. (There had already been a furore over the 1965 suicide of former ANP officer Dan Burros, following the *New York Times*' publication of evidence that he was Jewish.) What eventually brought Collin down, however, was not claims of his ancestry but the discovery in 1979 by some of his followers that he had engaged in sex with young boys in the party headquarters. The police were informed, and Collin was subsequently imprisoned.[27]

Both parties continued into the Reagan years. The NSWPP demonstrated against the administration's dispatch of American troops to Lebanon and picketed the White House, protesting at the dangers nuclear power and 'the nuclear arms buildup' posed to the Aryan race.[28] Under a succession of leaders, the NSPA also remained active. But it soon collapsed. (Indeed, in one pamphlet, Covington had lamented that party units had attracted 'drug addicts, tattooed women, total bums and losers, police informers, the dregs of urban life'.) But if the NSPA did not survive, nor, in the form that he had inherited from Rockwell, did Koehl's party. As we discuss in Chapter 5, Rockwell had shown some interest in Christian Identity, arguing that religion could prove a potent recruitment tool for the party. Koehl took this belief in a religious national socialism further, and in 1983 he dissolved the NSWPP and established in its stead the New Order, committed to creating 'a Hitlerian religious ministry'.[29]

In the years that followed, the New Order has continued, although with little impact. Harold Covington, who had briefly taken over the NSPA after Collin's removal, attempted in the 1990s to revive the NSWPP.[30] Another former NSPA leader, Gary Lauck, continued with its former publication, the *New Order* (which had no connection with the Koehl grouping of the same name), and while active in America, devoted much of his efforts to spreading Nazi propaganda materials internationally, including, most importantly, within Germany itself.[31] Other national socialist groups have emerged. In the 1980s, for instance, three ex-members of the NSWPP formed the West Coast-based National Socialist Vanguard, while the Michigan-based SS Action Group was particularly active, demonstrating in Nazi uniform and clashing with counter-demonstrators.[32] There are numerous other groupings that have emerged in the national socialist milieu since Rockwell's assassination. But it is two that do not describe themselves as national socialist which particularly deserve discussion. One, which we will discuss shortly, is the National Alliance. The other is the constellation of groupings organized by Willis Carto.

In 1955 Carto had established a magazine, *Right*, as a 'Monthly Bulletin of, by and for the American Right Wing'.[33] Two years later, the magazine announced the inception of a new grouping, the Liberty Lobby, which would work for patriotic causes in the nation's capital. Both the organization and the magazine urged greater cooperation on the right, the magazine giving favourable attention to the conservative *National Review* and the anti-communist evangelist Billy James Hargis, as well as to such groupings as the ANP and the National States Rights Party. *Right* argued that America was under attack by 'International Communism, International Finance and International Zionism'. It denounced 'the Invisible Government' that had forced America into the Second World War and called on the right to remember the 'patriots' who had been charged with sedition for telling the truth. It also called for the repatriation of black people to Africa. (In 1957 it published an article praising Garvey while in 1959 it included an article by the Nation of Islam leader Elijah Muhammed.)[34]

The nature of Carto's project became even clearer at the beginning of the following decade. In June 1960, just before Yockey's death, Carto had visited him in jail, and the following month the author of *Imperium* was the subject of a front-page article. Since the appearance of his book, the article declared, it had been the intention of 'International Jewry' to destroy the 'great creative genius' who had dared to oppose it. In the magazine's final edition two months later, it declared its support for both the National States Rights Party and the ANP. There was now, it declared, 'no more need to play tag with the Enemy'. The Culture Distorter had long been at work, and rather than blame the situation on communism, its rise was only an effect of what had gone wrong. It was Jews who had created the Soviet Union, who had forced America into war with Hitler, and who controlled the press. Indeed, it was Jews who would gain if America engaged in a new war, this time in the name of anti-communism, because while they ruled America, 'Jewish control of Russia has been broken'.[35]

In 1962 a new edition of *Imperium* was published with an introduction written by Carto. If Yockey has a complex relationship to national socialism, then Carto does in a different way. Yockey had rejected what he saw as nineteenth-century materialism, holding that race was '*fluid*, gliding with History over the fixed skeletal form determined by the soil'. Carto, however, argued that 'the genetic interpretation of race' remained valid.[36] But Carto's greater proximity to national socialism than Yockey was complicated by a different characteristic. As with *Right*, he did not call for an overtly national socialist movement.

Right was succeeded by other magazines, first *Western Destiny*, then the *American Mercury*, each of which advanced similar ideas. (The NSWPP even reprinted an article from the latter describing the 'far better' world that might have resulted if national socialism had not been defeated.)[37]

In subsequent years, Carto was to remain active in a number of ways. One, as we will discuss shortly, was his launch of the Institute for Historical Review, the leading force in Holocaust revisionism. Another was his launch in 1975 of a weekly, the *National Spotlight*, subsequently the *Spotlight*, which sought to continue in *Right*'s tradition of promoting an 'anti-Zionist' politics while publicizing different sections of the right. During the early years of the Reagan administration, it attained a peak sale of over 300,000 issues.[38]

Carto also continued to devote much of his energies to Liberty Lobby. Again a policy of reaching across the right was highly evident. The Lobby's board of policy included figures who already had established a presence on the extreme right. Kenneth Goff, for instance, was a former associate of Gerald L. K. Smith who now led the paramilitary Soldiers of the Cross, while General Pedro Del Valle was the central figure in another group, the Defenders of the American Constitution. But the Lobby was also successful in attracting a number of conservative members of Congress to address its events. Liberty Lobby spokesmen testified before Congress on legislation concerning civil rights, immigration and trade with the Soviet Union. It also sought to involve itself in a range of issues. It organized against busing and in support of the Rhodesian government. In 1970, it organized a 'Tax Rebellion Rally' while in 1973 its 'Survival Seminar' included Robert DePugh, the founder of the paramilitary anti-communist group of the 1960s, the Minutemen. During the 1990s it was also highly visible as a supporter of the new paramilitary groupings that emerged in that period, the militias. (In 1995, for instance, John Trochman, one of the leading figures in the movement, addressed the Liberty Lobby Convention on 'The Militia Movement: Retaking Our Stolen Government'.) But, as we will discuss in Chapter 8, it also explored electoral possibilities. In 1996 and 2000, it supported a maverick conservative presidential candidate, Pat Buchanan. In the 1980s, it sought to build a rival to the Democrat and Republican parties, the Populist Party.[39]

This attempt to build a third party involved a striking number of disputes between Carto and other leading activists, and the main grouping that ultimately emerged from the conflict, the American Nationalist Union, was led by opponents of the Liberty Lobby.[40] Both Liberty Lobby and the *Spotlight* continued to the end of the century when Carto lost a legal dispute with his former associates in the Institute for Historical Review. A bankruptcy court ruled against Liberty Lobby while the *Spotlight* was succeeded by another publication, *American Free Press*.[41] Carto has sought to forge an extreme right with a broader appeal than Rockwell or his successors could achieve. It would, however, be one of his initiatives which would give rise to the emergence of a crucial rival.

In 1968, in response to the growth of a militant left among students, a National Youth Alliance had been launched. What had long been needed, an article by its vice-chairman declared the following year, was a movement with the guts to 'smash the campus red front'. Now it had emerged, and 'the terror of the Left' would at last be 'met with the greater terror of the Right'.[42] Quickly, however, both the author of this article and the Alliance's chairman denounced the direction the organization was taking, claiming that it was being manipulated by a clandestine Nazi group committed to the ideas of Yockey.[43]

The allegations that adherents of the Yockey movement were seeking to control the National Youth Alliance included the claim that Carto had told a meeting of activists that followers of Yockey should 'capture the leadership of as many conservative elements as possible'. The furore resulted in a number of the Alliance's officers departing and was soon succeeded by another row, in which Carto accused another leading Yockeyist, Louis Byers, of stealing the organization's mailing list. For a period, more than one National Youth Alliance existed, with the grouping supported by Carto arguing that it was necessary to go beyond national socialism. Rockwell, it was suggested, had sought to root his politics in American conditions, but the Nazi groups that had emerged since his death were trapped in the German past. Those who adhered to national socialist goals, it was argued, should abandon national socialist forms.[44]

But it would be a different faction that was to gain from the split in the National Youth Alliance. In the later part of Rockwell's leadership, the party launched an ideological journal, *National Socialist World*. The editor was a former professor of physics at Oregon State University, William Pierce. Although he did not join the party until after Rockwell's death, he was a committed national socialist, responsible for a column in *White Power*, 'Lessons from Mein Kampf'. He was not able, however, to continue to accept Koehl's leadership, and a later reminiscence by a former NSWPP activist describes Koehl setting up 'a kangaroo court to drive Pierce out of the party'.[45]

Soon after, the National Youth Alliance abandoned the claim that Yockey represented the way forward, and sought to forge a politics that moved beyond national socialism in a different way. Its new leader was William Pierce. (The organization also inherited much of the stock from the NSWPP bookshop.)[46] Among the Alliance's key concerns was America's attitude towards Israel. In 1973 it testified before the Senate Committee on Foreign Relations, arguing that Henry Kissinger should not be confirmed as secretary of state. He would support Israel over America, it declared, and the previous year it had infiltrated a demonstration against the Vietnam war, opposing the provision of American arms to Israel. But in its early years, Pierce's group most distinguished itself by its support for a violent confrontation with the establishment. What America needed, it proclaimed, was the 'cleansing fire of total revolution'.[47] The National Alliance monthly published details of how to build bombs and how to use a sniper's rifle. It was not leftists who should be the target of violence, it declared, but federal judges and newspaper editors. Most significantly, in 1975 it began a serialization of what would become one of the most important extreme right publications, *The Turner Diaries*. As we discuss in more detail in Chapter 6, this book, written under a pseudonym by Pierce, vividly pictured a fictional future in which a racist group, The Order, bombed its way to a white America. What is crucial to note now, however, is that its writing coincided with a major shift in Alliance strategy. In 1974 the National Youth Alliance became the National Alliance, and as he subsequently wrote, Pierce was becoming increasingly convinced that a more long-term approach was needed.[48]

The objective remained a wholly white America. Blacks, the Alliance declared, were inferior to whites and responsible for much of the crime in America. (Immigration from the Third World also came under attack.)[49] But while the Alliance now believed in a more long-term strategy, this did not stop it from declaring at the end of the 1970s that the first signs of revolution were now apparent. Nor did it mean that violent rhetoric disappeared from its propaganda. In 1978, for instance, *The Turner Diaries* first appeared as a book. But what most marked the Alliance was Pierce's argument that in the period ahead, it should aim to recruit from 'an elite minority carefully sifted out of the overall White population'. The resulting organization would 'elaborate and elucidate the truth' and when mass mobilization at last became possible, it would be ready.[50]

Pierce did not describe the National Alliance as national socialist. On occasion, however, its propaganda expressed admiration for Nazism. In one article, it described the Third Reich as 'dedicated to the goal of racial progress', while in another it praised the 'volunteers, from thirty different European peoples' who had enlisted in the Waffen SS.[51] Denouncing plans for gun control, it claimed that in Nazi Germany there had been less restrictions on the possession of firearms than in contemporary America, and on the hundredth anniversary of his birth, the cover story of *National Vanguard* declared that Hitler had dared more and achieved more than 'any other man of our times'.[52] In 1993 the Alliance produced a *Membership Handbook*, and one of the questions it dealt with was the organization's relationship to national socialism. How, it asked, should members reply when asked if they were Nazis? In some cases, it suggested, this should be denied. But if the question came from a potential recruit, the idea needed to be distinguished from its manifestation in early twentieth-century Germany. Political uniforms, for instance, were alien to America. But it would be 'wrong, however, for us to shut our minds to the eternal truths embodied in the National Socialist idea: they are the truths on which our own creed is based'.[53]

To take a stance towards national socialism would also, for the Alliance as for other sections of the extreme right, necessitate taking a stance towards the Holocaust. As we noted earlier, Holocaust revisionism had already emerged before the creation of the ANP. Rockwell had espoused it, but it was a number of later authors and the promotion of their writings by Carto's Institute for Historical Review that were central to the spread of revisionism throughout the racist movement and beyond.[54] The Alliance, like much of the extreme right, sold materials on the Holocaust as well as arguing a revisionist case in its own publications. In a cover story in 1979, for instance, The Alliance's publication *National Vanguard* proclaimed '"Holocaust" Claims Exposed as Lies'. A leading revisionist, it reported, had visited concentration camps and analysed thousands of documents. He had concluded that German gas chambers had never existed. In a second article shortly after, however, a rather different emphasis appeared. To prove whether or not Jews had been gassed, it was suggested, might be impossible. There was no finer source on the issue than Arthur Butz's *The Hoax of the Twentieth Century*, which was sold by the Alliance. But it would not be right to condemn the Germans if they had carried out the Holocaust. Such actions had to be judged on the basis of a higher morality, and non-white immigration and the non-white birth-rate had to be seen in that light too.[55]

While much of the extreme right welcomed the rise of Holocaust revisionism, this was not true in every case. In one publication in the early 1990s, it was argued that promotion of Holocaust revisionism was a diversion from the proper task of national socialists. The cover of another publication showed a picture of a sniper with the caption, 'Firing Shots to Change the Future Is Better than Bitching about the Past'. The editorial that followed argued that Holocaust revisionism's contribution to the white cause was 'doubtful'. Most revisionists, it claimed, were appalled at 'real, get-down, racism' and were attempting to portray Hitler as a liberal.[56]

But Pierce was not arguing that Holocaust revisionism should be abandoned. When the National Alliance sought to recruit someone, its *Membership Handbook* noted, the subject of the Holocaust could come up. This 'myth' could be challenged, but the case should not be overstated. The Germans had killed groups of Jews on the Eastern Front, and in discussing what had happened, the Alliance should draw attention to the number of Europeans who had been killed by the Jews. This information, it was suggested, could be highly effective in reaching those who had believed in the Holocaust. 'They will come to understand that, regardless of how many Jews died during the war, it wasn't enough.'[57]

Pierce's vision of the future was one in which the race war would be won beyond America. The goals of the Alliance, its *Handbook* declared, involved a white living space, an Aryan society and a government 'committed to the service of our race'. In the past whites had occupied Europe, Australia, southern Africa and 'the temperate zones of the Americas'. They would do so again, and no non-whites would remain in those lands. Spanning the continents would be 'a strong, centralized government', at the head of which would be men and women 'whose attitude towards its mission is essentially *religious* ... more like a holy order than like any existing secular government today'.[58]

For the Alliance, there was no greater obstacle to its plans than the American mass media. In newspapers, it claimed, opponents of Israel were never portrayed favourably while in TV drama black characters were presented as admirable. Despite the appearance of debate, the media spoke with one voice, claiming races were equal, defending inter-racial marriage and encouraging immigration. This, the Alliance claimed, was the work of Jews, and their control of the media was 'the single most important fact of life, not only in America, but the whole world'. In response, the organization sought to build its own media. One approach was through fiction. After *The Turner Diaries* Pierce wrote a second novel, *Hunter*, in which the protagonist waged a campaign of terror, killing mixed-race couples. Another member wrote a third novel, while the Alliance also produced audio cassettes and comic books, and, in 1991, began weekly radio broadcasts.[59] It subsequently turned its attention to video games. The first, 'Ethnic Cleansing', was described as

about urban warfare between Whites and non-Whites. The number-one bad guy in the game is the Jewish prime minister and war criminal, Ariel Sharon. The player wins if he can find Sharon's secret hideout in the depths of the New York subway system and kill him without being killed by a non-White.[60]

The Alliance subsequently produced a second video game, 'White Law', in which a police officer purges part of a city of drug dealers and pornography distributors, starting by killing blacks and Latinos before moving on to kill Jews.[61] The most important Alliance propaganda initiative, however, was to move into the sale of racist music CDs. Music had been used by extreme right groups before.[62] In its modern form, however, it can be traced to a British band, Skrewdriver. Emerging out of the punk rock explosion at the end of the 1970s, Skrewdriver used a speeded-up and raucous music (known as Oi) to drive home a brutally racist message. Other bands emerged in a number of countries, and among the earliest groupings to attempt to popularize the music in America was one of the most radical, White Aryan Resistance (WAR).

Led by a former Klansman, Tom Metzger, WAR was established in the early 1980s. We discuss in Chapter 7 its attitude to violence. Here, however, we focus both on its ideology and the significance it gave to white power music. While vitriolic to racial minorities, WAR like the ANP before it argued that racists should cooperate with black nationalists to bring about the separation of the races, and in 1985 Metzger announced that he had been invited to attend a Nation of Islam meeting by its leader, Louis Farrakhan, and had given $100 to the organization as 'a gesture of understanding'. This was only one of the alliances that WAR envisaged as vital for the fight against what it, along with a growing number of other racists, were coming to describe as ZOG, the Zionist Occupation Government. Metzger described WAR as 'a working class movement', called for support for militant environmentalists and denounced 'monopoly capitalism'. White revolutionaries, he wrote,

> do not connect ourselves to reactionaries who think they are assisting their race by fighting for 'western traditions' or against 'socialism'. . . . White racial socialism is positive. Race mixing socialism is negative. . . . Socialist regimes seeking to overthrow coca cola 'culture' and zionism, and that are ruled by white men who keep their nations essentially white, have our support.[63]

WAR, he declared in one interview, had 'began to take on a lot of the positions of the left, and we started recruiting people from the left'. The group's stance towards national socialism was similarly radical. The development of the NSDAP had been marked by factional conflicts, and it is not only the victorious faction which has attracted the sympathies of some on the extreme right. The NSDAP, one article in WAR's paper declared, had originally been a revolutionary movement whose aim had been to overthrow German capitalism. Both the North German wing of the party, led by Gregor and Otto Strasser, and the stormtroopers of the SA had been radicals, but after national socialism had come to power, Hitler had sold them out. The result was the betrayal of the 'true Nazi Revolution'. An article in the previous issue described WAR's stance as 'a form of National Socialism' but 'like that brand promulgated by Otto and Gregor Strasser'.[64]

While WAR rejected mainstream national socialism, it was willing to adopt Nazi imagery. Thus in 1989 it reported on an Aryan music festival under the headline, 'REICH 'N ROLL'. Speaking at the event, Metzger declared that in Germany, whites had 'ceased to be divided and they began to kick ass'. Now it was Skinheads who were kicking ass, and their music was 'the most powerful message in the country today for the White race. . . . If the Jews can use music against us, we will destroy them with our music.'[65]

WAR created the Aryan Youth Movement which called for 'a new wave of Predatory Leaders among Aryan Youth. . . . Our Enemies understand only one message: That of the knife, the gun and the club.' Groups with such names as the Chicago Area Skinheads and the Reich Skins emerged, with whom Metzger built alliances. It was not, however, to be WAR which would play the most crucial part in the early spread of 'white power music'. In the early 1990s, Resistance Records set out to produce CDs as well as distribute them, and it subsequently produced its own magazine. While *Resistance* published articles by prominent racists, it concentrated on reviews of CDs and interviews with bands, and its website allowed CDs to be both sampled and ordered. In 1997, however, it was raided by Michigan state authorities on tax charges. Resistance Records was put on sale. Initially, it was purchased by Carto and a former Republican official, Todd Blodgett. Shortly afterwards, however, it was sold by Blodgett. The new purchaser was William Pierce.[66]

Following the purchase of Resistance Records, Pierce explained why he had bought it. It gave him a 'better opportunity than before to talk with young Americans' and see how their alienation was growing. 'There are hundreds of thousands of young, White Americans who would like nothing better than to rip out the throats of the people who have made their lives pointless and meaningless. ... The rage building now will find a way out.' His aim, he went on, was to 'help it find the right way' so that the throats that were ripped out belonged to the right people.[67]

Pierce's imagery fitted the music well. Many of the bands whose CDs were sold by Resistance Records made their attitudes all too clear. Nordic Thunder's album was entitled 'Born to Hate', while Berzerker's was 'Crush the Weak'. But if the titles were suggestive, the lyrics were clearer still. One band, The Blue Eyed Devils, for instance, released a CD entitled 'Murder Squad', the title track of which celebrated the murders committed by the Nazi Einsatzkommando:

> My orders are simple, plain and clear
> Murder on command and have no fear ...
> A cleansing wind throughout this land
> The final solution, the final stand

A later track shifted the scene from wartime Europe to contemporary America:

> Nonwhite scum we're gonna kill you
> Slit your throat and watch you die
> Time to crush the brown eyed subrace
> Strangle, beat and crucify[68]

While most white power musicians were young men, this need not be the case, and the novelty of one act gained considerable publicity. Prussian Blue, the twin teenage daughters of a prominent extreme right activist, April Gaede, initially performed acoustic covers of white power songs, then moved to writing their own material, one example of which proclaimed:

> Aryan man awake
> How much more will you take
> Turn that fear to hate.

Their music was released on CDs by Resistance Records and their photograph appeared on the cover of *Resistance*. 'We are hoping', their mother declared, 'to get the attention of young girls who are being bombarded with images like Britney Spears and the like'.[69]

The sale of racist CDs has brought Pierce's group both considerable income and access to a new generation of racists. In the same period, the

Alliance's deputy membership coordinator, Billy Roper, became particularly prominent in urging unity between the Alliance and other extreme rightists. In August 2002, for instance, members of different groupings joined an Alliance march from Washington DC's Union Station to the Capitol. Among the slogans, a subsequent Aryan Nations report noted, was 'Roses are red, violets are blue – for every dead Arab, another dead jew!' In July 2002, however, Pierce died of cancer and kidney failure. Six days later, his successor was announced. Erich Gliebe, a former professional boxer, was leader of one of the Alliance's local units and had been running Resistance Records. The result, however, was the rise of tensions both within the Alliance and between it and other groups. As with other extreme right groupings, the Alliance has been systematically opposed by the Anti-Defamation League, the Southern Poverty Law Center and other anti-fascist organizations. Shortly before Pierce's death, the Southern Poverty Law Center's *Intelligence Report* reported, Pierce had given a speech at a leadership conference of the organization in which he had declared that 'the Alliance has no interest at all in the so-called "movement". ... If anything, we would be grateful that the movement is out there to soak up a lot of the freaks and weaklings who otherwise might find their way into the Alliance'. Gliebe had also spoken, calling for the destruction of the 'make-believe world otherwise known as "the movement"', and the report had contrasted this scathing approach to Billy Roper's pursuit of racist unity. Pierce, it noted, had criticized the 'unity thing ... this idea that the freaks and sieg-heilers could somehow be a benefit to us'. If Roper was expelled, the article went on, he could form a rival grouping.[70]

The following issue of the Law Center's magazine reported that Gliebe had dismissed Roper on the same day as the previous article had appeared. The speeches made at the National Alliance convention had particularly inflamed skinheads who bought material from Resistance Records. The announcement that Roper had been removed for making 'very wrong decisions' and for not accepting Gliebe's leadership worsened the situation still further. While Gliebe denied the authenticity of *Intelligence Report*'s quotes, former Alliance members declared that they were genuine. (Indeed, Pierce had written along such lines in a members' bulletin two years before his death, proclaiming that rather than being the dominant group in the 'movement', the Alliance wanted to be no part of it.) Taking a very different stance, Roper launched a new group, White Revolution.[71]

Differing sharply from the Alliance, Roper's new group urged cooperation with other groups. In 2004, for instance, it called for other groups to support a demonstration to protest the 50th anniversary of the *Brown* decision. Using such slogans as 'Brown = Jewdicial Tyranny Over Whites' and 'Has Your White Girl Been Raped by Brown Yet?', White Revolution declared that integration had led to failing education and unsafe schools.[72] The appeal for cooperation was not wholly successful (the National Socialist Movement withdrew its support in protest at White Revolution's call for demonstrators to avoid wearing Nazi uniforms). In the aftermath of the White Revolution rally, however, another National Alliance dissident, Alex Linder, issued an extended discussion of *Brown* and its role in the evolution of America. The decision's real meaning, he claimed had not been to do with schools and segregation but had been to do 'with who will control our communities and run our lives: us or judeo-Washington'. That it was passed without those who did so being lynched was proof that America had ceased to be 'a nation of Aryan freemen. ... We fought a bit against *Brown*, but in the main we gave in.' 'Leaving the New Deal aside', *Brown* had marked the point where America had become a nation of slaves.[73]

White Revolution's hostility to blacks was particularly evident three years later when, in reaction to Hurricane Katrina, the organization called for aid to be collected for white victims and set up a 'Cartridges for Katrina' programme which would pay for the reimbursement of the ammunition used in the killing of 'every black looter'. The same year, he declared that 'the whole world is ours, and the only part of the earth that non-Whites should inherit is however much it requires to cover them'.[74]

The Alliance's travails had not ended with the departure of Roper. In 2003, *Intelligence Report* reported that the Alliance's membership had declined, earnings had declined from Resistance Records, and Alex Linder was publishing attacks on Gliebe on his website, Vanguard News Network.[75] Disputes spiralled, and shortly after his 2004 resignation, the Alliance's former Membership Coordinator, David Pringle, accused its leadership of having lost over half its membership and two-thirds of its income in the last year. But rather than Linder or Pringle, the key role in the developing crisis in the National Alliance was taken by veteran member Kevin Strom. Responsible for many of the Alliance's radio broadcasts, Strom was accused by Gliebe of conspiring to seize control of the organization, and expelled along with other dissidents. Soon after, however, the newly married Gliebe resigned from the chairmanship. He was replaced by his closest associate, Shaun Walker. Strom, meanwhile, announced the launching of a new group, National Vanguard.[76]

Both the National Alliance and National Vanguard continued to be hit by problems. National Vanguard has suffered the breakaway of some of its members and the resignation of Strom. (He was subsequently indicted on child-pornography charges.) In March 2007, the group dissolved. The National Alliance, meanwhile, has had to change its leadership again, with Gliebe stepping back into the chairmanship following Walker's arrest on charges of attacking racial minorities in bars.[77] Introducing himself to listeners to the National Alliance's broadcast, Shaun Walker had described the organization as having 'many beliefs that come from National Socialist ideology'.[78] But the explosion of the National Alliance represents only one of the crises that has affected groups in the national socialist milieu in recent years. Other groups which have drawn on national socialism have also entered into crisis. WAR, for instance, had been hit by legal action following a racist murder in

Portland, Oregon in 1988. The Southern Poverty Law Center argued that WAR's sending of an organizer to the area had been crucial in the subsequent death, and a jury ruled that WAR should pay $3.5 million and Tom Metzger $5.5 million. Amidst controversy over allegations by other extreme rightists that WAR's leader was now allowing correspondence to be opened by the Center, it has remained active but no longer as crucial.[79] Another organization, Aryan Nations, combines the promulgation of Christian Identity with profound admiration for national socialism. In the early 1990s, for instance, its 'HQ Staff Leader' and 'Propaganda Minister' were described as 'Col-Gruppenfuhrer' and 'Maj-Sturmbannfuhrer' respectively, while the invitation to its 1996 youth congress invited attendance from those Aryans 'who wish to honour the birthday of the greatest statesman our race has produced in 2,000 years, Adolf Hitler'.[80] In recent years, as we discuss in Chapter 5, Aryan Nations has suffered splits and the loss of first its headquarters and then its founder, Richard Butler. Neither Aryan Nations nor WAR retain their earlier prominence.

More recently, the Minnesota-based National Socialist Movement has become a key grouping. At the beginning of 2006, one of its leading figures declared that his organization's militant street activities had impressed others on the extreme right, and sections of different organizations, from chapters of the Klan and 'Aryan Nations congregations to National Vanguard, National Alliance and White Revolution units have simply been transferring their allegiance to the NSM.'[81] Unlike the National Alliance or the groups that have emerged from it, the NSM believes an unalloyed national socialism is the only way forward for American racists. As we will see later, however, it too has entered into crisis. But what of extreme rightists who have avoided identification with the politics of inter-war Germany? In this chapter, we have already encountered groupings to whom overt declaration of national socialism is anathema. In the next chapter, we will discuss those who look to the history of the South for their inspiration, and in the following chapter we will examine those who argue that the American Revolution should be the central reference point for an American movement. In Chapter 4 we will be considering too the question that our initial discussion of Willis Carto has raised in this chapter. What do we mean when we define a political grouping as on the extreme right, and how do we demarcate it from other sections of the right?

3 Out of the Southland

In the previous chapter, we discussed those sections of the extreme right which looked to national socialism for inspiration. But racists have not solely looked to inter-war Germany, and in this chapter we will look at some of those groupings who believe instead that it is aspects of the American experience which should be central. More precisely, they look to two particular aspects of that experience, the Confederacy and the subsequent rise and fall of Southern segregation. This belief in the South as the template of a white politics has taken a number of forms. The most important, however, has been the rebirth of the Ku Klux Klan.

As we have seen, the Klan was forced to suspend its national activities in the early 1940s. In 1953, a remnant of the group that succeeded it, the Association of Georgia Klans, launched the US Klans, Knights of the Ku Klux Klan. Interviewed on television in the late 1950s, the US Klans leader declared that its aim was 'maintaining segregated schools at any and all cost'. At this time, it was the strongest Klan group. But its dominance did not last long, and the most militant opposition to integration would be led by other groupings. In the late 1950s, the Alabama Grand Dragon, Robert Shelton, broke away and formed an Alabama Klan. Following the death of the US Klans' leader in 1960, most of his organization amalgamated with Shelton's grouping to form the United Klans of America. It was the UKA that would play a leading role in resistance to desegregation, but it would not be the only Klan of that period that we should consider. Some Klansmen resisted amalgamation into the UKA, launching first the National Association of Ku Klux Klans, then the National Knights of the Ku Klux Klan. Others avoided joining either national grouping, preferring to organize at state level, of which the most important example emerged in Mississippi in early 1964, the White Knights of the Ku Klux Klan.[1]

If the Klan was divided, it still retained a formidable capacity for violence. In 1961, for instance, a group of Freedom Riders stopped in the bus station in Birmingham, Alabama, and were the object of an organized attack by members of the UKA. In September 1963, four young black girls were killed when a bomb blew up a Birmingham Baptist church. A UKA member was subsequently convicted of the murders.[2] In June 1964, three civil rights workers disappeared in Mississippi and two months later their bodies were found in an earthern dam. The state never brought murder charges, but a subsequent federal trial on charges of conspiring to violate the men's civil and constitutional rights was told that the men had been killed on the instructions of the White Knights leader, Sam Bowers.[3] In July 1964, a black reserve officer was driving home to Washington DC from a period of duty in Georgia. Another car pulled alongside and the officer was shot dead. The car contained men with links both to the UKA and the National Knights. In March 1965 members of the UKA opened fire on a car containing a white woman and a black man. The two had taken part in a civil rights march in Selma, Alabama, and the woman was killed.[4]

For all three groupings, the very reason for the Klan's existence was the fight against desegregation. The UKA declared that it believed in God, the Stars and Stripes and white supremacy. America, it held, was 'a white man's country' and it declared that it was 'eternally opposed to the mixing of the white and colored races'. The National Knights declared that the only issue was whether the purity of the white race would continue. The Klan had 'already saved America from a Mulatto citizenship', and it stood ready to do so again.[5] The White Knights declared that it was working day and night to preserve law and order in the only way that it could be preserved: by strict segregation and the control of society by 'Christian, Anglo-Saxon White men, the only race on earth that can build and maintain just and stable governments'.[6]

All three of the major Klan groupings continued to espouse anti-Catholicism. The UKA claimed that 'Every Catholic holds allegiance to the Pope of Rome, and Catholicism teaches that this allegiance is superior to his allegiance to his country.' The National Knights declared it pitied 'all Catholics in their foreign papal enslavement', while the White Knights denounced 'Papists' for bowing down 'to a Roman dictator'.[7] For all three, however, behind the drive for integration stood a Jewish conspiracy. Speaking in the 1960s, one leading figure in the UKA declared that the Civil Rights Movement was funded by the Communist Party and 'the Zionist, Christ-killing Jews'. In the following decade, the UKA magazine, the *Fiery Cross*, described the *Brown* decision as the act of 'a Jew dominated judicial system' following which 'a Jew dominated federal government instituted a revolution to dispossess the majority'.[8] The White Knights, while declaring that it had no quarrel with 'the individual, ignorant and deceived "Jew"', denounced what it described as 'the Synagogue of Satan', while the leader of the National Knights attacked 'Jew Communism and Jew Bankers ruling the world'.[9]

Anti-Semitism does not mean Klan leaders always denounced a Jewish conspiracy for the challenge to segregation. In much of their propaganda, they emphasized the anti-communist aspect of their politics. The *Fiery Cross* quoted the right-wing writer, Revilo Oliver, describing communism as 'not a theory in which men may believe; it is a conspiracy in which men participate'. Communists were masters of subterfuge who would use any method 'to infiltrate every area of life ... to bring about their plan of world enslavement'. It published too a photograph of Martin Luther King at a Tennessee meeting in the late 1950s. The meeting, it declared, was a communist training school. The UKA was not the only Klan to claim that communists were manipulating those who were seeking to destroy segregation. The White Knights described the three civil rights activists who were killed in 1964 as 'Communist Revolutionaries'. Mississippi, it declared, was under attack by 'savage blacks and their communist masters'.[10] But however it ultimately framed the issue, the Klan concentrated its ire on the Civil Rights Movement. The killing of the three civil rights workers came after a decision to send volunteers to Mississippi to register black voters. The White Knights had declared that this could affect 'the fate of Christian Civilization for centuries to come'. The previous year, a UKA rally near Birmingham, Alabama, had described civil rights activities in the state as 'the greatest darkness this nation has ever faced'.[11] The Klan was similarly opposed to civil rights legislation. In 1964, the Civil Rights Act was passed, prohibiting segregation in public facilities and accommodations and barring job discrimination. The following year, the Voting Rights Act forbade the use of literacy tests and gave federal examiners the power to ensure the registration of qualified voters.[12] Unable to defeat either the Civil Rights Movement or civil rights legislation, the Klan was also harried by government. In 1965 the House Un-American Activities Committee launched an investigation of the Klan. When UKA officials refused to hand over membership records, they were charged with contempt of Congress, and Shelton and the leader of the South Carolina UKA were subsequently imprisoned. The Klan was also a target of the FBI. In 1964 COINTELPRO (the FBI's counter-intelligence programme) was extended from the far left to 'White Hate Groups' including the ANP, the National States Rights Party and the Klan. Activities included the sending of anonymous postcards to Klan members, informing them that their membership was no longer a secret, the cancelling of hotel reservations for attendance at a Klan convention and the encouragement of breakaways into Klan factions controlled by FBI informants.[13]

There were frequent attempts to recruit informants from within the Klan. Most dramatically, as a result of paying such informants, in the summer of 1968 two White Knights members, Thomas Tarrants and Kathy Ainsworth, were ambushed while attempting to bomb the home of a local Jewish leader. Tarrants was badly injured and Ainsworth killed. While the UKA and Venable's group continued into the subsequent decade, the White Knights ceased to exist.[14] But the continued drawing power of the Klan was most evident in the emergence of new groupings during the 1970s. The most important was the Knights of the Ku Klux Klan. Led by former national socialist student activist David Duke, some of its most prominent figures also had a national socialist background (its Alabama organizer was Don Black, its Louisiana organizer James Warner).[15] Its paper, the *Crusader*, emphasized the need for a firm ideological basis. Its list of books for sale included such works as *The Protocols of Zion*, *The International Jew* and *Mein Kampf*, while 'A Basic Reading Program for Klansmen' declared that while many members understood 'the Negro and Jewish problems', those who did not were recommended to read four books. The first looked at 'the Communist influence behind the Negro revolution' while the second concerned 'the lies behind the racial equality doctrine'. The third was described as exposing 'the Jewish lie that there was an extermination policy in Germany regarding the Jews'. The fourth, which claimed 'Jewish control and influence in Communism, organized crime, pornography and every other vice imaginable' was described as 'the best single book on the Jewish problem'.[16]

Following his period as leader of the White Student Alliance, Duke had sought to build a youth group independently of the NSWPP. He had then attempted to develop his own National Party.[17] In deciding to become leader of a Klan group, he was taking a very different approach from these. From its inception over a century earlier, the Klan had been marked by its use of ritual. In part, this involved the exotic names given to Klan officers, in part the use of robes and the carefully orchestrated nature by which prospective members were initiated into the invisible empire. While retaining all this (if in a modified form), the Klan that re-emerged in 1915 deployed its ritual in a different way. It organized rallies in which the central feature was the lighting of a cross, and later Klans retained this. In 1963, for instance, a newspaper account of an Alabama UKA rally described the setting alight of a sixty-foot high cross, while in 1965 a television documentary reported on a cross burning at an Ohio rally of the National Knights. Interviewed in the late 1970s, Shelton declared that Klan supporters preferred meeting in a field. 'In a building, you can't have your cross-lighting ceremony. You don't have the stirring activity that you have in the open-type field'.[18] Duke too held such events, but he increasingly emphasized a new approach. The Klan, he declared, had to 'get out of the cow pasture and into the hotel meeting rooms'. He began to use appearances on TV chat shows to argue the Klan's case. ('The media can't resist me', he told his followers. 'You see, I don't fit the stereotype of a Klansman.') He held an anti-busing rally in Boston and placed Klansmen on the California-Mexico border in an attempt to stop illegal immigration; he spoke on university campuses and attempted to gain election to the Louisiana state legislature. Challenging the image of the Klan, he disavowed anti-Catholicism and believed that women should play a more prominent part in the organization. Most importantly, he sought to argue Klan beliefs in a new way. All races, the Knights declared, had the right to self-determination, but discrimination in employment and education had made white Americans an oppressed group.[19]

Sometimes, the Knights declared, people who supported what the Klan believed asked why it did not change its name. The answer was that it was 'the first racialist group in the history of the world', and that the name attracted great interest and evoked 'a religious-like magnetism and strength'. But, frustrated at the people who were drawn to the Klan, Duke decided to abandon the organization and create a more 'high-class' National Association for the Advancement of White People. One of his lieutenants, Bill Wilkinson, had broken away in 1975, launching the Invisible Empire, Knights of the Ku Klux Klan. 'We tried the moderate approach in trying to halt the extravagant gains by blacks', he declared, 'but it failed. Now we are resorting to other methods.' In contrast to Duke, he frequently posed for cameras with heavily armed bodyguards. In 1981 the two men met, Wilkinson having apparently agreed to purchase Duke's membership list. Instead he secretly recorded the meeting and gave the tape to reporters. Duke declared that he was leaving the Klan 'because of its violent image and because of people like Bill Wilkinson'. Sending a resignation letter to members of the Knights, he invited them to join his new organization. Following his departure from the Klan, leadership of the Knights passed to Don Black.[20]

The Invisible Empire declared that civilization rested on 'the creativity of the white race' and called for 'the resettlement of the black race' in an African homeland. It argued that government restriction had had a devastating effect on business, but called for money to be only issued by authority of Congress. Wilkinson differed from Duke in his rhetoric ('You don't fight wars with words and books', he declared, 'You fight them with bullets and bombs.') But the Invisible Empire shared the Knights' anti-Semitism. It sold *The International Jew* and declared that 'American Jews so completely dominate our U.S. Senators and Congressmen that the State of Israel has a direct pipeline into the U.S. Treasury'. Wilkinson's leadership did not long survive, following the revelation in 1982 that he had passed information on the Klan to the FBI.[21] It continued under new leadership but was eventually dissolved in 1993 as a result of a court case over the violation of the civil rights of demonstrators in Forsyth County, Georgia. The UKA was also to fall victim to a 1987 court case, following the murder of a black teenager by some of its members. As for the Knights, Black's imprisonment for his part in an attempted invasion of the Caribbean island of Dominica led to a power struggle between rival factions, and the eventual emergence as leader of Christian Identity minister Thom Robb.[22]

The Knights has remained crucial to the development of the Klan. It has continued to attack affirmative action and immigration. A special issue of its paper, the *White Patriot*, intended to introduce new readers to the Klan, denounced international finance for enslaving Americans to 'their debt money system'. But it also proclaimed that 'homosexuals' should not be allowed to 'teach in our schools' or 'parade down our streets'. In 1986 its Illinois chapter sponsored what it termed an 'Anti-queer Rally ... to protest Gay Pride Week', while the previous year the *White Patriot* sought to win over beleagured farmers. Citing the *Protocols*, it declared: 'It's as plain as can be, the Jewish conspirators wrote in their own book what they intend to do. And to put it simply, THE JEW PLAN IS TO STEAL YOUR LAND!'[23]

Under Robb's leadership, his group claimed, the Klan was stressing 'love of one's race not hatred of others'. The organization was continuing the approach pioneered by Duke. (Indeed, following the election of Duke to the Louisiana state legislature, Robb announced his intention to train 'one thousand David Dukes' who would be 'taught to avoid statements that sound hateful and "turn people off"'.)[24] Yet the Knights were capable of sounding as radical as some of their rivals. In 1989, for instance, their Illinois newsletter published an article by David Lane in which he argued that those in 'the White resistance' who believed that they could keep 'all of what they call "our" land' would not succeed. Instead, Aryan Nations was right to call for the 'migration of our Folk to the northwestern United States'. Indeed, one of the Illinois Knights' organizers, Kim Badynski, had already relocated to Washington state, and in another Knights publication he described 'the Northwest Territorial Imperative as the last hope for the White Race within the present political system', and declared that if it was embraced, 'ZOG' would no longer 'feel as free to try to intimidate us by their non-White, anti-Christ hordes'.[25] Like Duke before him, Robb was keen to position the Knights as the Klan that was both more realistic and more effective than its rivals. But as an article in its Illinois publication noted, there were 'some elements in the movement that state they are more radical and that others are conservatives'. They accused them of being 'money-grubbers' too. The article did not name Robb as one of those who had been so characterized. The contents of a newsletter of the Missouri-based White Knights of the Ku Klux Klan, however, made it all too clear. Duke's continued prominence, it declared, was based on the ability to get 'well meaning but naïve people' to 'dig into their pockets to get conned again and again'. Robb, likewise, was guilty of 'fraud and treason'.[26]

The Knights has remained a significant Klan grouping. But it has both suffered breakaways and continued to be rivalled by myriad other Klans. One defector, Tom Metzger, was Duke's California Grand Dragon. Increasingly, however, he became convinced that Duke was an opportunist unfit to lead the Klan, and he launched instead his own California Knights of the Ku Klux Klan.[27] Another defector was Duke's Texas Grand Dragon, Louis Beam. A Vietnam veteran, Beam organized paramilitary training camps and subsequently led a campaign against immigrant Vietnamese fishermen which culminated in the burning of Vietnamese vessels and a court case in which he was enjoined from continued intimidation. Subsequently, however, he first joined with Robert Miles in launching the *Inter-Klan Newsletter and Survival Alert* and then brought together many of its arguments in his *Essays of a Klansman*.[28]

It was time, the *Newsletter* declared, for 'members of all the different Klans' to communicate with each other, and for 'time-tested and experienced Klansmen to guide their fellow Klansmen' through 'modern police state America'. The *Newsletter* proposed a chronology dividing Klan history into five eras, and, in doing so, laid out a critique of the organization's development. In the aftermath of the Civil War, the former Confederate states had been subjected to occupation. 'With a vengeance that only God-fearing men can exact, the Klan burst forth upon the Southland like first rays of the morning sun.' It had engaged in a 'secret struggle' against an enemy government, and had been victorious. In its second era, from 1915 to the 1920s, the Klan had achieved 'tremendous power' nationally, but had failed to channel it into a clear national goal. In its third era, it had reorganized, and the Supreme Court's 1954 decision gave it 'new impetus'. The enemy was the Civil Rights Movement, but 'heroic but desperate Klans' had failed to defeat 'the forces of evil' that secretly controlled it. In the fourth era, the Klan had sought a mass following. David Duke's Knights of the Ku Klux Klan had drawn many to its ranks. But there were other Klans, and in the new era this would be an advantage. 'In this age of the all seeing, all-knowing superstate, a single organization would only make it easier for the government to destroy the Klan.' All means short of armed conflict were now exhausted, and decentralization was vital for the success of an organization that could save America.[29]

But this was not the way that the Klan developed. Some Klan groups have no ambition to secure a national presence. The reasons for this could vary. Some Klans did not seek to expand beyond the area in which they emerged. Indeed, the leader of one group, the Georgia-based Southern White Knights, even told one interviewer that he had received a letter from 'a guy' in Wisconsin saying 'he had thirteen members he wanted to join up with us'. He had written back, refusing the offer. 'Hell, let those people in Wisconsin worry about the problems there and we'll worry about them here in Georgia.' Conversely, Dobratz and Shanks-Meile note, some Klansmen continued to organize at a regional level following the dissolution of the Invisible Empire.[30]

Unsurprisingly, such groupings rarely achieve notice beyond the area in which they were active, but this need not be the case. In the late 1970s, two North Carolina Klan groups linked up with the National Socialist Party of America. The following year some of the members were involved in a confrontation with members of the Communist Workers Party. It resulted in the fatal shooting of five of the leftists, and film of the clash was subsequently broadcast as part of a Public Broadcasting Service documentary, *88 Seconds in Greensboro*. One of the Klan leaders, Virgil Griffin, had declared that 'We can take our country back from the Communist Party; we'll take it back from the niggers. ... If we have to get in the streets and find blood up to our knees, by God, it's time to get ready, fight!' In a subsequent pronouncement, he declared 'I don't see any difference between killing Communists in Vietnam and killing them over here.' Both sides had been armed, however, and despite evidence that it was the extreme rightists who had fired first, they were acquitted.[31]

Many Klans, however, have looked beyond the area in which they emerged, and in doing so have pursued a variety of approaches. In the early 1990s, for instance, the Texas-based White Camelia Knights organized a rally to protest against the 'forced integration' of a federal housing project. Like a number of other Klans, it is particularly shaped by the belief that whites are the chosen race. Its Grand Dragon, Charles Lee, has described it as 'a Christian Identity Klan', and according to its irregular publication, *Crosstalk*, the belief that Jesus was Jewish was 'false and unscriptural'. Jews, it declared, were 'in control of most of the organized evil of the world, such as prostitution … international money-changing, profiteering on wars … corruption in politics, modernism in religion … promotion of lewd propaganda through theaters and picture shows etc.'.[32] The White Camelia Knights is not the only Klan to support Christian Identity. In 2003, for instance, Aryan Nations' leader, Richard Butler, visited the Alabama White Knights. It subsequently affiliated to his group, taking the name Aryan Nations Knights of the Ku Klux Klan.[33]

Whether Identity or not, Klan groupings have used a variety of different methods to try to win support. The Indiana-based American Knights of the Ku Klux Klan, for instance, attracted considerable attention in the late 1990s through what one account described as the 'foul speeches and trademark tough-boy style' of its Imperial Wizard, Jeff Berry. In 1996, for instance, Berry appeared on the *Jerry Springer Show*, and his organization's telephone number was shown on the television screen.[34] The White Camelia Knights produced material for showing on local public access cable TV systems, while the Imperial Klans of America has arranged for white power rock bands to play at its annual Nordic Fest.[35] Different Klan groupings have sometimes cooperated. In 1989, for instance, the Invisible Empire joined with the Southern White Knights, the Royal Confederate Knights, the Knights, the White Camelia Knights, the Christian Knights, and the Confederate Knights in a Georgia march against 'non-white immigration'. The following year, an Atlanta protest against Martin Luther King Day once again brought together the Invisible Empire, the Southern White Knights and the Royal Confederate Knights, with the US Klans and the Fraternal White Knights.[36]

The Imperial Klans has been particularly concerned to work with other groups. This could lead to conflict (at its 2002 festival, for instance, a dispute broke out with one white power music distributor, Panzerfaust, over the Imperial Klans' attempt to involve the Outlaw Hammerskins, a breakaway from the racist skinhead group Hammerskin Nation. Four years later, the Imperial Klans became involved in a physical confrontation between the National Socialist Movement and another skinhead group, the Vinlanders Social Club). But the Imperial Klans' ecumenical attitude to the different strands of the movement could also lead to winning over new recruits, and while in 2002 it had spoken of its intention to build its own Christian Identity church, in 2006 the IKA declared that it now would welcome

Odinists into its organization.[37] In the 1990s, the Northwest Knights had used White Camelia Knights material for its own cable TV programming. In 2006, the Imperial Klans announced that rank-and-file members of the American Knights were welcome at its events. But as the earlier accounts of cooperation between different Klans should remind us, fragmentation is the more predominant characteristic of the Klan. Indeed, the Imperial Klans' invitation was authored by a former American Knights Grand Dragon and included the suggestion that 'former and current members' of the American Knights should consider coming over to the group to which he now belonged.[38] Different Klans seek to win over dissident members of rival claimants to the name. But leading figures in the Klan have also ceased to be active in it, and turned instead to other forms of the extreme right.

Metzger, for instance, jettisoned the California Knights to create the White American Political Association. In 1983 he launched White American Resistance, which the following year became White Aryan Resistance.[39] Beam too, as we will discuss later, was also to abandon the Klan. Nor were they the only Klansmen to turn to other forms of organization. In 1980, for instance, a former member of the NSPA, Glenn Miller, had formed the Carolina Knights of the Ku Klux Klan. A participant in the Greensboro shootings, he had later proclaimed, 'I am more proud of the 88 seconds I spent in Greensboro on November 3, 1979, than I am of the twenty years I spent in the U.S. Army.' As his ambitions expanded, the group became the Confederate Knights. In March 1985, however, his group had become the White Patriot Party.[40]

The party described itself as 'the political party for Southern White People', arguing that once law and order broke down, millions of whites would 'flood into the Southland' and 'legions of White Patriot Soldiers' would be able to take power. They would create an independent Southern White Republic which would bring about an end to 'forced school integration', the restoration of school prayer and a sane financial system. In 1983, as the result of a lawsuit, the group was forbidden to engage in paramilitary training and in 1986, Glenn Miller and another leading figure, Stephen Miller, were found guilty of violating this order. Subsequently Stephen Miller was imprisoned for conspiring to buy stolen military explosives and blow up the Southern Poverty Law Center. Glenn Miller issued a 'declaration of total war' and went into hiding but was quickly arrested and agreed to plead guilty to one weapons charge and give testimony against other racists. The organization disbanded.[41]

Metzger, Beam and Miller all evolved away from the Klan in the 1980s. Most strikingly, so too did David Duke. In 1980, he launched the National Association for the Advancement of White People. As with its predecessor, it called for an end to affirmative action and busing. Whites, it claimed, faced widespread discrimination, and, just like other races, should defend their civil rights. It denounced immigration too. Along with 'nonwhite birthrates', Duke declared, immigration would make whites 'vulnerable to the political, social, and economic will of blacks, Mexicans, Puerto Ricans, and Orientals. A social upheaval is now beginning to occur that will be the funeral dirge of the America we love.'[42] Among the books the NAAWP sold were Yockey's *Imperium, The International Jew, The Protocols* and a pamphlet it described as 'documenting the Zionist control over the mass media'. It was succeeded by another organization, the National Organization for European-American Rights, subsequently renamed the European-American Unity and Rights Organization. In 2003, Duke would be imprisoned for filing a false tax return and mail fraud. (In part, this involved claims that he had used large amounts of the money sent to him by supporters to fund a gambling habit. He had pleaded guilty, he declared, because he did not expect to receive a fair trial.) Following his release, among those who attended an event to welcome him were Willis Carto of *American Free Press* and David Pringle and Kevin Strom of the pre-split National Alliance.[43]

As we have noted, in addition to launching the NAAWP, Duke was also able to gain election to the Louisiana state legislature. Other former Klansmen have also played leading roles in other parts of the extreme right. His successor as leader of the Knights, Don Black, for instance, subsequently launched 'the first white nationalist website', Stormfront.[44] But if one noteworthy feature of the extreme right of recent years is a shift from the Klan to rival groupings, another is the ability of the Klan to forge links with other racist groupings.

On occasion, this has involved links with national socialists. In late 2005, for instance, a row in the Cleveland Knights of the Ku Klux Klan reached its conclusion. Its leader, Klan veteran Virgil Griffin, came under fire for his links with the National Socialist Movement, but rather than break with the NSM, he expelled his critic. The following year, the NSM held a meeting with the leaders of several Klans to discuss increased cooperation, and followed with a membership meeting addressed by Virgil Griffin and speakers from the NSM, Aryan Nations and the National Knights, the Teutonic Knights and the Yahweh Knights. The NSM produced a document discussing its developing relationship with the Klan. Some Klan groups, it suggested, maintained 'high personal standards' while others were 'havens for criminals and ex-cons'. Many both subscribed to Christian Identity and believed that the American Constitution was sacrosanct, and they were intolerant of other 'white nationalist viewpoints'. Furthermore, the Klan was deeply split by different warring personalities, and many in its ranks held 'negative views of National Socialism'. The situation was yet further complicated, the document remarked, by the presence of expelled ex-NSM members in the Klan. Nonetheless, while recognizing the historic differences between the Klan and the NSM, it was in the latter's interest that out of cooperation arose 'a united, powerful and national socialist friendly Klan movement'.[45]

The Imperial Knights declared in 2006 that it no longer adhered to 'the long held KKK belief' that Klansmen could not also be national socialists. But as both the NSM document and the Imperial Knights' reference to its previous belief indicated, much of the Klan had long rejected any identification with national socialism. (Indeed, one interviewer noted that the Invisible Empire's Imperial Wizard had been 'indignant at being associated with neo-nazis and at pains to assure me that "you don't have to be a Nazi to be an anti-Semite"'.) Whether any long-term cooperation could be maintained was thus far from sure.[46]

But while an alliance with open national socialists has been relatively rare, more common has been connections with racialists who draw on national socialism. The Klan has published, for instance, material by William Pierce's grouping. In the early 1970s, for example, one issue of the *Fiery Cross* included an article describing how to make bombs. A well planned campaign, it observed, could create havoc, undermining the population's confidence in the authorities. An accompanying article, 'Why Revolution?', argued that the only government worthy of its citizens' loyalty was one dedicated to 'the preservation of one's own kind'. The present government had become completely alienated from 'the racial elements which originally created it and gave it life'. Every white student in the schools integrated by the government had experienced the terror which stalked the classrooms and hallways. Every responsible teacher understood the lies they were expected to plant in the minds of their charges. The Supreme Court's disastrous 1954 decision had not been an accident, and it would take a revolution to reverse it. Both articles were reprinted from *Attack!*, the paper of the National Youth Alliance.[47]

The following decade, the *Crusader* reprinted a National Alliance article on the rise and fall of the first Klan. It had been hit by government repression, the article noted, and its localized clandestine nature had led to different dens acting on the whims of their leaders. Eventually Reconstruction had been defeated and the struggle to bring this about had been 'the most inspirational political movement in American history.' But the segregation that succeeded it had still left millions of blacks in proximity to whites. The South had now been defeated again, and only geographical separation would suffice to protect racial integrity.[48]

The most substantial link between the Klan and another group, however, concerns neither the National Alliance nor open national socialists. Instead, it concerned another form of the extreme right which like the Klan had also emerged in the South, the National States Rights Party. From its inception, two veteran racists were central to the party. J.B. Stoner and Edward Fields had been the central figures in the Christian Anti-Jewish Party, which in August 1954 organized a picket of the White House. The demonstrators called for the overthrow of Jewish control and for the reversal of the Supreme Court decision on segregation.[49] In 1957, Stoner and Fields formed a United White Party and then the organization the two would lead for the next three decades, the NSRP. The party platform declared that it sought 'the creation of a wholesome White Folk Community', the separation of whites and non-whites and the setting up of 'a National Repatriation Commission,

to encourage the voluntary resettlement of Negroes in their African homeland'.[50] If blacks stayed in America, the NSRP declared, mongrelization
would destroy the white race. They should never have been brought into the
country, but 'it is never too late to correct any mistake. ... A White Supremacy Party must take over the U.S. Government and begin an immediate
program to ship all negroes to Africa.' This, the party held, was both
practical and urgent. They could 'easily be moved out of the cities in truck
and rail convoys' and then the navy, merchant marine and chartered ships
could return them to Africa.[51]

The NSRP saw itself as a national party. Calling on supporters to 'Fly
the Confederate Flag', it argued that it was 'no longer a sectional emblem.
It is now the symbol of the White race and White supremacy.' But it was
the people of the South, it declared, who could lead the struggle against
communism and 'race mixing'.[52] In 1963, for instance, it picketed a visit by
Robert Kennedy to Montgomery, Alabama, under the slogan, 'KOSHER
TEAM KENNEDY KASTRO KRUSHCHEV', while one of its most prominent activists, the Christian Identity minister Connie Lynch, spoke at a
Florida Klan rally shortly after the death of four black girls in the bombing
of an Alabama church. They were not children, he declared, but only 'little
niggers', and it 'wasn't no shame they was killed. Why? Because, when I go
out to kill rattlesnakes, I don't make no difference between little rattlesnakes
and big rattlesnakes ... I kill 'em all, and if there's four less niggers tonight,
then I say, "Good for whoever planted the bomb!"'.[53] The *Thunderbolt*
attacked the 'traitors who had plotted and planned' the *Brown* decision and
called for the execution of Supreme Court justices. In 1965, it called upon
Southern whites to fire their black employees. This, it declared, would
reduce black voting strength by forcing them to move North. But the party
had chapters outside the South (in New York in the mid-1960s, for instance,
it distributed 'Communism is Jewish' stickers) and while it concentrated
much of its energies on defending segregation and opposing communism, its
activity stretched far more widely. It organized petitions, for instance,
against the Supreme Court's 1962 ruling that mandatory prayer in schools
was unconstitutional.[54] Its propaganda ranged more widely still. It published proposals for the confiscation of Jewish wealth and its redistribution
to patriotic Americans. Lyndon Johnson, it complained in the late 1960s,
was planning gun control legislation to ensure the people did not resist
tyranny. In a cover article in the following decade, the *Thunderbolt* urged
that America should 'Mine the Mexican Border!' Over a million Mexican
illegal immigrants were crossing the border each year. Less than 10 per cent
of Mexicans were white, and the vast number of Mexicans and others
pouring into America was threatening to destroy the country's white
majority. But the planting of mines along the border with warning signs in
Spanish would soon bring the invasion to an end.[55]

Among the publications it sold was a pamphlet on 'Jewish Ritual
Murder' by Arnold Leese, the leader of an anti-Semitic group in inter-war

Britain, the Imperial Fascist League. Described in the *Thunderbolt* as explaining 'in detail the charges which had the Jews expelled' from 'every country in Europe', the pamphlet had accused Jews of murdering Christian children as part of a religious ritual. (The party also reprinted what it described as the Jewish ritual murder issue of the German Nazi magazine, *Der Stürmer*).[56] In the mid-1980s, the *Thunderbolt* published an article in praise of the Waffen SS. It had recruited some half a million non-German Europeans in its fight against Bolshevism. It had been, the paper suggested, a pan-European army, the finest fighting organization of the Second World War and perhaps in the whole of history.[57] The NSRP was an early champion of Holocaust revisionism. Attacking the Eichmann trial, in the early 1960s the *Thunderbolt* declared that since most Jews were communists, it was inevitable that some had been tried and executed. Eichmann had done 'his duty as a Christian patriotic German soldier in a war against world Communism, and against world Jewry'. But it was a 'great lie' that six million Jews had been killed by the Nazis.[58]

Despite its sympathies for the Third Reich, the NSRP was a bitter foe of the ANP. In 1962, the *Thunderbolt* accused Rockwell of only pretending to be a patriot while really working for Jewish interests. Fields refused to withdraw the claim, and Rockwell brought a libel suit. In 1965, the suit was settled out of court, and Fields published a retraction in the *Thunderbolt*.[59] But if the NSRP was hostile to Rockwell's group, it was considerably more favourable to the Klan. In the same period that he was initially organizing the NSRP, J. B. Stoner had organized his own Christian Knights of the KKK. In one issue of his *Klan Bulletin*, for instance, he had attacked the marriage of 'negro entertainer' Sammy Davis Jr to 'a blond white woman'. 'The Jews are happy to have mixed degenerate marriages', it declared, 'because they can use them as examples to innocent young White boys and girls'. As we have noted, Stoner had been an active Klansman in the 1940s. Between his two periods in the Klan, Stoner had formed the Christian Anti-Jewish Party. One of its local chairmen was the later leader of the National Knights, James Venable.[60]

Links with the Klan continued. In 1965, the *Thunderbolt* advertised a meeting in which Fields would speak alongside leading figures in the UKA, urging 'all Patriotic groups to Unite behind the KKK'. The same issue included an article asking what Nathan Bedford Forrest would do about the second Reconstruction of the South. After the Civil War, the article declared, 'the Negro' had taken over 'an occupied Southland', and it had been necessary to 'use force, pressure, and terror' to drive him out of office. Eventually 'the Whiteman was once again master of his own house', but now, a century on, 'the Blackman is once again taking control of the voting box'. If Bedford Forrest returned, he would fight to save America 'from Jewish-financed race-mixing and Communist treason'. Direct action was needed, and needed now, and with a thousand men like Bedford Forrest, the problem could be solved 'overnight'. In the early 1990s, Fields was included among the speakers at a rally organized by Dave Holland of the Southern White Knights and addressed by Thom Robb. Later in the decade, he addressed a dinner organized by another grouping, the Federation of Klans. But while willing to work with different Klans, he clearly had a preference. At the beginning of the decade, he discussed the splintered world of Klandom. Shelton and Duke had been among 'the many fine heads' the Klan had had since the Second World War. Today there was a large number of Klan groups. But only Thom Robb had built a real national Klan. (Indeed, in the mid-1990s, when Robb opened his new headquarters, the *Truth At Last* reported that Fields was 'the guest speaker and covered the subjects of non-White immigration and the dangers of interracial marriage'.)[61]

Throughout its history, the NSRP has been associated with the Klan. It has been linked too with violence. In late 1958, an Atlanta synagogue had been bombed, and members of the local NSRP were accused of the attack. None were convicted, and the author of the book on the case speculates if some of the accused were guilty and whether J. B. Stoner may have been involved. In the early 1980s Stoner was found guilty of the bombing of a church in 1958. During the three and a half years he served in prison, the party imploded. An earlier split in the 1960s had led to the creation of a breakaway American States Rights Party. This had left little after-effect, but twenty years later, the impact of internal tensions was more serious. Fields was accused of diverting his energies into another group, the New Order, Knights of the KKK, and lost control of the *Thunderbolt* and the NSRP. As a result of court action, he regained control of the paper, subsequently renamed as the *Truth At Last*. The party, however, passed out of existence.[62] Fields' paper continued to wield an influence within the Klan. Talking to one interviewer, for instance, the Southern White Knights' Dave Holland declared that the *Truth At Last* was valuable for its information on Jewish ritual murder. He produced an article which discussed an episode of the Oprah Winfrey show in which a young woman had spoken of the 'ritual murder of infants by Jews'. When 'you read it in Dr. Fields', Holland declared, 'you've got the real lowdown'.[63] But if Fields was both supportive of the Klan and had supporters within it, when he chose to join an organization, it was not the Klan. In 1993 he was elected secretary of the newly created America First Party. A decade later, the National Alliance published a letter from him. He had decided to become a member of the Alliance, and he intended to use his paper, the *Truth At Last*, to build the organization. The split in the organization, however, led to Fields' paper aligning instead with National Vanguard.[64]

In this chapter we have considered groupings shaped by the Southern fight against segregation, while in Chapter 2, we considered those most shaped by national socialism. Although a useful distinction, it is in no way a perfect one. As Fields' recent decision should remind us, a commitment to racism could draw an activist to both the Klan and National Vanguard. Likewise, both the United Klans of America and the Knights of the Ku

Klux Klan saw it as appropriate to publish material by the National Alliance. We will return to the vexed question of fluidity between national socialism and other strands of the extreme right in Chapter 9. In the next chapter, however, we will discuss a different question. The Patriot movement argues that neither the Klan nor national socialism should be the key reference point for its challenge to America's rulers. But only some of its components are on the extreme right, and it is not always easy to clearly demarcate them.

4   Not all Patriots

In previous chapters, we discussed both those who look to early twentieth-century Germany and those who look to the American South for the central reference points in their extreme right politics. In this chapter we will consider a movement which looks back to the American Revolution for inspiration.

Those who fought for America's independence were known as Patriots, and in recent decades, a new Patriot movement has emerged. The influence of the original Patriots is very clear. Some of the movement's adherents wear patches showing the Minutemen of the 1770s, and in one account, a Patriot writer recalls the American Revolution. At Lexington and Concord, citizen soldiers had used their muskets to begin the fight for America's freedom, and George Washington had declared that 'Firearms stand next in importance to the Constitution'. They were, he declared, 'the American people's liberty teeth'. What is needed now, the writer argues, is a struggle to protect what the original rebels had fought to secure.[1]

The American Constitution, Patriots hold, had sought to create a government that would preserve freedom. It had taken on powers, however, that were incompatible with what the Founding Fathers envisaged. This is linked, for instance, to Patriot concerns with the Second Amendment. Gun control, Patriots contend, is not intended to reduce crime or protect the innocent. Instead, its real purpose is to disarm the people and protect the over-mighty government. There are other fears. In mid-1994, for instance, one Patriot newsletter claimed that the government was planning to listen in to all telephone conversations. Anti-government feeling is linked too with opposition to environmental regulation.[2] But, as this example suggests, Patriots are not only opposed to what they see as the federal government's attacks on their rights. Often, they object too to what they see as the economic dispossession of Americans. In 1913, they note, legislators had set up the Federal Reserve. Americans believed that this meant that the government controlled the money supply. But it did not. What the Federal Reserve Act really did was give 'a handful of private international bankers the privilege to inflate and deflate the economy and enlisted for its enforcer – the government'.[3]

If Patriots frequently see the banking system as dispossessing Americans, they are often hostile too to the Internal Revenue Service. The *Communist Manifesto*, they argue, included a demand for a progressive income tax, and this is exactly what the IRS is enforcing today. It was seeking to plunder the people and its principal tool was fear, 'the tool of tyrants. . . . This is a direct violation of the Constitution.'[4]

Patriots link their opposition to government and international financiers to a wider conspiracy. Sinister forces, they declare, have set up a range of secretive organizations to undermine America. The Council on Foreign Relations, for instance, was set up in 1921, while the Trilateral Commission was established over fifty years later. The ostensible aim of such bodies was to promote international cooperation. The real objective, however, was to bring national sovereignty to an end and put a 'one-world government' in its place.[5]

Not all Patriots hold such theories. For some, only the tax laws or attempts to restrict gun ownership are at issue. But for those who oppose international finance, fight against secretive conspiracies and fear the coming of one world government, there are long traditions that can be called on. As early as the 1790s, some Americans were denouncing the Illuminati for seeking to subvert the new republic while in the following century, Populists were only one of several movements to mobilize against bankers. Both these concerns have continued into the twentieth century, and one Patriot pamphlet, for instance, quotes a magazine from the 1950s describing the efforts by 'The invisible Money Power' to enslave mankind. The pamphlet refers too to the formation of the Illuminati in the late eighteenth century. This organization, it goes on, was based on 'the very plan of world domination that is still in use today to enslave the world's masses'.[6] The same pamphlet also discusses the most important element of Patriot conspiracism. In 1990, it notes, President Bush had declared that the Gulf War made it possible 'to move toward an historic period of cooperation. Out of these troubled times . . . a new world order can emerge'. This pronouncement, the pamphlet declared, was proof of what had been 'long planned and covertly implemented'.[7]

The notion of a conspiracy to impose a new world order has long been in circulation. In the 1950s, Patriots have noted, the Council on Foreign Relations called for a 'new international order' in which nations would become interdependent. In the 1960s, they claim, the American government laid plans to give up its armed forces and allow the world to fall under the control of a UN Peace Force. For sections of the right, another force was of even greater importance. Communism, it was feared, could take over America and, as we will discuss, this was a fear that Patriots expressed in the 1970s and 1980s. But the Soviet Union eventually collapsed, and fears of a plot against America gravitated to other sources. Above all, there was the United Nations. In the 1990s, Patriots became convinced that vast numbers of 'combat ready' United Nations troops had been concealed on

American soil. Some were encamped in National Forests, others were stationed in US Army bases. Others still were stationed in Canada and in Mexico, and their purpose was all too clear. 'It doesn't take a genius to figure it out! We're being set up for a takeover by the United Nations – the enforcement arm of the New World Order!'[8]

If Patriots can believe in concealed UN troops, they often believe that plotters against America have already made other preparations. Reports of unmarked black helicopters in the skies over California or near the Canadian border are linked with plans for the New World Order. So too are reports that the government has set up large numbers of detention camps. Their purpose, they suggest, is to hold gun owners and anyone who will not cooperate with those 'who are trying to enslave America and turn it into a totalitarian cesspool'.[9] This belief in conspiracy permeates how Patriots understand all of the developments to which they object. President Kennedy, it is suggested, was not the victim of a single assassin but had been murdered by a secret group which controlled the CIA. Even natural cataclysms are seen by Patriots as proof of the conspiracy's ability to use secret weather modification technology to secure its sinister goals.[10]

In the decades that it has existed, the Patriot movement has taken a wide variety of forms. In the early 1970s, for instance, the Identity preacher William Potter Gale produced a 'Guide for Volunteer Christian Posses'. Since the formation of the Republic, he argued, the county had been the true seat of government for the citizens who lived in it. The county sheriff was 'the only legal law enforcement officer', and he had the power to mobilize men aged between eighteen and forty-five and form a posse. If he refused to do so, citizens could still form a posse. Officials who violated the Constitution should be arrested and put on trial before a citizen jury. If found guilty, they should be taken to 'a populated intersection of streets in the township and at high noon be hung there by the neck, the body remaining until sundown, as an example to those who would subvert the law'.[11]

In 1983, another leading Posse figure, James Wickstrom, was jailed for impersonating a government official (he had signed documents as an officer of a 'Constitution Township' in Wisconsin). Like Gale, Wickstrom was an Identity preacher. In 1980 he was also a Constitution Party candidate for the Senate. (Gale had been a Constitution Party candidate some twenty years earlier.) Wickstrom declared that the government, not the Federal Reserve, should issue money, and officials of the 'jew communist banks' could be tried for treason and, if found guilty, hanged. The same fate, he went on, would meet all elected officials who had 'upheld the unlawful banking practices'. His attack on the bankers was concentrated on the farm foreclosures that were devastating the countryside during the period. The government, he declared, had encouraged farmers to buy more land and equipment, plunging them into debt, but were now refusing to help them. The bankers were planning to seize the land, he went on, and 'the White Christian American' would have to surrender or fight back. In Wickstrom's account, Jesus had declared, 'Bring mine enemies before me and slay them', and in the early 1980s, he and Gale broadcast sermons over a Kansas radio station, in one of which Gale had declared:

> You're damn right I'm teaching violence! You better start making dossiers, names, addresses, phone numbers, car license numbers, on every damn Jew rabbi in the land. ... If you have to be told any more than that, you're too damn dumb to bother with.[12]

This combination of anti-Semitism and violence was particularly demonstrated by the fate of a North Dakota Posse activist, Gordon Kahl. In early 1983 he had attended a meeting 'to restore the power and prestige of the U.S. Constitution'. (Discussions had particularly centred on plans to create a Posse township.) On the way home he and his son became involved in a shoot-out with federal marshals, two of whom were killed. In a subsequent letter, he declared that one of the nation's Founding Fathers had predicted that if Jews were not excluded from the country, within 200 years Americans would be slaving in the fields for them. This had now happened and America was 'a conquered and occupied nation'. Four months later he was tracked to an Arkansas farm and both he and a sheriff died in the subsequent gunfight.[13]

Soon after Kahl's death, another Patriot paramilitary grouping emerged. In July 1984, forty-four Patriots gathered to establish a Committee of the States. 'We, the People', they declared, '... are the Lords and Masters of this self-governing Republic known as the United States of America', and Congress was subject to removal from office and replacement by the Committee of the States.[14] Gale was the central figure in the new group, and in an audiotape circulated the same year, he declared that the government was depriving Americans of their God-given rights and imposing unlawful taxation, and just as the colonists of the eighteenth century had risen in revolution, so a second revolution was brewing today. The 'shot at Concord Bridge hasn't been fired yet'. But it soon would, and when it did, 'the King's magistrates had better head for England, or they're gonna be hung by the neck'.[15]

The Committee of the States engaged in training in ambushes and attacks on buildings. It, however, did not survive. In 1985 a number of IRS employees had been sent documents declaring that the Committee was in session for the purpose of indicting officials who sought to subvert the Constitution. Any interference with the Committee's activities, the document noted, would result in a death penalty. In late 1987 Gale and other members were put on trial for a conspiracy to threaten IRS officials. They were found guilty and sentenced to terms of imprisonment.[16]

Patriots, however, have set up other armed groupings. In 1977 John Harrell launched the Christian-Patriots Defense League. He organized regular 'Freedom Festivals' on his estate in Illinois, one of which included classes on Guns and Ammunition, First Aid, Taxation and 'the Communist Conspiracy and the Real Enemy Behind that Conspiracy'.[17] America, he believed, would fall prey to a communist invasion, and the only area that could be held would be a 'Golden Triangle' stretching from the Canadian border to Texas and northern Florida. God's punishment for 'a wayward nation', he declared, was to let it be taken over by its enemy. But 'a remnant of patriots' could then rebuild America.[18]

The CPDL involved prominent Christian Identity figures. One, Jack Mohr, was National Defense Coordinator of its affiliate, the Citizens Emergency Defense System. Another, Sheldon Emry, reporting on the League's 1979 gathering to supporters of his ministry, declared that he agreed with the organization's policy. At least 80 per cent of those who attended, he reported, were Identity believers. The CPDL was not the only armed Patriot group of the period. In 1976 another Identity preacher, James Ellison, set up an encampment on the Arkansas-Missouri border. Two years later he launched another paramilitary group, the Covenant, the Sword and the Arm of the Lord. The purpose of the group, it declared, was 'to build an Ark for God's people during the coming tribulations on the earth'. The Arm of God would 'administer judgment in the days to come', when God would raise up 'a remnant out of the nations ... to be manifested as mature Sons of God, who walk in His image upon this earth, and who will rule and reign upon earth as His Elect'.[19] The Jews, the CSA observed, were 'constantly gaining power and influencing our people into bondage' and the economy was almost bankrupt. 'Many Patriots', it declared, were expounding the Constitution but few were 'prepared to make war with the Beast'. War, however, was inevitably coming to America.[20]

The CSA took part in the CPDL's Freedom Festival. But it also organized its own Endtime Overcomer Survival Training School, in which attendees received training in urban warfare, wilderness survival and 'Christian martial arts'. Its 1982 annual convocation, addressed by three non-CSA figures, Jack Mohr, Robert Miles and Richard Butler, was advertised as being for 'White Patriotic, *Serious* Christians', with classes on weapon shooting, nuclear survival, 'Racial truths' and 'The Jews'. The CSA was also involved, however, in other activities, and in 1985 its compound was raided by federal officers. After a three-day siege, a surrender was negotiated, and a large number of illegal weapons was discovered. In the subsequent trial, a CSA plan to attack the Oklahoma federal building was revealed. (Members had also stolen cars, carried out arson attacks, and bombed gas pipeline and electricity transmission lines.) Ellison received a twenty-year prison sentence, subsequently reduced to five years following his agreement to testify against other racists.[21]

Patriots were extensively involved in paramilitary training in the 1980s and, as we will see, they have continued to engage in it. It would be a mistake, however, to assume that Patriots necessarily organize or engage in such activity, or that, if they do, it is their greatest priority. Many, for instance, have been involved in seeking to change the legal system. The courts, they argue, are seeking to impose unjust laws on those who come before them. On occasion they seek to challenge court proceedings from within. Another approach has been to seek to organize a wholly separate legal system. Gale had argued in his 'Guide for Volunteer Christian Posses' that the existing courts were unlawful and had called instead for the creation of Citizen Juries. In the early 1970s, Posse activists in Michigan announced they had established a grand jury 'in accordance with ... the CHRISTIAN COMMON LAW', and Patriots continued to organize along these lines subsequently. The Common Law Supreme Court of Oregon, for instance, was set up in 1995, declaring that in possession of rights which they would not 'waive to any government', citizens had the authority to establish their own courts. The same year a 'Supreme Court in common law' in Idaho described itself as 'pursuant to our organic law under Magna Carta'.[22]

Common law courts have often been involved in issuing property liens in an attempt to enforce their judgements against officials. Patriots have also created their own monetary system in which specially created 'certified bankers checks' are paid into banks and the consequent balances used to purchase items or pay debts. In 1995 one group, the Freemen, occupied the Montana farm of one of their members who had lost it to auction as a result of failing to make payments on federal loans. The group declared themselves to be a township with their own judges and law officers, and in the words of one admiring Patriot, 'deposited billions of dollars in liens' and had then written checks to pay off credit card companies and purchase computer equipment from a local wholesaler. They organized seminars in how to do likewise, and ultimately, were the subject of a protracted federal siege and terms of imprisonment.[23]

If the Patriot movement involves a wide variety of groups, it involves too a rich array of publications. Originally published by the Oregon-based Citizens Bar Association, the *CBA Bulletin*, subsequently the *American's Bulletin*, has recommended *The Protocols of the Learned Elders of Zion* and published material by Identity writers.[24] In recent years, however, it has concentrated on challenges to the legal system, disputing the validity of driver's licenses and arguing that Americans should reject federal citizenship and reclaim their rights as sovereign citizens.[25] Another publication, the *Patriot Report*, is produced by an Identity believer, George Eaton. It has made reference to the belief that whites are God's chosen race, but has focused on the new world order and the need to resist it. (One issue, for instance, discussed how 'conspirators for global government' had been at work for decades. Another reprinted an attack from the late 1960s on 'the Invisible Government' threatening America's freedom. The author was General Del Valle.)[26] A third periodical, the *Free American*, has reprinted *The Protocols* but has also publicized other conspiracy theories. It has claimed, for instance, that a key role in the conspiracy was being played by the Vatican, but has been most concerned with attacking government. Part of the plot, it claims, is the hypnosis of vulnerable subjects so that they become mind-controlled assassins.[27]

The periodical which has been most popular among Patriots, however, has been the *Spotlight*. Its first issue reported on a gathering of Posse Comitatus and anti-tax activists. It quoted a Posse spokesman (and Liberty Lobby activist) as arguing that 'the only obstacle' to communist world domination was private gun ownership by Americans, and later editions have given wide circulation to Patriot concerns. Its hostility to banking is expressed, for instance, through Christian Identity pastor Sheldon Emry's *Billions for the Bankers Debts for the People*. Instead of Congress creating money, he declared, the Federal Reserve Act had passed the power to the bankers. They had deliberately brought about the Depression in the 1930s, and today America was ruled 'by a system of Banker-owned Mammon that has usurped the mantle of government ... and set about to pauperize and control our people'. In the 1990s, one Patriot publication remarked, it published 'excellent' stories on 'UN troops in America' and 'Russia's men and equipment in our country' while, in the aftermath of 9/11, its successor, the *American Free Press,* was vociferous in its claims that the American government was concealing the truth about the attacks.[28]

The *Spotlight*'s importance has been particularly noticeable in the emergence during the 1990s of the most important Patriot grouping, the militia movement.[29] The Second Amendment had not only defended 'the right of the people' to bear arms but placed it in the context of the necessity of a 'well-regulated Militia' for 'the security of a free state'. In time, a distinction arose between the idea of an organized militia, the National Guard, and other citizens, the 'unorganized militia'. It is unclear when Patriots first became convinced that the unorganized militia needed to be revived. As early as 1968, one Patriot document, *The Declaration of the Third Continental Congress*, called for the creation of a parallel government, one element of which would be state militias based on 'family units of honest citizens'. That Congress was linked with a faction of the Constitution Party, one of whose members was Gordon Kahl.[30]

In 1979, at the first conference of the Citizens Emergency Defense System, a resolution was passed declaring that 'as free men' they would 'exercise our Constitutional rights' to organize 'the unorganized militia'. Certainly the idea had spread by the late 1980s. A militia was active in Oregon while in a 1987 sermon at Gale's church, the speaker had declared:

> Pay attention you Unorganized Militiamen ... Jesus Christ has ordered you to arm yourselves ... you should keep your ammunition dry, and be ready to go. Just like your ancestors were at Concord Bridge ... we'll take this nation back. And we won't lose it this time.[31]

It would take, however, developments in the early 1990s to spread the idea across the nation.

Just as the death of Gordon Kahl in the early 1980s did not lead to the creation of a militia movement, this was likewise true of the violent death of another Patriot at the beginning of the 1990s. Randy Weaver, an Idaho Identity believer, had failed to attend a court hearing on firearms charges, and when federal marshals were discovered on his land, both one of them and Weaver's fourteen-year-old son were killed. The siege that followed resulted in an FBI sniper killing his wife.[32] Among the Patriot responses to the Weaver shootings was a gathering of '160 Christian leaders' at Estes Park, Colorado, organized by Identity pastor Pete Peters. A series of committees was set up, which discussed a range of possible measures, ranging from the circulation of petitions to the setting up of Grand Juries. The meeting called for establishment of a 'Christian civil body politic', and considered what could be done about the government's 'police-state tactics'. Among the speakers were former Klansman and Identity believer Louis Beam, and Baptist pastor Greg Dixon. The Identity paper, *Jubilee*, had offered to serve as 'an information distribution center' for the Estes Park gathering, and in its subsequent report described Dixon arguing that churches should set up militias and some of the participants discussing 'leaderless resistance – a concept where Yahweh gives each man his inspiration for defensive action'. Neither the Weaver siege nor the Estes Park gathering, however, would spark the creation of a militia movement. It would take another confrontation with the federal government before this would come about.[33]

In 1993 in Waco, Texas, a fringe religious group, the Branch Davidians, was raided by the Bureau of Alcohol, Tobacco and Firearms searching for illegal weapons. The raid resulted in the death of four federal agents and a protracted FBI siege. After fifty-one days, the authorities pumped CS gas into the building, a fire broke out and over eighty adults and children were killed. Already angry over proposals for gun control, Patriots saw Waco as proof of their fears that the federal government would use force against gun-owners and religious believers.[34] In 1994 militias began to emerge, and opponents noted the involvement of extreme rightists in their launch.

This was particularly true in the case of the Militia of Montana. Its most prominent figure, John Trochman, was once again an Identity believer who in 1992 had declared himself 'a free white Christian man' who had never 'knowingly been a citizen of the United States'.[35] The organization he subsequently launched produced its own newsletter, *Taking Aim*, and sold a variety of publications, ranging from books revealing UN troop locations or exposing the Illuminati conspiracy to paramilitary training manuals. Among its own publications was a version of the Declaration of Independence, in which new accusations were added to those made by the original Patriots. In the 1770s, the British monarchy had been accused of stationing foreign troops on American soil, protecting them from prosecution and waging war upon Americans. In the revised version, the American government was accused of bringing in UN troops and launching attacks on Waco, the Weaver family and elsewhere.[36] At the beginning of 1995, the

Spotlight published an article by the Patriot writer J. B. Campbell. As long ago as 1989, he declared, he had called 'for a rising of the militia against the criminals who have usurped the United States government'. Now, with the assault first on the Weaver family, then on the Branch Davidians, this had finally come about. The Militia of Montana had helped thousands to form militias in other states and provided many of the photographs that the *Spotlight* had published of foreign military equipment on American soil. Campbell had moved to Montana, he declared, to help the Militia. 'Our friend Louis Beam recently pointed out that a man can join the armed forces and serve the United Nations or he can join the militia and defend America. Montana is probably where the fighting will begin.'[37]

Identity believers were active in other militias. One militia in Washington, for instance, was led by Mark Reynolds, an Identity adherent, while in 1998, the Michigan Militia Corps split over an attempt to rewrite the organization's rules, in part to give the leadership the power to exclude Christian Identity believers who were accused of having infiltrated the Corps.[38]

For sections of the militias, as for the Christian-Patriots Defense League or the Covenant, the Sword and the Arm of the Lord, extreme right politics and preparing for guerilla war are bound together. But is this true of Patriots as a whole? We have already noted that not all Patriots engage in paramilitary activity. But a more important question is whether the Patriot movement as such should be seen as part of the extreme right.

From an early stage, a number of writers have argued that it should. The American Jewish Committee's Kenneth Stern, for instance, argued in the mid-1990s that anti-Semitism was central to the militia movement. John Trochmann was crucial, as was the *Spotlight*, and it was all but impossible to attend a militia meeting without encountering racist publications. Furthermore, militia conspiracy theories were 'rooted in the *Protocols of the Elders of Zion*'. In the same period, another author, the Southern Poverty Law Center's Morris Dees, focused his attention on Estes Park. The Weaver shooting had 'ignited the militia movement', but Peters' gathering had produced 'a unified strategy'.[39] This argument has continued to be raised in later publications. In one recent study, the militias are portrayed as descended from the Patriot paramilitary groupings of previous decades. Another writer has suggested that such groups as the Order and Aryan Nations 'provided a template of paranoia and anger from which the militias drew their ideas'. The belief in a New World Order, he claims, was 'tightly linked' to the theory advanced in the *Protocols*, while the Estes Park gathering 'laid the groundwork for the new militia movement'.[40] In part, this argument focuses on the activities of racists in the militia movement, in part on the influence of the *Spotlight*. But it also revolves around the prominence of conspiracy theory among Patriots, and in particular their attacks on international finance.

But is this convincing? As we implied at the beginning of this chapter, Patriots hold different beliefs. Unlike Nazis or Klansmen, they are not defined by adherence to a particular body of thought but see America's problems in very different ways. They do not all believe in a particular conspiracy theory, and those who believe in an overarching conspiracy hold diverse theories of what it entails.

To understand this, we need to go back to the roots of such theories. The belief that the Illuminati are the master conspirators first emerged in the 1790s among French counter-revolutionaries. It did not have an anti-Semitic colouration and only took this on, first, when one of the early writers on the Illuminati, Abbé Barruel, reworked his original theory and second when an early twentieth century British writer, Nesta Webster, produced an interpretation of events which linked both the French Revolution and the Russian Revolution to the Illuminati and the Jews. As we have seen, an anti-Semitic rendering of the Illuminati theory was taken up in the 1930s by Gerald Winrod. (In the 1950s, it was also taken up by another extreme rightist, William Carr.)[41] But the Illuminati theory was most importantly taken up by the leading force of the post-war radical right, the John Birch Society.

The French Revolution, the Society's leader claimed in the mid-1960s, had been a rehearsal for what the world would face in the twentieth century. Whether communism was a continuation of the Illuminati was unclear but likely. Such a far-reaching theory could easily be expanded yet further, and a 1971 book by Society author Gary Allen emphasized the involvement of bankers in the conspiracy. It attacked the Rothschilds, but also criticized 'Anti-Semites' who, it declared, were playing 'into the hands of the conspiracy by trying to portray the entire conspiracy as Jewish. Nothing could be further from the truth.'[42] As we discuss in Chapter 8, it has come under fire from the extreme right for refusing to accept its approach. Instead, the Society claimed, the conspiracy was raceless, and this confrontation between rival conspiracisms has continued in the Patriot movement. When we examine Patriot writings, we can find both radical right and extreme right sources, even in the same volume. This is true, for instance, of James Wardner's *The Planned Destruction of America* or Gurudas' *Treason. The New World Order*. Both are sold by the Militia of Montana and the latter drew on both Gary Allen and British extreme rightist A. K. Chesterton. But neither of these books argue a Jewish conspiracy theory and Gurudas explicitly rebuts it. The real conspiracy, he argues, is money. 'There is no Jewish conspiracy', and when some people use anti-Semitism to attack the bankers, this not only slanders a race but discredits conspiracy theory in general.[43]

The conviction that the Trilateral Commission or the Council on Foreign Relations are planning to destroy America's independence need not then be an indication of identification with the extreme right. Nor need the belief that the ultimate enemy is the Illuminati, the Money Power (or both) prove that Patriots are necessarily anti-Semites. What has to be present is an explicit link between the alleged conspiracy and the race of the conspirators, and this has been expressly excluded by some Patriots.

More strikingly, the Patriot movement has been divided by the presence of racists in its ranks. Two years to the day after the Waco conflagration, a devastating explosion killed 167 people at a federal building in Oklahoma City. The man initially arrested for the attack, Tim McVeigh, had gone to Waco during the siege. He did not give racial reasons for the bombing, but he had been an enthusiastic promoter of *The Turner Diaries*, William Pierce's portrayal of a racist group's terrorist campaign against the government. He had also tried to contact the National Alliance shortly before the attack, as well as contacting an Identity compound at Elohim City with the apparent intention of fleeing there after the bombing. Another Patriot, Terry Nichols, was found guilty of involvement in the bombing and a third man was convicted of concealing the conspiracy.[44] As we will discuss in Chapter 7, some on the extreme right have praised McVeigh's actions. Within the Patriot movement, however, it has been common to believe that McVeigh was only part of a wider conspiracy involving both the government and a number of extreme rightists. Much of this speculation has centred around Elohim City, but there are important differences as to how it is understood. The Militia of Montana, for instance, has claimed the existence of a conspiracy centred around Elohim City, while *Patriot Report* has criticized the circulation of such allegations by 'so-called Patriot journalists'. What some Patriots have done, however, is cite such a conspiracy as part of a case against the extreme right. In late 1996, an officer in the Alabama militia, Mike Vanderboegh, was joined by a number of other militia figures in signing the Alabama Declaration, which accused government agencies of having had advance information of the Oklahoma bombing while describing McVeigh and Nichols as part of an anti-Semitic terrorist group which hoped to 'destroy the American Republic' and bring about 'a Nazi American Reich'. Both white supremacists and the Clinton administration, it was argued, could seek to gain from a terrorist incident but militias were opposed to both.[45]

This view of the incompatibility of true patriots and the extreme right was not an isolated one. In 1997, for instance, the Virginia Citizen's Militia published an article on 'The Basics of Resistence'. It was vital, it argued, to work with 'every possible ally'. However, this did not apply to neo-Nazis, the Klan or other groups that believed in oppressing or destroying other ethnic groups.[46] As one racist website later reported, another militia officer, Southern Oregon Liaison and Intelligence Officer Carl Worden, has written more graphically. It was impossible, he claimed, to uphold the Constitution and believe in racism. 'Go fuck yourselves, Klan brothers.'[47]

In turn, extreme rightists have attacked many in the Patriot movement for refusing to pursue a racial policy. WAR, for instance, has published an attack by imprisoned Order member David Lane in which he claimed that the response of militia leaders to accusations of racism was to 'piss all over themselves as they hasten to recruit coloreds into their rainbow coalition'.[48] The National Alliance has also criticized Patriots. William Pierce has argued that the New World Order feared racial consciousness, not constitutionalists who avoid the issue of race. Such attacks are linked with criticisms of the priorities many Patriots often have adopted. Thus in one broadcast, Kevin Strom attacked 'Delusions on the Right'. Among the 'delusions' he attacked were ones associated with the Patriot movement. One was to rely on legal action, another to campaign for the abolition of the Federal Reserve. Strom attacked too 'the wilder "patriot" theories', from claims about common law courts to the rejection of driver's licenses, but he saved particular derision for claims that foreign troops were massing on the American border.[49]

But these criticisms are still not a sure guide to the boundaries between the extreme right and the radical right. If WAR or the National Alliance have been critical of the militias or the Patriot movement of which they are part, other extreme rightists have been favourable. This is true of the *Spotlight*, but is true too of others. Harold Covington's NSWPP, for instance, saw the militias as 'a very promising development'. They expressed white anger at 'the criminal regime in Washington', and as such were one more step towards Aryan revolution. Only some, he stated were 'openly racial nationalist'. Some were religious, many were conservative and some were 'even multi-racial'. But if the militia movement survived and prospered, some might form 'the future nuclei of the armed forces of the revolution'.[50] The NSWPP was not the only national socialist group to hope that at least some militias would advance the racist cause. National Socialist Vanguard saw one of its tasks as reporting on developments in the racist movement as a whole, and in mid-1994, it noted that there had been considerable discussion of the militias at the Aryan Nations Congress. Militia leaders ranged from Identity Christian to libertarian, and Aryan Nations members had even been asked to leave a Militia of Montana meeting. But if militias were not openly racist now, racists would either take them over or they would be torn apart. Early the following year, the group reprinted a Briefing Paper on the militia movement issued by the Bureau of Alcohol, Tobacco and Firearms. The Bureau noted the influence of Waco and opposition to gun control in their formation, but the National Socialist Vanguard's discussion focused on the role of racism. The militias, it commented, were 'becoming somewhat of an embarrassment' because of its leaders' attempts to convince people that they were not racist. But whatever the 'imperfections' of militias, it was important to keep them alive. Their members might already fear that a One World Government would enslave them for the benefit of international bankers. They could come to realize, however, that where communism was their enemy, national socialism was not. The militias would not only be a recruitment pool, but bring together those who were already racist and could become the leaders of 'future racial White Nationalist Militias, neighbourhood defense groups and even vigilante groups'.[51]

If National Socialist Vanguard saw promise in the militias, it had hopes for others in the Patriot movement. In the late 1980s, it wrote about an organization 'that specializes in tax reform and money matters, was against big business and was pro-Constitution. The organization's publication was not racial and did not discuss the Jewish problem.' It had purchased the organization's mailing list, and national socialist material had been sent out. The letters it had received in reply had included attacks on national socialism for being anti-Christian and unconstitutional. Some, however, were pleased to receive a document from a fellow-opponent of Zionism. The group went on to cite another example of what it saw as 'the potential support for the White Nationalist Movement that lies just below the surface'. The Citizens Bar Association, it commented, had recently undergone a metamorphosis. The speakers at its 1987 annual gathering had said nothing 'to promote the welfare of the White race', and its bulletin had called for restoring a constitutional republic. The 1988 gathering, however, was recognizably an Identity event, the bulletin now describing itself as 'A Voice of Opposition to Tyranny', and its book list included material by Pastors Pete Peters, Sheldon Emry and Jack Mohr.[52]

But in discussing differences on the right, diverse extreme right attitudes to the Patriot movement are just one complication. Extreme rightists, as we have seen, are also divided over national socialism. For Emry, for instance, Nazi Germany's financial policies had enabled it to recover from depression and 'it took the whole Capitalist and Communist world to destroy the German power over Europe' and bring it back 'under the heel of the Bankers.' Others, however, have even claimed that in reality national socialism had served Jewish interests. In the 1950s, Kenneth Goff published *Hitler and the 20th Century Hoax*, in which he argued not only that it was a lie that millions of Jews had been killed by the Nazis but that Hitler himself had been Jewish and a tool of communism. Goff had been an early Identity believer, and more recently, another believer, the Christian-Patriot Defense League's Jack Mohr, has argued that 'decent Christian Patriots' are being misled into supporting 'the discredited policies' of national socialism. As Goff had shown, however, Hitler had served Jewish interests and had been Jewish himself.[53] These ideas have spread to others on the extreme right. But there are still further complications in distinguishing between radical right and extreme right. If some extreme rightists can be bitterly hostile to national socialism, it is also the case that claims that foreign troops are already present in vast numbers on American soil or just over its border are not restricted to the radical right. Indeed, one of the leading exponents of such claims has been Jack Mohr. For over five years, he declared in the mid-1980s, he had been warning of the dangers of a communist take-over in Mexico. He had printed eye-witness reports on Soviet armour near the border, and photographs had been taken of heavy equipment transports capable of moving tanks. Soviet vehicles could be being concealed underground, and both Mongolian and North Korean troops had been reported. Another Christian Identity believer, Earl Jones, similarly claimed in the late 1980s that 'there is increasing evidence that the North Koreans have actually dug an elaborate system of tunnels' in the Mexican countryside 'and are living underground in them'.[54] Such claims have been harshly attacked by the prominent extreme rightist David Lane. He was particularly hostile to Mohr. In one speech, he asked his audience, 'Remember the story about millions of Commies hiding in tunnels near the Mexican border waiting to attack America?' He had told 'the particular deceiver that millions of Mexicans had walked across the border and were mating with many of our last White women, but retired colonels get big government checks, so they will never destroy our executor'. On another occasion, he made the same contrast between the supposed communist invaders and the actual Mexican ones, before declaring that 'the Colonel ... loved his money, his fairy tale religion and his false hero status more than the survival of his race'. But his argument was not with one particular Patriot. Long ago, he observed, he had 'coined the acronym C.R.A.P. for Christian Rightwing American Patriots', while Christian Identity had been created by government agents to neutralize resistance and mislead 'people to believe Christianity and America' were 'sacred entities of their race'.[55]

Not only are some Patriots on the extreme right, some on the radical right, but both radical right and extreme right have their own internal disputes. The real dividing line between extreme right and radical right lies around the nature of the conspirators each claims to detect. Yet even here we still have to be cautious.

That the Militia of Montana was led by an Identity believer did not mean that it only put forward an extreme right argument. (If so, it would not have sold Gurudas' book.) Even the *Spotlight* is more complex than we might assume. It has, for instance, published an article in the early 1990s claiming that the Waffen SS was a European army which had transcended petty nationalism to fight against communism.[56] But the *Spotlight* is not a typical extreme right publication, and one reason for its success in the 1980s and, to a lesser degree, in the 1990s, was its ability to take up Patriot concerns, whether with taxes, concealed UN troops or the need for militias, and play down the racial concerns so graphically displayed in the final issue of *Right*. The *Spotlight* is tailored to an audience that believes in conspiracies but would in many cases reject the language of a Pierce or a Rockwell, and as such it is tempting to see it not as an overt voice of the extreme right but as a bridge, intended to carry Patriots from a resentment of bankers or a fear of the New World Order to the belief that the enemy was Jewish.

If a fondness for the *Spotlight* may not be a sure guide to the politics of its readers, even a belief in the *Protocols* is not a sure guide to someone's political identity. Not all anti-Semites believe that it is genuine; William Pierce, for instance, believed it to be written by an anti-Semite who was attempting to imaginatively portray what the Jewish conspiracy was seeking to achieve. More importantly, some on the radical right believe that the *Protocols* were deliberately created by the conspirators to mislead those who sought to expose them. Thus one prominent Patriot, William Cooper, reprinted the full text of the *Protocols* but with a warning declaring that whenever it referred to the Jews, this was a ploy to disguise the identity of the real conspirators. This claim, that the *Protocols* is both true and false, that it reveals a plot but seeks to camouflage the plotters, has been made by other writers. It is not, however, an argument that reveals a hidden extreme right agenda. Indeed, in commenting on Cooper, one Identity grouping complained that he was misleading Patriots.[57]

As this chapter has sought to demonstrate, the Patriot movement is an extraordinarily diverse phenomenon. It exists because of profound distrust of the direction that the American government has taken for decades. But it is also embittered at the power of international finance. This has propelled some Patriots towards creating common law courts and their own monetary systems. It has motivated some to form armed groups. And, whatever their organizational strategy, it has drawn them towards conspiracy theory. When asking why the political system has veered away from its eighteenth-century origins, or why farmers have been faced with bankruptcy, Patriots are drawn to explanations that uncover the power of a hidden elite. Often, that elite is taken to be international finance. But that theory is not an identifying mark of the extreme right. It is widespread among radical rightists, and the Patriot movement is a battleground between the two strands.

5   Race and religion

The American extreme right does not take one form. Where some look to the Third Reich, and others to the South, still others look to the American Revolution for inspiration. But the extreme right does not only differ on the moment in history with which it most closely identifies. As we will discuss, it differs too on how that moment can be recaptured, a disagreement which comes out both in its attitude to violence and its stance towards other sections of the right. But it also has other disputes. One, which we will turn to shortly, concerns the role of women. First, however, we will look at another area of contention. The American extreme right is divided on religion, and in the discussion that follows, we will examine a number of the different religious systems that have attracted its adherents. The first, and arguably still the most important, is Christian Identity.

As we noted earlier, the original Ku Klux Klan had seen itself as Christian. It believed in a Bible that had been understood to justify slavery before the end of the Civil War, and which justified segregation in the post-bellum South. In the twentieth century, this reading of Christianity continued to hold sway among many on the extreme right. As the century progressed, however, a new interpretation of how the Bible sacralized racism arose in extreme right ranks. This was Christian Identity, and to understand what it argues, we need to go back to nineteenth-century Britain.

It was here in the 1870s that the movement known as British Israelism came into existence. In the heyday both of the British empire and Victorian Christianity, it should not surprise us that the achievements of the first could be seen as integrally connected with the second. What was distinctive about British Israelism, however, was the proposition that the British were more than a particularly favoured nation. Its proponents claimed that Jews were only part of the people that had once inhabited Israel. Many Israelites, it was claimed, had been taken captive by the Assyrians, 700 years before the birth of Christ, and instead of returning to their homeland, they had seemingly disappeared from history. Yet at almost the same moment as they had been lost, another people had just as mysteriously sprung into existence. The British had become 'the greatest race on earth', but they had not known their true identity. Now, however, 'the lost are found', and the Saxons could be recognized as the Sons of Isaac, 'the national sons of God'.[1]

As Michael Barkun has noted, British Israel was initially challenged by a rival interpretation, that God's promise to Israel was not inherited by Britain but by Germany. In the context of the rivalry between the British empire and the German, this competing claim was defeated.[2] Yet space remained in the British Israel argument for the claims of other nations. The Israelites were described as leaving settlements behind as they trekked across Europe towards their ultimate destination (thus Denmark was supposedly where the tribe of Dan had tarried). An important role was also given to the United States. Israel had been described, one key writer declared, as having lost its first children. This should be seen as a reference to America's break with Britain, but in the future the mother country and the land that had separated from it would come together in pursuit of their rightful dominion.[3] British Israel privileged the British, supported the return of the Jews to Palestine and believed the United States to be crucial in God's plan. In the 1930s and 1940s, however, the doctrine underwent a mutation. In what was eventually to become known as Christian Identity, Britain diminished in theological significance, the Jews were now seen as the enemy and the United States was depicted as the promised land, the 'NEW JerUSAlem'.[4]

In the creation of Christian Identity, the central figure was a Klan organizer and close associate of Gerald L. K. Smith, Wesley Swift. In California in the mid-1940s, Swift created the Anglo-Saxon Christian Congregation which in 1956 became the Church of Jesus Christ, Christian.[5] Swift was not the only figure of significance in the early Christian Identity movement. In the mid-1960s, for instance, one figure, William Potter Gale, began to produce a periodical, *Identity*, and in a pamphlet which appeared earlier in the decade, he argued that the struggle against segregation was the result of a Jewish plan to put blacks 'in the same schools with Adam's young children', the ultimate aim being to 'destroy the Holy seed'. One of Swift's earliest associates, Bertrand Comparet, was also particularly important in the development of Identity. But it has proved to be highly fissiparous, and this was particularly noticeable among Swift's co-workers. One dispute in the 1960s, for instance, led to Gale breaking away. Comparet took Gale's side, while an argument following Swift's death in 1970 eventually resulted in a figure originally recruited by Gale, Richard Girnt Butler, moving to Idaho where later in the decade he would launch the most important Identity grouping, Aryan Nations.[6]

While predominantly organized through different ministries, Christian Identity has also exerted an influence on a number of extreme right political groupings. The National Knights of the Ku Klux Klan's periodical, for instance, declared that 'JESUS CHRIST WAS NOT A JEW' and recommended a key Identity text, *Tracing Your Ancestors*, to those who wanted to understand the rightness of segregation. Indeed, the later founder of Aryan Nations has described touring the South after his conversion to Identity, organizing those who had already heard Wesley Swift's taped preachings and bringing the message to Klan meetings. Nor was the Klan the only Southern racist grouping to show sympathy for Identity. The National States Rights Party claimed to be led by Christ, and some of the leading activists in the early party were Identity ministers. One figure, the Rev. Oren Potito, was president of the Eastern Conference of Swift's church while a particularly prominent NSRP activist, the Rev. 'Connie' Lynch, had ministered at several of Swift's churches.[7] In the late 1960s, the *Thunderbolt* announced the publication of a reprint edition of a classic racist text, *The Negro a Beast*. It contained an introduction by Stoner in which he declared that while the Christian religion was the religion of whites, the Jewish religion was 'Satan's religion'. Satan's forces included both 'his children, the Jews' and 'the black beasts'. When Carroll's book had been first published, no church in America preached that only whites were human. But now Wesley Swift's Church of Jesus Christ, Christian taught not only that blacks were beasts but that Jews were imposters and it was white Christians who were the true Israelites.[8]

Despite such interest, much of the Identity movement remained independent of pre-existing political groupings, and the American Nazi Party eventually sought to take advantage of its growing following. In 1962, the party magazine had declared that the ANP did not allow religion to enter its affairs and that 'the majority of our people are, shall we say, unreligious'. In 1964, Rockwell described himself as believing that there was some higher power but being agnostic as to what it was. But the party's *Stormtroopers' Manual*, while declaring the party's belief in religious freedom, had also declared that it supported Western Christian traditions, and the ANP subsequently described itself as standing for Christianity. Having been introduced to Identity by Richard Butler, he forged an alliance with Swift and encouraged one of his leading officers, Ralph Forbes, to create a Christian Identity ministry. 'You can gather in a nucleus and form a Church, which will seize all the little outfits trending this way already.' Forbes was long to remain active in Christian Identity circles. Rockwell's vision of winning over Christian Identity as a whole to his party, however, came to nothing.[9]

Instead some Identity ministers created their own political groupings. In the early 1970s, for instance, James Warner, formerly prominent in both the National States Rights Party and the American Nazi Party, launched the New Christian Crusade Church, revived the Christian Defense League (a group that had originally existed in the 1950s) and began producing *Christian Vanguard*, an explicitly Christian Identity publication that publicized Holocaust revisionism and offered free copies of *The International Jew* to new subscribers.[10] He was later to play a key role in Duke's Knights of the Ku Klux Klan, functioning both as its Louisiana Grand Dragon and its National Information Director. The California Grand Dragon, Tom Metzger, was also a minister in Warner's church, and the Knights' subsequent leader, Thom Robb, was likewise an Identity minister. The most important Christian Identity political vehicle, however, was Butler's Aryan Nations.[11]

In the first issue of its newsletter, Aryan Nations declared that 'The very foundation of faith and worship is Racial Truth, for with the Aryan, Christianity and Race are one. ... True Christianity seeks above all the preservation and increase of Aryan man.'[12] Aryan Nations was crucial in the spreading of Identity belief among extreme rightists, but this was not its only role. It was central in disseminating the idea that America was now under the control of ZOG, the Zionist Occupation Government.[13] It was crucial too to the spread of an idea that was to influence others on the extreme right: that instead of taking power in America as a whole, extreme rightists should instead migrate to the overwhelmingly white northwest of the country, and create a white nation there. Its most articulate exponent was former Klansman Robert Miles. 'White racialists', he declared to one Aryan Nations gathering, should move to Idaho and neighbouring states, 'buying land together or adjacent to each other and having families consisting of five and ten children'.[14] Aryan Nations was crucial too in bringing extreme rightists together. For many years it organized an annual congress attended by activists both from Identity groups and other sections of the extreme right. In 1982, for instance, it gave 'Aryans of Outstanding Valor' awards to Robert Miles, Louis Beam and J. B. Stoner. At the 1984 gathering, one speaker spoke on 'the unorganized militia' while another gave a lecture on intelligence gathering. After speeches by Miles and Beam, night exercises took place.[15]

Aryan Nations congresses were attended by such figures as the Christian Patriots Defense League's Jack Mohr and James Ellison, patriarch of the Covenant, the Sword and the Arm of the Lord. But these events were not only crucial in bringing together a range of activists, some of whom belonged to paramilitary groups. They also brought together some who were prepared to launch violent campaigns immediately. In Chapter 7 we discuss the robberies and murders carried out in the 1980s by one such grouping, the Order.[16]

Subsequently, members of the Order and a number of leading activists, including both Butler and Beam, were put on trial in Fort Smith, Arkansas. In the words of the indictment, the accused had 'Willfully and knowingly ... conspired ... to overthrow ... and to destroy by force the government of the United States and form a new Aryan nation'. The authorities had raided the Covenant, the Sword and the Arm of the Lord, and Ellison had been amongst those who subsequently testified against the accused. As Robert Miles was later to gleefully report, however, the jury did not believe that the prosecution had proved that he and the others had engaged in a seditious conspiracy, and the trial resulted in acquittal.[17]

While the Covenant, the Sword and the Arm of the Lord did not survive the 1980s, another Identity compound, Elohim City, provided a home for Ellison following his release from prison, and was also central to the emergence of yet another armed group, the Aryan Republican Army. (The group was responsible for a series of bank robberies in the mid-1990s.)[18] Aryan Nations continued to be active. Following an incident in 1998, however, in which Aryan Nations security guards assaulted a mother and son outside its compound, the organization was hit by a lawsuit brought by the Southern Poverty Law Center. The result was an award of $6.3 million in damages, and the consequent loss of the compound.[19] By then, however, the group was splintering.

A former Klan member, August Kreis had adopted Christian Identity and become a leading figure in the group which retained the name Posse Comitatus. He was subsequently appointed as Aryan Nations webmaster and coordinator of its activities in the Northeast. When the Southern Poverty Law Center lawsuit put Butler's possession of his Idaho compound under threat, Kreis offered his plot of land in Pennsylvania as a new base. Denouncing Butler's group as made up of 'weirdos, winos and clowns', at the beginning of 2002 Kreis and others launched a rival Aryan Nations.[20]

It was not the only splinter (other dissidents launched the Church of the Sons of Yahweh). In 2004 Butler died and both his group and that of Kreis moved location. Kreis announced that his faction had a new World Chaplain, the former leading Posse Comitatus activist James Wickstrom.[21] But if Aryan Nations has long been in crisis, Identity has been promoted by many other groupings. Some, for instance, continued to follow an early Identity leader, Dan Gayman, who had been among those who testified for the government in the abortive Order conspiracy trial. Others have looked to a Colorado-based pastor, Pete Peters, and his Scriptures for America or to an Idaho-based preacher, Dave Barley, and his America's Promise Ministries.[22] Beam himself became a prominent figure in *Jubilee*, an influential Identity bi-monthly which published articles on subjects ranging from 'Israeli terror' to the killing of abortion doctors. Identity groupings differed on a number of points, ranging from whether God should only be described as Yahweh to whether the Sabbath should be celebrated on Sunday or Saturday.[23] One area of difference, however, split the movement into warring factions. Both sides shared the belief that Jews were the enemy. The division, however, was over how this was to be understood in Identity theology.

For key thinkers, Jews were children of Satan. This belief was already evident in early writings by Swift and Gale.[24] The most important early discussion, however, was first published in the 1970s. C. L. Mange's *The Two Seeds of Genesis 3:15* describes how having failed in his revolt against God, Satan had decided 'to incarnate himself into the seed of Adam and bring forth a counterfeit seedline'. He had appeared to Eve in the Garden of Eden, and where Adam had placed his seed in Eve to produce Abel, Satan placed his seed in her to produce Cain. She had been deceived into thinking Cain had come from God, but he was 'the Seed of the Serpent' and the source of 'Black Magic. ... Secret societies and subversive movements'. During Israel's captivity among the Assyrians and its subsequent passage through Europe, the seed of Satan had come to control religious life in Palestine and it was the descendants of Cain, now known as Jews, who crucified Christ. They continued to conspire against the white race. The truth was revealed both in the Bible and in *The Protocols of the Learned Elders of Zion*, and as the final battle approached, it was 'no time to white-wash the offspring of Satan'.[25]

This notion of Jews as literally Satan's seed has continued to be crucial for Aryan Nations and other Identity groupings. A number of Identity figures, however, have come to reject the idea. As early as 1978, America's Promise Ministries published Stephen Jones' *The Babylonian Connection Between Ancient and Modern Religion*, which criticized unnamed figures 'who believe that the serpent sexually seduced Eve'. Other writers took up this argument, of which the key text is *Eve. Did She or Didn't She? The Seedline Hypothesis under Scrutiny* by Nebraska-based preacher Ted Weiland. Mange, he revealed, was really the veteran Identity preacher Dan Gayman, and he attacked his book as well as the writings of a number of other seedline authors. Cain, Weiland insisted, was described in the Bible as the son of Adam, not of Lucifer, while when John the Baptist described the Pharisees as a 'generation of vipers', he been using a metaphor, not revealing their descent from Satan. The seedline hypothesis, he declared, was not needed to distinguish true Israelites from 'today's Israelite impersonators'. It was not only a perversion of the Bible but it was more. The claim that Eve and Satan had had sexual relations had originated in ancient Jewish writings, and rather than basing themselves on Scripture, seedline believers had adopted the teachings of 'antichrists'.[26]

Defenders of the seedline doctrine have struck back fiercely. Much of the response has come from an Arkansas-based group, Kingdom Identity Ministries. In one of the pamphlets produced by its American Institute of Theology, it accused Pete Peters and David Barley of playing a leading role in 'Judaising Identity'. Much of the attack, however, centred on Weiland. His work, the author suggested, 'had all the marks of a considerable effort by a committee of Rabbis to destroy the most important anti-Jewish, Christian Doctrine'.[27] If this attack went unanswered, the pamphlet declared, then the ultimate result would be that the Identity faith would be undermined and Jews would be seen as fellow Israelites. But they were not; they were 'the progeny of Satan' and behind every conspiracy against Christian societies. It was right to see the Bible as containing a multitude of metaphors. But to describe Jews as descended from Satan was to speak literally, and when the Messiah returned Satan would be defeated and the Jews would be destroyed.[28]

It is not only advocates of the seedline doctrine who identify Christian Identity with an apocalyptic anti-Semitism. Charles Weisman, another writer attacked in the American Institute of Theology pamphlet, has portrayed Jews not as Satan's seed but as the products of Israelite intermarriage with women of other races. The Bible had described the descendants of these relationships as Edomites, named after the land to the south of the Dead Sea which they inhabited. But it had also said that Edom would know God's vengeance. What such prophecies foretold, Weisman declared, was that one day the white race would wipe out the Jews.[29] Supporters and opponents of the seedline doctrine are both capable of believing not only that they are God's chosen race but that Jews must be eliminated. Nonetheless, they are bitterly opposed to each other, and represent a fundamental schism in the Christian Identity movement.

Christianity, whether it takes an Identity form or not, is not the only religion on the American extreme right. As we will see, there are a number of other spiritualities which appeal to racists. Of these, the most important is Odinism. In 1930, an Australian writer, Alexander Rud Mills, published *The Odinist Religion: Overcoming Jewish Christianity.* Both before and after the Second World War, he attempted to organize a Church of Odin and in 1959 published an article in *Right.* The rise of Christianity, he held, marked a victory for Jews and the defeat of the ancient religion of the Nordic people. But the hammer of Thor, he declared, would bring the natural order back. (This was not the view of *Right* itself, which editorially presented Mills' view as an extreme response to liberal Christianity.)[30]

Odinism did gain adherents, however, most notably around the short-lived extreme right publication, the *Free American.* Odinism, it argued, was the only religion that fully supported the white race. It taught nobility, courage and race pride, and was the faith of the Nordic people before they were 'contaminated' by Judeo-Christianity.[31] Published by dissident national socialists, the *Free American* involved James Warner, who also published his own Odinist magazine, *Viking Age,* in which he announced that the leading figure in the *Free American,* Dan Burros, had become a believer. Following the failure of the magazine, Warner passed his Odinist material to a Canadian-based activist, Else Christenson.[32]

The belief that the true racial religion should be pre-Christian, however, has continued to be argued on the American extreme right. At the beginning of the 1970s, Christenson, now based in Florida, launched the *Odinist* which promoted both Norse religion and white nationalism. Others argued for a different understanding of Norse religion, Ásatrú (Icelandic for a belief in the gods). Here, however, a bitter conflict broke between those who understood paganism racially and those who believed it was relevant to anyone seeking religious truth. But this did not simply polarize Odinism and Ásatrú. Differences also emerged among Ásatrú adherents. In the 1980s and 1990s arguments along these lines appeared in the leading Ásatrú publication, *Vor Tru,* while in the late 1970s the main organization, the Ásatrú Free Assembly, denounced national socialism, declaring that white men were being driven to extremism because there was no 'well-known responsible organization working for white ethnic awareness'. Ásatrú continued to attract racists, but it was Odinism (or Wotanism, as it is sometimes called) that appears to exert more influence among them.[33]

The Order contained both Identity adherents and Odinists, and having been a leading figure in Aryan Nations, a leading Order member, David Lane, later converted to Odinism. It would be a group, Wotansvolk, run by his wife, Katja, which would be especially crucial in the spread of Odinism. David Lane, who had driven the car in the murder of radio talk-show host Alan Berg, was found guilty of racketeering, conspiracy and violating Berg's civil rights. He is serving a sentence of 150 years and has become known to much of the extreme right for what are described as his '14 Words', 'We must secure the existence of our people and a future for White children'. In 1994 he and his wife set up 14 Word Press and the following year, with another figure, Ron McVan, they established Wotansvolk. In 1999, 14 Word Press published *Deceived, Damned and Defiant. The Revolutionary Writings of David Lane*, in which he argued that whites could not share gods with other races. Wotan was 'the best blended representation of Allfather, the Creative force, and folkish needs for the White race today'. Christianity taught that the meek would inherit the Earth; Wotanism believed that fortune smiled on the brave. Christianity taught 'Love your enemies'. Wotanism taught 'Smite your enemies. ... Feed their bodies to vultures in the market place, that your next enemy depart in fear.'[34] Two years later it published McVan's book on Wotansvolk's beliefs, in which he argued that a race without its own belief-system could not prosper. The gods gave the people purpose, and while Wotanism had been 'forced underground by point of sword', it had revived among the Germanic peoples in the late nineteenth century and 'became manifest' during the world wars. Wotan symbolized the cosmic life source of the Aryan folk, and by recapturing the strength portrayed in the 'old myths', the people could regain the desire to seize control of their lives. No oak tree grew without soil and root, and through 'Wotansvolk and the 14 Words we can rebuild the foundation towards our highest potential and our destiny as Nature's finest'.[35]

Christian Identity and Odinism are not the only religions which have secured a following on the American extreme right. Some racists, for instance, have been drawn to occultism. In the late nineteenth century a Russian mystic, Helena Blavatsky, claimed to be have been initiated into a secret doctrine by hidden masters. She had founded the Theosophical Society, which claimed that those who would now guide the Aryan race had once ruled in Atlantis. We have seen earlier how William Pelley had carried ideas of an Aryan Atlantis into the racist politics of the 1930s. In the post-war extreme right, the NRP was particularly wedded to a racism which claimed legitimation through its knowledge of hidden mystical truths. In the early 1970s, reacting to early signs of what would later become known as New Age thinking, the NRP greeted what it described as the swing away from Judeo-Christianity to the ancient wisdom of the Aryan race found in such beliefs as Theosophy, witchcraft and Druidism. Judaism, Christianity and Islam had arisen in the Semitic deserts and had nothing to do with Aryans. Their religion had come from Atlantis, passed to India and Tibet and then travelled to Egypt and to Greece before manifesting again in the modern occult revival.[36]

In a series of later articles, NRP leader James Madole argued that Aryan man needed to understand his racial heritage and 'his forthcoming Divine Mission to create a higher type of humanity'. In the future, a New Atlantis would rise in America, in which 'the union of physical science with occult science' would create a new human race. The great Russian occultist Helena Blavatsky had sought to bring the truth to millions of Aryans whose minds were shackled. But as long as they remained Christian, they would remain 'a slave to the Jew who imposed this Semitic heresy upon the Aryan mind'.[37]

This attraction to religious belief systems that disavowed Christianity brought the NRP close to the most controversial of occultist manifestations, Satanism. As Jeffrey Kaplan has noted, the NRP had a friendly relationship with the Church of Satan and the party's Michigan organizer organized a Satanist group in Detroit, the Order of the Black Ram.[38] The party itself, as we have seen, passed away in the 1970s. Extreme right attraction to the so-called dark side of occultism did not, and in the 1990s re-emerged in the form first of the Black Order, then the White Order of Thule. For these groupings, if Christianity was the enemy, Odinism was not yet the answer. It needed to be blended with occultism. The White Order argued that those who stood for 'troth with the Old Gods and resurgence of the Tribes' should not exclude from their ranks 'those who profess loyalty to "Satan," the one true archetype of *defiance* and *rebellion* that this dying old Aeon has given us'. Young people, it suggested, were more likely to read Anton LaVey's *Satanic Bible* than *Mein Kampf*, and many of those already Satanists were racially conscious. Tapping into the latent energy of such a symbol could help the birth of a new order.[39]

Thus the Black Order argued that national socialism was essentially modern conscious paganism. It expressed how Aryans were and what their destiny was. It showed how to build a pagan warrior society and a race of higher beings. An article subsequently published by the White Order of Thule argued that national socialism was more than a political movement. Hitler had shown how Aryans could evolve 'towards the gods' and restore the connection between the race and the cosmos. But he was yet more than that. National socialism stood for the development of the human species as a whole, and the chance of any race to evolve. 'Adolf Hitler was the cosmos striving to evolve, in consciousness.'[40]

Following bitter disputes, the White Order of Thule dissolved in 2001. More recently, bitter disputes have broken out over the allegation that one of the National Socialist Movement's leading figures, Cliff Herrington, was involved with an occultist grouping led by his wife, the Joy of Satan. Another of the NSM's leading figures, Bill White, made public a wide range of allegations while a rival group, the American Nazi Party, expressed outrage at its receipt of a message from an NSM supporter signed 'HH &HS!',

the first denoting Heil Hitler, the second Heil Satan. Eventually, an increasingly bitter dispute led to the emergence of four breakaway groupings.[41] If a number of forms of extreme right occultism have emerged, other racist spiritualities have taken different directions. Writing in the NSWPP paper in the 1960s, William Pierce had argued that it was 'the spiritual nature' of national socialism that set it apart. During the 1970s he created a new doctrine, Cosmotheism, as the spiritual basis of the new order he sought. In 'Our Cause', a speech in the latter part of the decade, he argued that no individual or race existed as an end in itself. They were only parts of a whole, and this whole was continually evolving. This evolution involved the development of different races, and for the white race, 'this upward urge, this divine spark' had brought the potential for a new understanding. It was an understanding of why the earth had been born, the first amphibian had crawled out of the sea and why Jesus had fought the Jews. It was 'the path of the creator's self-realization' and 'if we ... heed the inner knowledge engraved in our souls ... we will once again be on the upward path ordained for us, and our destiny will be godhood'.[42]

Pierce attempted to persuade supporters to join him in West Virginia and build a Cosmotheist Community. He wrote pamphlets to describe what this would entail. In one pamphlet, *On Society*, he pictured a community which would be both church and state. It would be led by a hierarchy which would keep it moving forward toward higher levels of consciousness. In another publication, *The Path*, he pictured a 'community of Divine Consciousness, the Awakened Ones' who would be 'conscious agents of the Creator's Purpose' and resume the ascent towards Godhood.[43] In some ways, Pierce's ideas had been anticipated by Madole. In 1972, the *National Renaissance Bulletin* had argued that all life was a struggle to achieve Godhood, and had gone on to refer to the 'upward path' of evolution. But one crucial difference was that the NRP, influenced by Theosophy, believed in an ancient wisdom of the Aryan rulers of Atlantis, India and Egypt. Pierce did not.[44]

Yet if there were affinities between Madole's occultism and Pierce's belief that humans, particularly whites, were part of a greater whole, another link is more surprising. In the early 1970s, another racist doctrine, Creativity, was created by Ben Klassen. *Nature's Eternal Religion* would be the first of what would be a series of books espousing his beliefs, and its appearance was marked by Madole's declaration that where he had been unable to find the opportunity to write a book, an NRP supporter had written a book that reflected the essence of the party's philosophy.[45]

But instead of providing a new basis for the NRP, Klassen's writings underpinned a new grouping, the Church of the Creator. At its core was a fiery rejection of what it described as the 'whole "spooks in the sky" story'. There was no evidence, Klassen insisted, that gods or spirits existed, and any such belief was a swindle. Christianity, he argued, had been created by Jews to destroy the Roman empire and the white race, and even Christ's existence should be doubted. While rejected by Jews, Christianity served their interests by claiming that they were the chosen people and promoting such ideas as love of one's enemies. Instead, they should be hated.[46] At its most strident, Klassen declared that 'Racial Holy War', RAHOWA, encapsulated the programme of the church. 'We gird for total war against the Jews and the rest of the goddamned mud races of the world. ... We regard it as a holy war to the finish. ... No longer can the mud races and the White Race live on the same planet and survive.'[47]

Originally based in Florida, in the early 1980s the Church of the Creator established its headquarters in North Carolina and launched a monthly paper, *Racial Loyalty*. Klassen sought to persuade leading extreme rightists of the need for building a new organization based on Creativity. The *Spotlight*, he complained, failed to frontally attack the Jews while Hitler had failed to break with Christianity and had seen himself as a leader of Germany, not of the white race. The subsequent history of the Church of the Creator was a stormy one and following the death of his wife, Klassen committed suicide in 1993. But his faith was continued both through several rival Creativity groupings and through the efforts of a Canadian follower, George Burdi, who both headed a white power band, RAHOWA, and founded the racist music magazine, *Resistance*. In 1996, however, a twenty-five-year-old law student, Matt Hale, was declared leader of the World Church of the Creator. The Illinois-based church established itself as one of the leading forces on the extreme right, and in early 2002 the Anti-Defamation League noted that it had been forging links with the National Alliance. William Pierce, however, had just declared that the Alliance should not engage in joint activities.[48] In the long run, such collaboration had been doomed. The Alliance had long believed that it would lead a white revolution. But Hale's group also envisaged a leading role. If its adherents remained loyal, its *Membership Manual* likewise declared, it would 'one day rule the world'. In 2003, however, the church was hit by a court judgement in favour of a rival religious group's claim to exclusive use of the name Church of the Creator. Shortly afterwards, Hale himself was charged with soliciting the murder of the judge responsible for implementing the decision. Found guilty in 2004, Hale was imprisoned, and remnants of the church were forced to compete with groupings that had emerged earlier after prominent figures in the church had come into conflict with Hale's leadership.[49]

If Christian Identity and Odinism have been the strongest spiritualities within the American extreme right, the other manifestations we have discussed have not been the only alternatives to have emerged. In the 1950s, for instance, a veteran atheist publication, the *Truth Seeker*, attacked Christianity as a 'Jewised' religion that wrongly believed that races were equal. In 1957, *Right* published what it described as 'perhaps the most controversial article ever to appear in an avowedly Rightwing publication', in which the *Truth Seeker*'s editor, Charles Smith, argued that not only could a rightist be an atheist, but the two went logically together. The *Truth Seeker* organized Racist Forums addressed by such figures as NRP leader James

Madole and published articles by a number of activists, including Robert Kuttner, Matt Koehl and Eustace Mullins. Mullins, in turn, was linked with a Chicago group, the Institute for Biopolitics, which attacked religion in general and held that the 'Christ Myth' in particular was contrary to white barbarian virtues.[50]

During the 1980s, Robert Miles espoused a very different faith. As a Dualist, he wrote, he believed in the existence of a war between the forces of God and those of the Devil. As revealed in Genesis, God had sent whites to Earth to fight against evil. At first sight, this appeared to be espousing Identity, and, as we discussed earlier, he spoke at Aryan Nations events. But his religion was crucially different. It long predated Christianity, he argued. It had believed in God and 'His Royal Son' long before ancient Israel existed. He did not, he wrote, dispute the right to believe that whites had come to Europe from the Middle East. But while he did not wish to emphasize his differences in the presence of Identity believers, Dualism focused on what it saw as the original home of God's chosen people. At times he was willing to suggest that some whites might have eventually moved southward from their frozen homeland. But at other times he ruled it out. 'We never were in Israel. ... We came out of the North. We were there since we arrived on earth. We are Aryans, not desert wanderers.'[51]

Matt Koehl has pursued yet another path. After the death of Rockwell, he had inherited the NSWPP only to decide that it was the wrong vehicle for national socialism. In an account of Rockwell's life published when he was still in Koehl's movement, William Pierce had described the ANP founder placing a swastika banner on the wall of his living room shortly after becoming a national socialist. He had then placed a bust of Hitler in front of it, drawn the blinds and lit three candles. He had experienced

> a religious experience that was more than religious. ... He felt the awe-inspiring awareness for a few moments, or a few minutes, of being more than himself, of being in communion with that which is beyond description and beyond comprehension. ... One may call that Something by different names – the Great Spirit, perhaps, or Destiny, or the Soul of the Universe, or God – but once it has brushed the soul of a man, that man can never again be wholly what he was before.[52]

Years later, Pierce would unveil his Cosmotheism. Koehl, however, took the notion of an 'awe-inspiring awareness' in a different direction. As noted in Chapter 2, in 1983 he launched the New Order as a specifically religious national socialist grouping. In 'Hitlerism: Faith of the Future', published the previous year, he argued that the Germanic peoples had seen Christianity as alien when they had first encountered it. They had valued courage and respect for the natural world, and even though Christianity had eventually become dominant, it had remained Semitic. Luther, in defending an individual's right to interpret the Bible, had begun the long process of ending Christian hegemony. Now, the final stage was at hand. Aryan science had shattered Jewish myths, and the Promethean spirit had to look elsewhere. The Third Reich had failed militarily and politically but not spiritually. Hitler had been 'a god in human form', and those who continued to serve him had found 'our redemption'.[53]

Just as with the political groups of the extreme right, there has been a frequent interchange of leading figures between the different religious belief systems. James Warner, for instance, shifted from Odinism to Identity while Ron McVan had been editor of the Church of the Creator paper before embracing Odinism. David Lane, as we have seen, was an Identity adherent before defecting to Odinism.[54]

Tom Metzger, however, has evolved from playing a key role in Warner's New Christian Crusade Church to the belief that religion was a secondary issue (indeed, he has described himself as an atheist). *WAR* has been edited by an Odinist. But it has also published Creativity material, and at one gathering, he wrote in *WAR* at the end of the 1980s, Odinists, Identity Christians, atheists and others had come together only to have one Identity grouping raise their sectarian differences. Warriors could believe what they wished on religion, but they should never allow a 'priest class' to divide them.[55]

As we have seen with the National Alliance, others on the extreme right envisage the coexistence of different religions. In the late 1980s, for instance, National Socialist Vanguard argued that it was 'the nature of our race to believe in at least one god and an afterlife' and neither Matt Koehl's religion nor the Church of the Creator could be expected to prosper. The racist movement, however, included many different forms of religion, and all were acceptable. The Stormfront site even has a special section devoted to theology, in which 'Traditional Christianity', Christian Identity, 'Pre-Christian Indo-European Religions' and 'Agnosticism/Atheism' have their own separate discussions.[56]

Others, however, have responded differently. In 1998, for instance, one Identity group denounced NSWPP leader Harold Covington for saying that in order to avert religious conflict in the party, 'We are probably going to have two Hitler's Birthday celebrations and eventually build what amounts to two parties, one Christian and the other non-Christian.' Both views, he had stated, 'were perfectly legitimate currents of belief within the National Socialist world view and were represented in the Third Reich'. This, the Christian Separatist Church Society replied, was unacceptable. A national socialist could not be a non-Christian, and Covington was not a national socialist but an antichrist.[57]

There have been attempts too to synthesize different traditions. We have already seen this with the White Order of Thule, and Gardell has noted the existence of an Institute of Creativity-14 Words Coalition which sought to bring Creativity and Wotansvolk together.[58] There have also been attempts to bring different religions into alliance. Gardell has noted that Aryan Nations events have been addressed by Katja Lane. More recently, following a split from the Church of the Sons of Yahweh, the breakaway group denounced attempts at 'seeking unity with idolatrous pagan Odinists'.[59] More strikingly still, Aryan Nations has attempted to cooperate with followers of Islam. It has published material by the British national socialist David Myatt. He knew, he wrote, 'the reality of Islam ... as a noble, civilizing Way of Life'. It was not an enemy of the West but a natural ally against Zionism. Another posting on the Aryan Nations site, 'Why Islam Is Our Ally', praised 'the Islam of Al-Qaida, of the Taliban, of Hamas'. It was 'authentic Islam' which rejected any compromise with Zionism or the decadence of the West, and Aryans should respect them just as Hitler had respected the Grand Mufti of Jerusalem. Aryan Nations' sympathy for Islam even included accepting that Aryans could follow the religion. In 2005, Aryan Nations published an Aryan Muslim's announcement of his acceptance of the post of the group's Minister of Islamic Liaison. Like Islam, he declared, national socialism was a way of life with a profound spiritual awareness and promoted a warrior ethic. They shared the same foes, from Zionism and communism to feminism and capitalism, and it was vital the two worked together.[60]

The development of an Aryan Nations alliance with radical Islam is the most striking example of cooperation among different religions. More common, however, is continued dispute. In part, the conflict is highlighted by attempts to identify the Third Reich with a particular religion. Asking 'Was Adolf Hitler a Bible Christian?', Aryan Nations answered in the affirmative. The NSDAP programme, it noted, had declared support for 'Positive Christianity'. Luther had written extensively on 'the danger of the Anti-Christ Jew', and German Christians were far more informed about conservative theology than most Americans. Hitler had supported the German Christians' Faith Movement which had called for a new translation of the New Testament which would accord with national socialism. He had been continuously in contact with scholars well versed in its views. He knew that the New Testament in its original form was 'uncompromisingly racist' and 'certainly knew that Christ and His Apostles were Galileans and racially pure Aryans'. Christ had called for a Christian nation. Peter had called for a holy nation. 'Hitler's National Socialist German nation was a fulfilment of this Christian vision in Germany.'[61]

If some extreme rightists see Nazi Germany as essentially Christian, others have seen it as pagan. For the White Order of Thule, to understand Christianity's relationship to national socialism, the private pronouncements of Nazi leaders deserved particular attention. The actual practice of the Third Reich towards the churches also needed consideration. For the first, it argued that one should turn to the records of Hitler's conversations made by prominent Nazis. According to one, he had declared that it was not possible to bring national socialism together with Christianity. Christianity was a rebellion against natural law, Bolshevism its illegitimate offspring.

According to another, he had described both the Old and New Testaments as part of a Jewish swindle. 'We don't want people to keep one eye on the hereafter. We want free men who know that God is in themselves.' The SS epitomized the conflict between Christianity and the Third Reich. Himmler had prepared for what was described as 'the final showdown with Christianity', and his right-hand man, Heydrich, had declared the crucified Christ was an image of suffering and surrender. 'The Gods of our ancestors looked different; they were men, and each had a weapon in his hand'.[62]

Ron McVan has likewise claimed Nazi Germany for his faith, declaring that in the 1930s the 'Wotan Spirit' had united the German people and transformed them 'in an arcane and spiritual way that stunned the world!'.[63] As we have noted earlier, some racists have rejected the Third Reich. But whether they seek to claim it or not, they are concerned with attempting to gain legitimacy for their spirituality as distinct from others'. The Church of the Creator, for instance, rejected Christian Identity. There was no evidence, Klassen insisted, that Yahweh or Abraham or Moses had ever existed. Figures like Richard Butler espoused 'White racism' but he believed too in 'Jew-concocted spooks'. Whites had to have their minds purged of 'all this Jewish trash and rubbish', and it was only those whose minds were still open who could be won to Creativity. But 'the Identity crowd' were a lost cause. They only pretended 'they are on our side ... we are their enemies, and they are ours'.[64]

This hostility did not only apply to Christianity. At the beginning of the 1990s, the Church of the Creator paper published Klassen's declaration that Creativity should 'replace Odinism, Identity, and all other myth-based pseudoreligions of the White Race'. Odinism, he went on, was 'a primitive, infantile, spook-chasing religion ... that failed to withstand the Jewish-Christian onslaught a thousand years ago'. It could not 'be expected to roll it back now, under conditions a thousand times more adverse'.[65] Its successor paper continued this hostility. Thus in one issue an article declared that 'gods were born from the undeveloped mind of the brute'. It mattered little 'whether one calls a god "Odin", "Zeus", or "Yahweh"'. None existed, and the very idea of gods had to be destroyed 'so that our people can thrive in a land of reason, logic, and common sense'.[66]

But while the Church of the Creator rejected any belief in gods, most of the dispute on the extreme right has concerned the specific claims of Christianity. In the early 1980s, for instance, *White Power* published an attack on Christian Identity. Some 'good Aryans', it noted, claimed to be the true Israel. But Identity was 'a sad case of *mistaken identity*'. Aryans had not come from the Middle East some 2,500 years ago but had been settled in Northern Europe for far longer. Furthermore, the cruelty and depravity portrayed in the Old Testament were incompatible with the ethos revealed in the Aryan sagas. 'In the critical struggle in which we are engaged, we cannot afford any confusion as to who we are. Our true identity is that of Aryans – *not* ... Israelites.'[67]

Some on the extreme right have not only attacked Christian Identity's view of ancient Israel, but argued that Christianity itself is plagiarized from pagan sources. Thus one writer in *WAR* praised a study of 'Bible Myths and Parallels in Pagan Religions'. The story of the infant Moses being placed in the water, for instance, was taken from an ancient Sumerian story. *WAR* has also published an article on 'The Christian Plague' which argued that Easter, Christmas and the Christian cross itself were all taken from paganism. For his part, William Pierce has been particularly critical of Christianity. In its *Membership Handbook*, the Alliance argued that it was not an Aryan religion. Like Judaism and Islam it was Semitic, and 'its centuries of partial adaptation to Aryan ways' had not changed this.

> Its otherworldiness is fundamentally out of tune with the Aryan quest for knowledge and progress; its universalism conflicts directly with Aryan striving for beauty and strength; its delineation of the roles of man and god offends the Aryan sense of honor and self-sufficiency.

A religion or philosophy of life was needed that was an expression of Aryan nature and conducive to its racial mission. Christianity was neither.[68]

This had not been the only example of Pierce's hostility. In the early 1980s, one critic of the later Alliance noted, he had written on religion in the members' bulletin. There had been complaints, Pierce had noted, about 'anti-Christian bias' in Alliance publications. The Alliance had long avoided criticizing Christianity, but any member who belonged to a Christian organization which supported 'racial mixing or Zionism' should choose between that body and the Alliance. Some members belonged to small churches which had 'pro-White doctrines', but when they called on the Alliance not to attack Christianity, it could not be accepted. Their religion had originated in 'the Levant', and the Sermon on the Mount or the creation myth of Genesis could not be accepted. Nor could the claim that the ancient Israelites were the ancestors of today's whites be believed. They were Semites, and any thought to the contrary 'was demonstrably false'. Some members or potential members might still consider themselves as Christians. If by this they meant that they valued 'the specifically White elements of Christianity which have been added since its origins', then the Alliance would 'be proud' to have them as members.[69]

It was a policy that National Vanguard continued. Kevin Strom, when still in the National Alliance, had described himself in one broadcast as a non-Christian. Christians, he declared, were welcome to join the organization. He believed, however, that the divine existed not in ancient writings or on another plane of existence, but in 'the upward development of our race'. The group he subsequently formed described itself as a secular organization. National Vanguard understood, it declared, that Christianity was the faith of many whites. But it believed that members could adhere to other religions as long as they did not clash with the survival of the race.[70]

No more than national socialism has Christian Identity been an identifying feature of the American extreme right. Unlike national socialism, Identity is an American creation. It appeals both to the religious identity of most American extreme rightists and to their belief that not only they or the white race but America is special. But its efforts to disentangle Christianity from the Jews it so loathes have not only failed to persuade the vast numbers of Americans who continue to think in terms of Judeo-Christianity. It has failed too to persuade many who desperately seek a racial religion, and in that failure a startling diversity of racist spirituality has arisen among those who make up the American extreme right.

6 Fighting for women

For the extreme right, America is a white nation threatened by integration and immigration. Both, it insists, endanger racial purity, and in several ways this concern with race touches upon another subject. The movement is centrally concerned with white women, seeing them as both vital for the future of the race and in danger from the race's enemies. It sees itself as fighting for women, but it is fighting to possess them, and part of the rage that motivates it is entangled with sexual rivalry between men. But no more than race is male anger the only factor we should be considering. Women are playing an increasingly important role in the extreme right, and for some of them, and even some men, for too long the movement has only been concerned with the interests of white men. It is vital, these activists argue, that the extreme right should fight for women in a different sense, as the champion of a white womanhood not controlled by men, but fighting alongside them.

The American extreme right draws from national socialism in its views of women, and it is this debt that we will first consider. As we will discuss, there are also indigenous roots for the movement's concerns about women. But, as we have indicated, American extreme rightists do not all hold the same view of the subject. Some believe that racists have to break with misogyny, and it is to that dispute that we will subsequently turn.

In Nazi Germany, women who withdrew from employment upon marriage received a marriage loan, a quarter of which would be forgiven for every child born. Aryan women who bore four or more children received an Honour Cross of the German Mother, and abortion, already heavily restricted in pre-Nazi Germany, was limited still further in the Third Reich. But the regime did not believe that all children were welcome. It believed in eugenics, and the Nazis not only sought to restrict marriage to those it deemed free of hereditary disease, but carried out large numbers of sterilizations of those it saw as unfit to reproduce.[1]

If national socialism gave particular attention to the Aryan birth-rate, this was not the only reason why it was concerned with women. In *Mein Kampf*, Hitler had portrayed Jews lying in wait for Aryan maidens, and entangled with the priority Nazism gave to the fecundity of Aryan women was the conviction that other races sought to rob them of women who rightfully belonged to Aryan men. One of the leading Nazi newspapers, *Der Stürmer*, specialized in presenting Jews as preying on German women, and the Third Reich passed legislation forbidding sexual relations between Aryans and other races.[2] As we might expect, the idea of woman as above all mother is crucial to the American extreme right. But so too is the idea of her as either the victim of an 'alien' rapist or as committing racial treason by choosing to have sexual relations with a non-white. As we will see, the influence of German Nazism on such thinking has been all too clear. But there are other roots too. Testifying before Congress in the 1870s, General Bedford Forrest had declared that one of the reasons for the rise of the Ku Klux Klan had been black rapes of white women. The Klan that re-emerged in the First World War was still shaped by those fears. In the 1920s, it claimed the National Association for the Advancement of Colored People's advocacy of social equality was leading black men to 'lust upon women of the white race'. The Imperial Wizard declared that women should be mothers and should not see child-bearing as a burden, and one Klan leader even envisaged that 'the methods employed in stock-raising' could be used for 'developing a super race'.[3]

If we examine the extreme right in recent decades, we continue to find a central concern with motherhood. The NRP, for instance, called for the introduction of marriage loans that would have to be paid back more quickly if the woman remained in employment (as in the Third Reich, the amount that had to be repaid fell with each child born). For the NRP too, only those who were physically and mentally sound would be allowed to marry.[4] Other groups have been similarly committed not only to raising the white birth-rate but to ensuring that children were eugenically fit. One of the first articles in the World Union of National Socialists journal, *National Socialist World*, was a collection of extracts from *Mein Kampf*, in one of which Hitler declared that only the healthy should have children. The NSWPP's twelve-point programme had at its fifth point the elevation of motherhood to a position where it was seen as 'the noblest profession to which any White woman can aspire'. The eleventh point held that the state should seek the continual betterment of the race through positive eugenic measures and prohibiting the spread of genetically defective or racially impure genes.[5]

Other national socialist groupings took a similar stance. The *New Order* called for 'a massive eugenics program' and 'a vastly increased White birth rate', while the programme of the National Socialist White Workers Party both promised to take measures to restore to mothers the status they deserved and included a proposal to establish a National Eugenics Commission to discourage 'the unlimited breeding of the least desirable elements' and to encourage 'the reproduction of our best human stock'.[6]

Groupings that defined themselves as national socialist have not been the only section of the American extreme right to advance eugenic views. Part of the National Alliance's admiration for the Third Reich included both its encouragement of large families and its 'sterilization of congenitally defective Germans', and its *Membership Handbook* declared that the central task of the government it called for would be 'a long-term eugenics program involving at least the entire populations of Europe and America'.[7] One writer in the *Thunderbolt* declared that 'No racialist can overlook the importance of a healthy eugenic policy', while another argued that eugenics should be used to breed 'higher men among our race'.[8]

Eugenics has been promoted from different religious standpoints. In the late 1970s, for instance, Aryan Nations declared that 'The Aryan honors the science of eugenics' while in the same period *Christian Vanguard* published 'Ten Commandments for Choice of a Mate'. Originating in Nazi Germany, it called upon readers to choose a mate of kindred blood. The 'supreme aim' of marriage was 'the raising of healthy offspring', and having made sure of the worthiness of a prospective partner's ancestors, at least four children should be brought into the world.[9] But if advocates of Christian Identity have espoused eugenics, it has also been espoused by the anti-Christian Church of the Creator. Such a policy, it held, could 'easily' raise the average IQ of whites and future generations could be born free of hereditary defects. An international Jewish network, the church claimed, was trying to 'down-breed' the white race while Christianity had long agitated for the halt and the lame and against 'the fit and the competent'. It should be made 'a religious virtue', however, for the 'best White people to have larger families'. The 'less desirables of the White Race' should be induced to have smaller families.[10]

Given the centrality of raising the white birth-rate, extreme rightists have been particularly concerned to oppose abortion. In 1973, the Supreme Court struck down restrictive abortion legislation, ruling that in the early stages of pregnancy the decision to terminate a pregnancy was a medical one. The Court, the UKA paper declared, had decided on a 'Death Penalty for Unborn CHILDREN'. The *Thunderbolt* too denounced the Court's decision. A foetus, it declared, was a human being with the right to life. This argument was already being made by the burgeoning anti-abortion movement, which in the years ahead would become a crucial ally for American conservatives. The NSRP, however, linked opposition to abortion to race. There was, it declared, a shortage of white babies and in comparison with non-whites, a falling white population. The Supreme Court was guilty of legalizing the future murder of hundreds of thousands of white babies.[11]

For the Catholics and subsequently the evangelicals who made up the anti-abortion movement since 1973, abortion is the killing of an unborn child, and much of the extreme right has often adopted this 'pro-life' rhetoric. The Identity grouping led by Thom Robb, for instance, declared that 'Abortion is Murder' while *Jubilee* described abortion as 'the American Holocaust'.[12] But extreme rightists have been more than willing to link abortion with their belief in a Jewish conspiracy. In 1973, for instance, one group, the American White Nationalist Party, claimed that international bankers were using abortion as a way of destroying the white race. Whites, it argued, were the almost exclusive users of abortion, while the black race, which did not use abortion, was growing. In the following decade, the White Patriot Party declared that every year a million 'White infants' were being 'murdered thru Jew-engineered legalized abortion' while *WAR* published a cartoon in which a young white woman asked readers if they knew that most abortionists were Jewish or other non-whites. 'JEWISH RITUAL MURDER IS ALIVE AND WELL IN THE UNITED STATES OF AMERICA ... AND IS VERY LEGAL'.[13]

Nor has racist opposition to abortion been necessarily against all abortion. The Church of the Creator and the NSRP both published a cartoon contrasting the provision of abortion clinics for whites and maternity clinics for blacks, and some extreme rightists drew the conclusion that they should only oppose white abortions.[14] In 1978 the *Thunderbolt* attacked a leading anti-abortion campaigner for arguing that black people should be particularly opposed to abortion because it would destroy their race. The paper argued that abortion should instead be seen as a threat to the white race. It should be used, however, to 'eliminate the hundreds of thousands of illegitimate blacks'.[15] In the 1980s, the National Alliance attacked Christian conservatives for being equally opposed to abortion for 'Black welfare mothers as for healthy, productive White women', while more recently WAR has argued that while abortion should be opposed among whites, it supported abortion among non-whites.[16]

Seeking to stop abortion, at least among white women, was not the only initiative that American racists have taken to raise the white birth-rate. Under the headline 'Homosexuals Leave Women Without Men!', the *Thunderbolt* declared in the mid-1970s that hundreds of thousands of white women were without a husband because of the 'large number of men who have been taken out of circulation by the rapidly growing homosexual cult in America'. Desperation was leading some women to 'compromising their racial instincts and moral values by marrying a non-White', and it was part of the party's programme to see to it that 'every racially fit woman' had the opportunity to marry 'a wholesome man'. The NSRP attempted to matchmake between white men and women, something that both WAR and the Church of the Creator also took up in subsequent decades.[17]

But if racists sought to promote marriage between white women and white men, they were even more concerned at the danger of sexual contact between white women and black men. This has often taken the form of the fervent denunciation of the rape of white women. The Klan, as we have seen, has long been driven by such concerns. In the 1980s, for instance, the Invisible Empire, Knights of the Ku Klux Klan, declared that 'A Black man's dream is to make it with a White woman'. If he failed to achieve this by consent, then he would use rape. Other groups have shared such views.

In 1972, the cover article of one issue of the *Thunderbolt* proclaimed, 'Daily Press Suppresses News of Nation Wide Rape Epidemic of White Women', while in the 1990s its successor publication declared that almost 50 per cent of black rapes had been committed against white women.[18] The National Alliance has claimed that there are about 20,000 'Black-on-White rapes every year' in America, while in the late 1960s the NSWPP encouraged its activists to use a poster, 'The Black Plague', which depicted a knife-wielding black male and a prostrate white woman and declared that every thirty minutes, a woman was raped in the USA. 'The Negro', the party paper subsequently declared, was 'a sex-oriented creature' who sought 'to indulge in his favourite crime: RAPE'.[19]

But extreme rightists do not only fear the rape of white women. The National Alliance has accused the 'Jew-controlled entertainment media' of 'persuading a whole generation' that there was nothing wrong in white women dating or marrying black men. An Aryan Nations leaflet was illustrated by a photograph of a white woman with her arms around a black man, under which were the words, 'THE ULTIMATE ABOMINATION'. Not only, it declared, was the white birth-rate low and the non-white birth-rate high, but 'thousands of our young people (especially our women) desert their Race every day to marry non-whites'.[20]

The result of such views was that extreme rightists have attempted to oppose such desertions. One method has been the issue of stickers denouncing inter-racial liaisons. In early 1976, the *Thunderbolt* declared that it would take only a minority of white women to 'drown our race in a sea of color'. Whites were duty bound to discourage such marriages, and the paper had produced stickers calling for integrated couples to be 'shamed into disgrace'. More recently, one Identity grouping, Kingdom Identity Ministries, has distributed stickers declaring: 'Only inferior White women date outside of their race. Be proud of your heritage, don't be a race-mixing slut!'[21]

More brutally, both the *Thunderbolt* and Thom Robb's Christian Identity paper, the *Torch*, reprinted a comic strip by the National Alliance in which the 'hero' sprays tear-gas in the faces of a black man and his white female companion.[22] But racist reaction can be more brutal still. In 2003, White Revolution declared that the actress Nicole Kidman should be soaked in gasoline and burned to death for engaging in a inter-racial relationship, while in *The Turner Diaries*, those whites who engage in sex outside their race suffer the 'Day of the Rope', in which placards reading 'I defiled my race' are put around the necks of 'thousands of hanging female corpses. ... They are the White women who were married to or living with blacks, with Jews, or with other non-White males.'[23]

For the extreme right, a high birth-rate is crucial. Which race will be victorious is closely connected with which race has the greatest fertility, and the bitterness of racial feeling is intensified by anger that white women are being raped and a fury that they are voluntarily engaging in intercourse outside the race. Overwhelmingly, this is a male rage, and it is connected with another source of bitterness. During the NSDAP's struggle for power, leading members had argued that women were secondary to men and in 1934 Hitler had told the National Socialist Women's Organization that 'man's world' was the state while woman's smaller domain was 'her husband, her family, her children, and her home'. A decade earlier, one Klan minister had declared that every man should rule his own household and one of its writers had condemned women who 'blaspheme God by disobeying their husbands'.[24] When we turn to the American extreme right from the 1950s onwards, we find such ideas still strongly evident.

Rockwell, for instance, held that it was the Jews who were responsible for a growing belief 'that the specialization of women in child-rearing' was wrong and that instead they should pursue careers. If you looked at youth gangs, he declared, girls who belonged to them did not demand their rights. 'They glory in their roles as females, as "belonging" to and proudly helping a powerful male. And this is precisely the role of females in wholesome and happy societies.'[25] Both in pre-war Germany and since, extreme rightists have reacted against the existence of a feminist movement. In pre-war Germany, the prominent Nazi, Alfred Rosenberg, attacked feminism as alien to the nation, and called for men to decide political issues and for women to be freed from the idea of emancipation. In the 1960s the ANP called for the return of full-time mothers and 'the restoration of the father as master of the home', while at the beginning of the following decade one columnist in *White Power* declared that the nation was on 'the verge of matriarchy'. The American male had abdicated, but there was only one way to deal with an Aryan woman who wanted to get involved in 'women's lib'. If you suspected 'your mate' of such a thing, you should 'grab her by the hair of the head, drag her home and get her pregnant! It's good for her, good for you, and good for the White race!'[26]

Extreme right opposition to feminism has been particularly evident among adherents of Christian Identity. In 1979, in the first edition of its newsletter, Aryan Nations had declared that every child that an Aryan mother brought into the world was a battle waged for the existence of her people. 'The program of the National Aryan Women's Movement', it held, had a single point, the child, and it was far better to be 'the mother of healthy Aryan children than to be a clever woman lawyer'. Although unacknowledged, this was taken from pronouncements by Hitler.[27]

In later issues, Aryan Nations argued that a Satanic conspiracy had made women independent and put them into the workplace 'to compete with their men'. It was to a conqueror's advantage, it declared, to make a woman feel like a second class citizen and then 'do battle with her mate'.[28] Similar views were espoused elsewhere among Identity believers. *Christian Vanguard* declared that 'there is no biblical or historical question that this world was intended by God to be ruled by men', while Scriptures for America announced that women should be wives and mothers while men should lead.[29]

Anti-feminism can be found in other elements of the extreme right. The National Alliance has been bitterly opposed to the direction that relations between the genders have taken in recent decades. In the late 1970s, Pierce's organization began to promote a book which sought to trace the ills of the West. Written by one of its members, it argued that women's entry into the workforce had increased unemployment and undermined men's role while female enfranchisement had lowered the intelligence of the electorate. Women, it held, could only be mistresses of the home while it was men that must rule in society. What real women wanted was motherhood and a master, and they had always to be controlled by a male. In part, this was because a woman 'cannot be counted upon to keep her sexuality under control'. But it was also because if they attempted to change society, the result would be damaging or even disastrous. If women did not accept their place, then men would have to put them there.[30]

A later article in the Alliance's magazine related this argument more closely to race. Western males, it lamented, were losing their masculinity. They were supposed to be both provider and protector, but increasingly women were aggressively asserting themselves, robbing man of his role of 'master in his house'. The result was that Western women were reacting against the weakness of their men by turning towards 'non-White males, who are perceived as more masculine'. This was not solely because of the rise of feminism. But there could be 'no doubt that the Jews fully understand the destructive effect on Gentile society that their wielding of the feminist movement is having'.[31]

Subsequently, Pierce elaborated on his views. White men, he complained, had extended the vote to women, but he was not being male chauvinist in pointing this out. Women tended to see issues differently from men, and this had contributed to the nation's decline. Women did not belong in politics, and in the society of the future they would be 'the wives and helpmates of farmers, craftsmen and merchants' and 'make motherhood their principal occupation'. They would not be stopped from pursuing careers. But they would be encouraged to be what Nature had intended them to be.[32]

More strident views still have been put forward by Vanguard News Network. In 'On Women and Their Proper Relation to White Nationalism', its founder, Alex Linder, argued that men must lead the racial struggle. Women could 'chip in sensible remarks, in modulated tones, from time to time. And make everything happy and smooth running by providing offspring and sex and cookies and iced tea.' But only men were rational, and they should not allow themselves to be influenced by women.[33]

Linder's website has been a particular source of such views. One writer, for instance, denounced the marginalization of white men as providers and fathers. They were losing high-paying manufacturing jobs, the divorce rate was escalating and men were being demonized. Above all, the sons of white men were growing up fatherless, lost in 'a feminized culture' that hated them and sought to change their essential masculinity. Another writer denounced the women who were 'competing with us in the marketplace'. To accept even some career women was to surrender to Jewish conditioning.[34] His more recent launch of a print publication, the *Aryan Alternative*, has taken up this argument. In one issue, it accused 'Jewish culture wreckers' of putting 'gullible women' off marriage. 'Now women want it all. They want a career, self-actualization, man-as-sperm-donor-and-diaper-changer. ... What more do they offer in return for all the additional expectations they impose upon men? ... less attention, less gratitude, less sex and less respect'.[35]

Amidst the different extreme right anti-feminists, perhaps the most antagonistic has been David Lane. In a pamphlet published shortly after his imprisonment, he lamented the percentage of child-bearing white women who were married to white men. The Jews, he proclaimed, were using 'their media to insult and emasculate the White man while depicting non-white males to be heroes so White women would desert their Race by the millions'. His concern with white women's sexuality and white men's access to them continued after he abandoned Identity. In a collection of essays published in 1999, he argued that a race whose men would not fight to the death to keep and mate with their females would perish. The most fertile source for recruitment to the movement was 'young, disenfranchised young males', and Nature's way to raise armies was by the promise of seizing women. White women were being enjoyed by aliens, and they were 'not coming back by friendly persuasion'. They had been captured by money and deceit, and white men were 'going to take them back the way it has been done through the ages'.[36]

Subsequently he produced a novel, published on a extreme right website. In it, Lane pictured a future in which white women were kidnapped by racist warriors. The main story concerns the abduction of two strippers from a Jewish-owned club, both intended as polygamous wives of the main protagonist. In another element of the tale, the warriors learn of the intention of a schoolgirl to engage in inter-racial sex and raid her house, carrying her off as the intended mate of a second fighter. Through 'the aeons of time', the reader is told, women had 'adjusted to their captors, and usually come to love them'.[37]

To understand extreme right attitudes to women, it would be a mistake to only focus on the pronouncements of prominent activists or writers in movement publications. Much of the evidence for male chauvinism in the American extreme right comes from how it is organized. Those recruited by racist organizations bring with them ideas from the wider society or from sub-cultures within it. Some, for instance, already adhere to the views dominant in traditional Christianity. Others belong to skinhead gangs which, as Kathleen Blee has noted, often see women as 'little more than sexual partners or submissive partners of male agendas'.[38] Anti-feminism can be found across the extreme right, and we might assume that its exponents spoke for the movement as a whole. Closer examination, however, shows this is not the case. Even in the NSDAP, there was controversy on the issue. Although the party championed male primacy, banning women from standing as electoral candidates, it had recruited significant numbers of women (as well as receiving the votes of millions of women). One result of this was to open up differences within the party, in which some women argued that the belief that women were inferior was an alien belief and that true Aryans believed in women's equality. Another effect was the party's denial in its propaganda that it intended to remove women from employment.[39] The Klan of the 1920s also reacted to the changing role of women in complex ways. If, as we saw earlier, it could condemn women as disobedient to their husbands, in 1924 the Commander of the Klan's women's organization told the Klan convention that it had 'never been the purpose of God that woman should be the slave of man', while one Klan paper published an article acknowledging that women's economic freedom was leading to 'an entirely new conception' of 'the relation of men and women'.[40]

The existence of differences on the role of women both within the movement and in the society it seeks to bring about has become particularly evident in recent years. In part, this can be observed in the rise of racist women's websites. One site expressed sympathy for the National Alliance while criticizing its founder's 'derogatory generalizations about women'. On a second site, Elisha Strom, an activist in her own regard and wife of Kevin Strom, argued that while women had changed, many racist men refused to acknowledge this. Motherhood should be encouraged, but for the movement to give the impression that it wanted all white women barefoot and pregnant gave it a misogynist image that had to be destroyed.[41] A third site, Her Race, published a statement by a woman declaring that she did not 'intend to solely raise children and be a house-wife'. Nature, she contended, 'intended that women use their brains to advance their race' and for 'comrades to suggest that women squelch this natural instinct' was to act in an un-Aryan way. Instead, it was a Jewish view to see 'women as breeding tools and property'.[42]

Such charges have not only been advanced on women's websites. Elisha Strom had been among the signatories of the document that led to the emergence of National Vanguard. The organization's subsequent statement of beliefs included the statement that it would not accept any 'misogynist-type degradation of women' in the organization. While women's role as mothers was vital, they could be leaders and activists 'in keeping with the particularly high status of women in non-Semitized White countries'.[43]

National Vanguard was not the only extreme right grouping to denounce male chauvinism. One of the most forceful interventions in this area has come from WAR. At first sight, this might appear impossible. WAR's propaganda has often placed a high value on the most bellicose masculinity. In 1989, for instance, it published an article declaring that in a natural state, all men were warriors. Industrial society, however, sought to destroy masculinity but manhood could be restored by the revival of aggressiveness.[44]

Indeed, one essay has suggested that WAR is fundamentally opposed to women's rights. 'WHITE MEN *Built* This nation!! WHITE MEN *Are* this nation!!', one of its cartoons had declared, and the organization had claimed too that 'One of the characteristics of nations which are controlled by the Jews is the gradual eradication of masculine influence and power and the transfer of influence into feminine forms.'[45] But an examination of its views on women reveals a very different view. Judaism, it claims, has oppressed women and Christianity has continued to promote a 'negative regard for women'. So too did much of the racist movement. Yet women in the past had not only borne children but, on occasion, had been warriors. The same religion that falsely claimed all men were equal was wrong too in its denigration of women, and what the struggle needed was millions of women who could work, fight and mother. In 2000, *WAR* published a cartoon with the caption 'ARYAN WOMEN BRAVE, STRONG, BEAUTIFUL'. Beside it was a 'Declaration of White Womanhood'. Some racists, it claimed, wanted 'a return to the days when women were submissive and silent'. It was true that feminism had damaged the white race. But 'the bearers of the future' of that race were not weak. 'Stop whining about strong White women and look to them as partners in the struggle rather than just ovaries with tits who provide meals, sex, housecleaning, and child care for you.'[46]

Opposition to the subordination of women even exists among extreme rightists who explicitly define themselves as national socialists. Nancy Jensen, the woman cited earlier on the Her Race site, described herself as 'a staunch National-socialist female', but national socialist groups led by men have also made arguments critical of male chauvinism. In one issue of its newsletter, the SS Action Group called on men to show more respect for women, declaring that it supported 'the equality of the sexes', while the National Socialist Movement has declared that feminism would not have seemed so attractive 'to our women if there wasn't a lot wrong with the treatment they had been receiving'. Men had been poisoned by Jewish propaganda to see a woman as 'a dispensable pleasure object, a baby making machine, or a maid' but women should be given every opportunity to achieve their goals, and the Movement strongly opposed 'any racism that would hold over 50% of our people in contempt'.[47]

Even groups that have published particularly male chauvinist pronouncements have given space to contrary arguments. In one issue of the Aryan Nations magazine it was argued that Aryan women had 'served in every capacity, outside the home, from prophetess to queen and presidential adviser', while an article in *White Power* by Koehl's second-in-command, Martin Kerr, lamented that his male co-thinkers did not see rape as of concern to racists. The movement was infected by the belief that women's issues were not important, and any discussion met 'the unchallenged assertion' that the subject had been conceived by Jews to divide the race. But such an attitude was 'fundamentally un-National Socialist'. Men and women had distinct roles, but women deserved 'a high degree of freedom'. Feminism had not always been led by Jews, and male racialists were wrong to believe women's place was solely in the home. Under national socialism, while mothers would not have to work outside the home because of economic necessity, women would be free to pursue a career instead of motherhood.[48]

If finding such views espoused by a leading national socialist man is surprising, equally so is finding criticisms of patriarchal assumptions on the Vanguard News Network website. In 'Women and White Pride', a female writer noted how men in the movement often wondered why it did not attract more women. Yet movement women were 'made to feel that we should be kept barefoot and in the kitchen, constantly pumping out good White children, cooking, doing laundry etc.'. This would be fine, but not, she declared, until she was older, and no longer wanted 'to go out with the guys' to bars and white power concerts. For now, she wanted the same role in the movement as men. Websites had to be created for young women, and it would be a good idea too to have a novel like *The Turner Diaries* or *Hunter* but with a woman as the protagonist. The Germanic tribes had had women fighting alongside men when it was needed. Now was such a time.[49]

Rather than be united on the question of women's role, extreme rightists are divided, and the two views have come into direct confrontation. In one thread on the Stormfront website, correspondents discussed 'What is a Productive Attitude towards White Women'. The subject, the first writer observed, was 'a point of great disagreement' within the movement. But it was wrong to treat women as a reward or 'a breeding machine'. Instead, they should be companions and the mothers of intelligent, healthy white children. The response was wide-ranging. One respondent attacked women who took the roles that Providence established as belonging to 'the dominant male'. Any racist, it was argued, also adhered to a 'healthy' sexism. Another described his relationship with his wife who had no problem with obeying him and 'would never think of challenging anything I say in public'. Another post, however, insisted that feminism had not originated as a Jewish movement but a white one, while yet another recommended readers look at the 'only positive, very clearly-stated position on women', that of WAR.[50]

Debates elsewhere in the movement have taken a different direction, even attacking Stormfront as succumbing to the lures of the enemy. Thus in one of Vanguard News Network's forum discussions, one writer enquired if it was true that 'the final battle will be White males vs. everyone else'. Judging by 'the jew-dazed feminists' on Stormfront, this appeared a possibility. Another respondent, however, declared that it was hard for women to fight beside the men if they believed this. A second thread asked why white women engaged in sex with non-whites. One respondent declared 'White women hate White men.' In school they read the feminist material the teachers pushed on them. Race-mixing, he continued, happened because they hated white men. 'And it's for the same reason that Jews hate White men. We're superior to them.'[51]

If the movement is divided over women's role, sections of it have become even become divided over abortion. Stormfront has carried debates on the subject. One correspondent suggested that activists disagreed on the issue, and that it might be best to stay away from it. A key figure on the site joined in, declaring that the 'spectrum of opinion' tended to be 'almost as wide' among white nationalists as it was in 'the general society'. White people should be encouraged to have more children, and financially assisted to do so, and if particular groups among the white population wished to ban abortion, they could. But it would not be right to ban abortion for whites as a whole. One contributor declared 'I am Pro-Choice', while another contended that the 'communitarian' principle should trump the individualist. Abortion was too important to leave to the choice of a woman. But if extreme rightists disputed whether abortion should be a woman's right, they also argued whether abortion should play a role in the future racial state. Thus one correspondent attacked the idea that any white abortion was wrong as absurd. Not only should handicapped foetuses be terminated, but in a white society any foetus with an IQ below the mean should be aborted. It was a proposal which came under attack from others. There was no way, another contributor declared, that the future society would use abortion for eugenic ends.[52] In another exchange, one correspondent declared that as a man he could not fully understand the impact of an unwanted pregnancy on a woman. But he supported her right to choose.[53]

If not only the movement but the men within it are divided on the role of women, women on the extreme right do not speak with one voice either. In recent years, in addition to women's websites, there has been a rise of different women's print publications, and they vary considerably in their view of women's place in the struggle. In the early 1990s one periodical, *Today's Aryan Woman*, called for the recognition of the 'natural differences' between men and women and the 'proper roles' each should occupy, and reprinted William Pierce's call for a society in which women would be encouraged to pursue motherhood not careers. Conversely, another publication, *Valkyrie Voice*, called for women to study both Aryan history and weaponry. Women should not be expected to 'play a passive role with their main interest being that of their man's comfort, satisfaction, and approval'. Instead they should 'take an active role within our resistance'. Another magazine, the strikingly named *Rational Feminist*, praised *Valkyrie Voice* for its portrayal of 'a fine balance between the ultra-feminist, home-destroying path and the issue of women using her talents to the utmost and still being an integral part of the maintenance of home and family.'[54]

But it is not only women's websites or print publications that have emerged in recent years. Some women joined the Aryan Women's League, an affiliate of WAR. Others took part in an effort in the World Church of the Creator to build two women's chapters, the Women's Frontier and the Sisterhood.

The Aryan Women's League was founded in the late 1980s. Through leaflets, recorded phone messages, its own newsletter, *White Sisters*, and special pages in WAR's paper, the League argued that women had 'a definite place in the struggle for White victory'. They were both warriors and bearers of the future white race. The League's task, it declared, was to act as a support group which promoted family cohesion and the proper education of children. Its work included education in first aid and self-defence, protection of the environment and the provision of assistance to Aryans in need.[55]

Declaring his support for the initiative, one prominent WAR man observed that the biggest problem that the new group faced was men not accepting 'their women as counterparts in the race struggle'. They wanted women who were subordinate and feared their working with other women. But 'White racially conscious women are most beautiful when they are in battle', and any man who felt threatened when 'his woman' fought some battles of her own was not a man at all, 'let alone a White Warrior'.[56]

White Sisters described itself as a 'quarterly publication dealing with the problems and victories of women warriors fighting to save our noble Aryan race'. It would attempt to draw together white women throughout the world, and in its first issue it welcomed the contribution women were making to the advance of the Front National in France. It reported too on white women's struggles within the United States, publishing photographs of women rallying against integration in Boston and 'Baltic-American girls' demonstrating outside the Soviet Embassy in Washington. But in a later issue it published too an account of the life and death of Kathy Ainsworth. It remained 'a mystery', it claimed, whether she had been engaged in a bombing when she had been shot. But she had been, the AWL proclaimed, 'a fine soldier in the fight for the Aryan race'. *White Sisters* also emphasized the importance of the 'Aryan woman' as 'the bearers of our future, strong army', and one article by a male activist insisted that 'our racial battle' was really 'a battle of the groin'. The only way the race could survive, he declared, was 'to have as many babies as we can'. If motherhood was crucial for the Aryan Women's League, so too was the need to 'stand by our men' when they were imprisoned. One article declared that as 'the wife of a warrior', she celebrated his achievements and nursed him when he was wounded, recognizing he 'fights for me'.[57]

If the Aryan Women's League believed in women's role both as mother and warrior, two groupings that subsequently emerged within the World Church of the Creator also saw more than one role for women. Established in 1998, the Women's Frontier described itself as 'dedicated to spreading the word of Creativity to White women worldwide', while a later group, the Sisterhood of the World Church of the Creator, had the task of 'Encouraging Female Activism in the Worldwide White Racialist Creativity Movement'. Among the Sisterhood's activities was the publication of a newsletter, the running of a website and the production of a newsletter for 'Racial Parents' while the Women's Frontier's activities included running a website, distributing a newsletter by email and publishing an audiotape on 'The Women's Frontier – A New Chapter in Church History'. It also issued a Declaration of the Women's Frontier.[58]

The Declaration set out the duties of 'Proud, White Women'. They would create a world in which white women could safely walk the streets, white children would grow 'free and strong' and society would be freed from Jewish control. They would forge a link with 'our White Sisters worldwide', and in the world of the future white women's achievements would be honoured. But the Declaration did not agree with what it described as 'the twisted, unnatural Jewish feminist concept of womanhood'. Rather than being equal, men and women had their own special roles, and the Women's Frontier pledged to 'lovingly work as devoted wives, mothers, Sisters, helpers, friends, and Comrades-in-arms by the side of our Male Comrades'.[59]

Another document on the group's website reproduced the views of a number of male racist leaders. These included both extracts from a speech by Adolf Hitler, prioritizing women's role as childbearer, and the call by Alfred Rosenberg for German women to be freed from feminism. But it also included a quotation praising the contribution of his women followers by the pre-war British fascist leader, Oswald Mosley, and WAR's denunciation of Christianity's 'negative regard towards our White women'. The Jewish-controlled media, the site remarked, claimed that racist men did not respect women. These quotations would demonstrate the falsehood of such claims.[60]

The Women's Frontier had been set up by the Church's Women's Information Coordinator, Lisa Turner. Women's chapters, she declared, were one of the most controversial issues in the movement. There were both men and women who opposed them. But it was wrong to see them as divisive. The Jews were pleased when racialists discouraged the recruitment of women. Yet white women knew what it was like to have 'HONKY BITCH!' yelled at them when they were in the supermarket or picking up kids at school. Many were saying 'Enough is Enough', but more could do so, and women's chapters were vital to reach them.[61]

The Women's Frontier, Turner declared, had been formed because women's role in 'our Cause' had been overlooked. While most importantly, this was as wife and mother, they could also be fighters alongside men. This was not the same as believing a woman could be wife, mother and guerilla fighter at the same time. While Kathy Ainsworth and others had 'fought just as men have', most women did not fit into 'this rare category', and to pursue a strategy based on the recruitment of an elite of woman warriors would drive away large numbers of women. But women must use their abilities as best as they could including as leaders.[62]

It was this insistence on a greater role for women that drew the attention of the Anti-Defamation League. Such arguments as Turner's, it suggested, was a perversion of feminism.[63] Turner's response, however, was outrage. The Jews, she declared, were frightened by the growth of women's activism, and by claiming that racist women were feminists were trying to divide them from their male comrades. The Church of the Creator believed that motherhood was a woman's most important role and did not believe that men oppressed women, and to call 'a proud, strong White woman' a feminist was an insult.[64]

The Aryan Women's League did not survive the 1990s. In 2001, both Lisa Turner and the leading figure in the Sisterhood of the World Church of the Creator, Melody LaRue, broke with the church. Turner attempted to continue with the Women's Frontier as a non-aligned grouping while LaRue has continued with *Sisterhood* as an independent magazine. Other extreme right women, however, have taken yet other directions. Some have joined another group, Women for Aryan Unity, whose mission statement declares that its key task is 'reinventing the concept of "feminism" within the parameters of Race and Revolution'. Some, for instance, have joined the women's division of the National Socialist Movement while yet others have joined an Oregon skinhead group, Volksfront, which having originally been unwilling to recruit them, subsequently came to argue that instead of being treated as objects, the movement needed women activists.[65]

When we examine how extreme right women have organized, or what extreme right organizations have argued about women, what we see is not uniformity, but diversity. While the extreme right is defined by its stance on race, it is divided on gender. Many on the extreme right believe that motherhood is women's central role and that men's role is to be warriors and leaders. Some go further, arguing that just as whites are the superior race, so men are the superior sex. But others, and not only women, have argued that women are often devalued on the extreme right, and that they can be not only activists but leaders too. In some ways, understanding the role of women as secondary might be described as traditionalist, representing both the dominant tradition on the extreme right and what for a long time was the accepted understanding of women's role within society at large. In turn, the view with which it is in conflict might be described as feminist. But is the dispute best caught in these terms?

The very phrase traditionalist is arguable. Much of the extreme right has been particularly vociferous on the subject of eugenics, something which sits uneasily with what we might describe as a traditional view of the family. Furthermore, a wariness about the applicability of the term seems called for, considering the enthusiasm shown by some racists for polygamy. We have already come across this in the case of David Lane. A number of extreme rightists have engaged in polygamy. James Ellison, the leader of the Covenant, the Sword and the Name of the Lord, did so, for instance. So did Chevie Kehoe, the leader of the Aryan People's Republic, while Mike Hallimore of Kingdom Identity Ministries has written in defence of the practice.[66]

Only some extreme rightists advocate polygamy (a leading Identity publication has even published a debate on the subject).[67] But given some support for polygamy, and the more widespread advocacy of eugenics, the first view can be termed traditionalist only with caution. But can the second view be described as feminist? As Kathleen Blee has suggested, one factor in the diversity of views of gender on the extreme right is the discontent of some women activists with what is expected of them and how they are treated within the movement. Another is an attempt by racist leaders to 'broaden' the appeal of their group.[68]

If we concluded that feminism need not necessarily be racially egalitarian, then we might call those who argue for equality within the race feminists. To apply that term to those who wish to recruit more women is more in doubt. Some men on the extreme right do appear to agree with the equality of white men and white women. Others, however, may well be merely attempting to maximize their group's membership, and for either men or women, there are evident tensions between arguing that women can be activists as well as mothers and emphasizing that (some) women can fight or lead. What terms we should use for the different camps is far from certain. Feminism may be a useful term. What is clear, however, is that the extreme right is divided on women, and that this divide is not likely to recede.

7   A call to arms

The American extreme right has long been associated with violence. In the 1960s, in response to the burgeoning Civil Rights Movement, the Ku Klux Klan bombed churches and attacked Freedom Riders, while in the 1980s the Order engaged in a series of robberies and two murders. This is not to say that the American extreme right as a whole is to be identified with violence. It has been noticeable, however, that throughout the period we are discussing, violence or the threat of it have been a prominent feature of major sections of the extreme right. But it has also led to considerable disagreement among activists, and it is those disputes on which we will focus in this chapter.

These arguments have broken out among Klansmen, national socialists and Patriots, and one of the most important figures has been active in both the Klan and the Patriot movement. Having been prominent in the Knights of the Ku Klux Klan, by the early 1980s Louis Beam had become persuaded that the Klan needed to enter a new period. Rather than court publicity, it would once again have to operate clandestinely, and it would need to be highly violent. Initially arguing these views in the short-lived *Inter-Klan and Survival Report*, he became involved with Aryan Nations, and elaborated his arguments in *Essays of a Klansman*.[1]

America, he argued, was approaching terminal illness, and the only medicine that could save it came under such brand names as Colt and Smith and Wesson. 'Paradoxically, only by administering death to anti-Christ enemies can there be life for all that we hold dear.' Aryans needed to take up the sword. This could be 'an M-16, three sticks of dynamite' or whatever proved suitable, and what was needed was a point system so that patriots could 'intelligently judge the effectiveness of proposed acts against the enemy'. The killing of an ordinary non-white would be worth only a thousandth of a point, a Jewish demonstrator twice as much, an FBI director or a federal judge a sixth of a point, an egalitarian religious leader a third of a point. At the apex of Beam's scheme stood the leaders of the 'satanic anti-Christ conspiracy for the control of the world'. To gain a thousandth of a point, Beam held, was only to be cannon fodder. Only gaining a whole point would give a militant the status of Aryan Warrior.[2]

While Beam had been a Grand Dragon in Duke's Klan, the co-publisher of the *Inter-Klan and Survival Alert* was a former Grand Dragon in the United Klans of America, Robert Miles. In 1971, Miles had received a nine-year sentence for the fire-bombing of ten buses intended for the transportation of white children to black schools. Subsequently, he launched his own publication, *From the Mountain*, and spoke at Aryan Nations and other gatherings. At one meeting, he declared that far leftists had robbed armoured cars and racists should emulate them, at another that racist activists needed to put together files on the enemies of their race ready for the day when 'the racial armed party' emerged.[3]

Writing in 1981, Miles denounced the Klan's setting up of paramilitary training camps. If racists needed training, they should join the armed forces or sporting clubs. The movement was not yet ready for guerilla warfare. It needed to be able to pay its fighters, to set up safe houses, to secure lawyers, doctors and nurses. It would be folly, indeed treason, 'to enter into an armed action until the preparatory work has been done'. But at 'the right time, more than just the moon shall rise'.[4]

It would be tempting to portray Miles as calling for an organization along the lines of the Order. But organized guerilla warfare was not the only form of extreme right violence he was prepared to defend. In the latter part of the 1970s, a former member of the National Socialist White People's Party, Joseph Paul Franklin, had engaged in a protracted campaign of individual terror. He had travelled around the country, carrying out attacks, particularly on individual black men and racially mixed couples (he is believed to have killed some twenty people). He was ultimately apprehended, and writing in mid-1984, Miles asked what did the 'Resistance' mean when it talked of an Armed Party? It did not necessarily refer to a centrally controlled group. It could refer to an individual such as Franklin, 'roaming the nation at will, and striking blows where he alone sees fit'. Whether the act of an individual or a group, the Armed Party was an expression of the recognition 'that the only propaganda that finally awakens a people is the propaganda of the deed'.[5]

But if former Klansmen were influential in making a case for the centrality of violence in the racial struggle, a particularly important part was played by a former member of the NSWPP. William Pierce's leadership of the National Youth Alliance had taken it in a particularly militant direction. In the early 1970s, *Attack!* argued that revolutionary action should be directed against 'the creatures' who comprised and collaborated with the System. Judges should be assassinated, TV transmitters dynamited and whites who had sex with non-whites must be harshly punished.[6] In another article, *Attack!* declared that rather than reason with the System,

> we need to put a bullet into its brain and hammer a stake through its heart. If that means blood and chaos and battling the alien enemy from house to house in burning cities throughout our land – then, by God, it is better that we get on with it now than later.[7]

Nor were such views restricted to agitational articles. As we noted in Chapter 2, the Alliance's paper also serialized Pierce's first novel. *The Turner Diaries* took the form of two years of diary entries in which the protagonist, Earl Turner, describes his part in the guerilla war that eventually led to 'the Great Revolution'. In response to government raids on white gun-owners, the group to which he belongs, the Organization, launches a war against 'the System'. A truck packed with explosives is used to devastate the FBI's national headquarters, and after an unsuccessful attack on the *Washington Post*, one of its editors is gunned down. Other actions include a mortar attack on Congress, and Turner is initiated into the Order, the group that, unbeknowst to him, had set up the Organization. As part of the initiation, he reads the Order's central text, and realizes the real meaning of the Organization's struggle. 'We are truly the instruments of God in the fulfillment of His Grand Design', he writes, and he is told how members of the Order are 'bearers of the Faith', and that its existence must remain a secret until the System is no more.[8]

Soon after, Turner is captured, tortured by an Israeli interrogator and betrays his comrades. The Organization breaks many of its prisoners out of captivity, and in a subsequent hearing Turner is told that when he is instructed, he must undertake a suicide mission. The remainder of the novel continues to depict the guerilla war, from a mortar attack on the Israeli embassy to the blowing up of power plants and gas pipelines. As we noted in the previous chapter, white women who had lived with non-whites are publicly hanged. So too are politicians, judges and teachers seen by the Organization as race traitors. Non-whites are forced out of white areas, and missiles are launched at New York, Israel and the Soviet Union. A combination of radiological, biological and chemical weapons are used to destroy life from the Urals to the Pacific and the Indian Ocean to the Arctic, and the Order spreads its 'rule over the earth for all time to come'. But Turner is not alive to witness these last events. He has flown an old crop-duster containing a nuclear warhead into the Pentagon, and by his death assured the Order's victory.[9]

In the years that followed, Pierce's book sold in large numbers, and among its readers were the members of a group that emerged in 1983, the Order. Formed by National Alliance activist Robert Mathews and named after the group in Pierce's novel, members pledged that as Aryan warriors, they would 'do whatever is necessary to deliver our people from the Jew'. They would not lay down their weapons, they proclaimed, until they had reclaimed their land. Later it issued a declaration of war, in which it declared that 'in a land once ours, we have become a people dispossessed'. The cities were swarming with 'dusky hordes', farms were being 'seized by usurious leeches' and whites were taking non-whites as their mates. Yet still the people did not awake. But by 'ones and twos', then 'by scores and legions', the enemy would be driven into the sea.[10] The Order engaged in counterfeiting and the robbery of three armoured cars. It also bombed a

synagogue and murdered two people, one of them an over-talkative sym-
pathizer, the other a Jewish talk-show host who had insulted two of his
guests, Identity preachers Pete Peters and Jack Mohr.[11] Before being captured and sentenced to long prison terms (Mathews himself was killed in a
shoot-out with the FBI), members of the Order also planned to rob an
armoured car company's vault and drew up an assassination list which
included Henry Kissinger and members of the Rockefeller and Rothschild
families.[12]

Order members were indicted in April 1985, and in a *National Vanguard*
editorial at the beginning of the year, the National Alliance commented on
the group. Its aim had been an armed revolution, and it did not matter
whether its actions were ill advised. What mattered was that the Order had
raised the stakes and set a new basis for future resistance. Mathews had
taken up arms, knowing that he had no chance of success. But he had stood
up to do battle against the enemies of his race, and the Jews would not
know what to do when 'a hundred good men' rose up to take Mathews'
place.[13]

Shortly before the creation of the Order, Mathews had addressed the
National Alliance convention, declaring that he brought a message from the
Pacific Northwest where farmers, hit hard by 'the filthy, lying Jews and their
parasitical usury system', were being radicalized. 'The task is not going to
be easy', he stated. 'TV satellite dishes are springing up like poisonous
mushrooms. ... The electronic Jew is slithering into the living rooms of even
the most remote farms and ranches.' But, he stated, 'The signs of awakening
are sprouting up across the Northwest.' Pierce later recalled that when he
began to realize what Mathews might be planning, he had tried to dissuade
him. Mathews believed that the country was in a revolutionary ferment.
Pierce, however, had told him that this was not typical of the country, and
that people were not yet desperate enough to rise.[14]

This did not mean, however, that the Alliance rejected the Order. Under
the title 'A Call to Arms', it published an audiotape of Mathews' speech to
the Alliance convention. It also published a tribute to him. He had sought
to begin the Second American Revolution, and some had argued that he
was premature. If anything, the danger had been that he was too late, but
the people had not been ready. To better understand Mathews, it was
important to listen to his 1983 call to arms. One day he, and his fellow
patriots, would be seen as 'the equivalent of the embattled farmers' who
had begun the original American Revolution.[15]

As we noted earlier, in the years following the demise of the Order, others
have attempted to systematically break the law. The Aryan Republican
Army had been influenced by *The Turner Diaries*. So too was the terrorist
group led by Chevie Kehoe, the Aryan People's Republic.[16] Pierce, however,
neither praised McVeigh for bombing the Oklahoma Federal Building nor
believed that the attack was a government conspiracy. Instead, he believed
the attack 'didn't make sense politically'. Terrorism only made sense, he told

a journalist, if it could be sustained over a period. 'One day there will be real, organized terrorism done according to plan, aimed at bringing down the government.'[17]

If Pierce rejected the Oklahoma bombing, another leading extreme rightist did not. Tom Metzger argued that McVeigh had 'been instrumental in the most effective message' ever sent to America's rulers. The militias, he complained, had ceased opposing the System and turned instead to defending it, claiming that the attack had been launched by 'dirty racists' as part of a System conspiracy. But Middle America needed a 'wake up call', and the Oklahoma Federal Building had been a highly appropriate target. WAR would not join those who claimed the bombing had been a System plot. It hoped that McVeigh's action would win support, for he had 'gone further than any Aryan thus far in striking back at the Beast'.[18]

Subsequently Aryan Nations' August Kreis declared that the day of McVeigh's execution should henceforth be treated as a special day. Many believed that he could have been a tool of the Jew World Order, but he had struck a blow against the 'beast system'. He had refused to apologize for what he had done, and now, rather than rotting in jail for the rest of his life, he would be 'back with our Father'. But the fight to free the land from Jewish occupation would continue, for there would always be 'another Christian Soldier' to take the place of those who fell.[19]

Despite his enthusiasm for *The Turner Diaries*, McVeigh had pursued a very different strategy from the one Pierce espoused there. Metzger and Kreis, however, supported the Oklahoma attack, and to understand how they could do so, we need to turn our attention to an article written by a figure we have already encountered, Louis Beam.

It appeared first in the early 1980s in the pages of the *Inter-Klan and Survival Alert*. A version was subsequently published in the early 1990s in his later publication, the *Seditionist*. Federal tyranny, he declared, threatened to eliminate freedom in America, and those who sought to resist this needed to find a method that would prove effective. This should not be composed of a leader above and a mass below, a structure whose chain of command could be uncovered by electronic surveillance before the organization was infiltrated and destroyed. The alternative was the Phantom Cells or Leaderless Resistance proposed in the early 1960s by a veteran anticommunist, Colonel Ulius Louis Amoss. During the American Revolution, patriots had formed secret cells, and they had functioned without central direction. In fighting the federal government today, individuals and groups should also operate independently. Newspapers, leaflets and computers would keep them informed, enabling them to 'act when they feel the time is ripe', and while a single organization could be destroyed, in the future there would be 'a thousand points of resistance'.[20]

As with our earlier discussion of militias, there is a pre-history too to leaderless resistance. In the mid-1960s it was being promoted by Richard Cotten, a far right radio broadcaster (and subsequently a key figure in the early National Youth Alliance). In late 1965, his newsletter recommended a recent broadcast in which he had discussed phantom cells and leaderless resistance. The following year, a report of a conference of a far right group, the Congress of Freedom, described him discussing '"Phantom Cells" as outlined by Col. Amos'.[21]

The idea appeared too among the Christian-Patriots Defense League. In February 1984, Jack Mohr wrote a letter to supporters of the group and the affiliated Citizens Emergency Defense System, describing the latter as operating on the basis of leaderless resistance. This meant, he wrote, that each unit was self-sustaining and that it was almost impossible for an infiltrator to destroy the organization as a whole.[22] But it was Beam's article which led to the spread of the idea. WAR advocated leaderless resistance while a San Diego-based militant, Alex Curtis, was an enthusiastic exponent both on his website and in print. Beam had argued not only for separate cells but for individual action, and Curtis praised so-called lone wolf attacks. In July 1999, World Church of the Creator activist Ben Smith launched a series of attacks in Illinois and Indiana in which two people died, while the following month Aryan Nations supporter Buford Furrow opened fire on a Jewish day-care centre in Los Angeles and also killed an Asian-American postal worker.[23] Curtis himself was subsequently imprisoned for violating the civil rights of several people in his locality, but enthusiasm for decentralized violence continued, as was demonstrated by the response to a campaign by another individual terrorist, Eric Rudolph. In 1996, he set off an explosive device at the Olympic Games in Atlanta, Georgia. He subsequently bombed two abortion clinics and a gay nightclub before hiding for five years in the North Carolina countryside. Eventually apprehended, he was sentenced to multiple life sentences. In a statement handed out after he had decided to plead guilty, he described the Olympic Games as a celebration of 'global socialism'. The killing of millions of the unborn, he declared was a 'holocaust', while attempting to legitimize homosexuality was 'another assault upon the integrity of American society'. Force was justified against all of them.[24]

The Anti-Defamation League reported that following his arrest, extreme rightists had been vociferous in his support. One posting on the Aryan Nations website had declared that there would 'always be another to fill the shoes of a fallen hero', while a message on the White Revolution message board had declared: 'He rid this world of some degenerate scum. ... That is all that really matters to me.' A conservative website reported that messages on the Stormfront site were more direct still. One poster suggested that if there were more Rudolphs, McVeighs and Furrows in America 'we'd have a much nicer place to live', while a second declared: 'another good solid white warrior becomes another prisoner of war. We need more lone wolves ... WAY MORE!'[25]

As we shall see, such views are not shared throughout the extreme right. But if *The Turner Diaries* did not advocate leaderless resistance, the situation has been complicated by Pierce's authoring of a second novel. Published in the aftermath of the defeat of the Order and the attempted prosecutions at Fort Smith, *Hunter* was dedicated to Joseph Paul Franklin, whom he described as 'the Lone Hunter'. Franklin, Pierce said, had seen 'his duty as a White man and did what a responsible son of his race must do'. Immediately following this dedication, the book opens with a description of the murder of a black man and his white female companion. The killer is a white engineer, Oscar Yeager, who has already carried out five similar attacks, and he does so because such attacks would be readily understood, because they had 'therapeutic value' for him and, above all, so they could be imitated by others. He meets, however, a member of 'the National League', an organization dedicated to raising racial consciousness and ultimately bringing about 'a White World ... governed by eugenic principles'. The man explains to Yeager that the media is controlled by Jews, but Yeager is not persuaded. He subsequently bombs a meeting of leading anti-racists and is then held at gunpoint by an FBI agent.[26]

But instead of arresting him, the agent wants him to kill to order. His first target is a Jewish FBI official, and once again Yeager is lectured on the nature of the Jewish conspiracy, and this time he reads a number of works on the subject and begins to be persuaded. He meets the National League activist again, who sets out the organization's beliefs, and then meets the FBI agent, now promoted to a senior position. The agent pours scorn on Yeager's new conviction that whites can be brought to understand the truth about race, but Yeager nonetheless joins the League.[27] Subsequently, the FBI man reveals to Yeager that he intends to establish a dictatorship, and Yeager's response is to kill him. As the racial tension grows worse, he returns to building the League, but after a few days, he comments, 'it would be time to do some more hunting'.[28]

Where Pierce's first book argued for central direction, his second was more confusing. It continued to argue for centralized leadership but accepted its leading character's efforts to emulate Franklin. Asked by a later interviewer if *Hunter* advocated leaderless resistance, he denied it. Where Earl Turner had remained unchanged in Pierce's first novel, his second was intended to show how Yeager developed in understanding. He started as 'a typical idiot conservative' who was racist but did not understand 'the Jewish angle'. But he also started as a lone wolf. He came to realize this was 'no way to get things done ... if you really wanted to have an effect it would have to be in an organizational context and that's completely contrary to the leaderless resistance thesis'.[29]

In 1993, a collection of articles concerned with the subject appeared in the pages of the *WAR Eagle*, a paper which described itself as 'A Voice and Forum for Revolutionary Pan-Aryanism'. It opened with Louis Beam's article, and one of the other contributions was a short piece in support of the tactic by White Aryan Resistance. A longer article by another activist, Art Jones, drew on his experiences first in Vietnam, then in the NSWPP to argue that without centralized discipline, the struggle could not be won.

Hitler and Rockwell, he argued, showed the way forward, in which the path of legality should not be abandoned unless it became impossible. Leaderless resistance represented an abdication of leadership, and all it led to was activists planning 'mindless mayhem' or even their manipulation into acts of violence by federal informants and their subsequent imprisonment.

Another article focused on what it saw as a growing trend for activists to indulge in dreams of guerilla warfare. Anybody who wanted to study this form of warfare, he suggested, should read works by Guevara and Mao, not *The Turner Diaries*, and they would see what was crucial was popular support, something racialists did not have. Jews had obtained power by slowly building up their influence. They had not wasted their time with fantasies of revolution, and Aryans should distance themselves from the 'irresponsible losers' who called for immediate revolution.

The article's author, Jost, was the founder of the National Socialist Kindred, a group that had tried to set up a white separatist enclave on the West Coast. Like Jones, he was a Vietnam veteran.[30] But both men rejected an extreme right guerilla strategy, whether leaderless or not. A further contribution, by Pierce, reiterated the argument for a centralized organization of political violence. He saw no evidence that leaderless resistance was yet happening. 'I wish we had even one Oscar Yeager stalking the streets of Washington. ... It would be an enormous moral boost for all of us, and it would help greatly with recruitment.' But the 'message of *Hunter*' had not been that Yeager's initial actions had been the way forward. He had realized that he wasn't 'stimulating imitators to a significant degree' and he changed 'his whole approach'. Centralized leadership was what was needed, and while for now this could still be treated as a subject for debate, the time would come when a definite choice would have to be made.[31]

In a broadcast in the late 1990s, commenting on the shooting at the Los Angeles Jewish community centre, Pierce recalled again his sense of 'rage' when working in Washington. 'I wanted to blow up government buildings and kill the politicians and bureaucrats. ... I wanted to use a machine gun and sweep the streets clean of all the non-Whites'. White men should feel this rage. But it was time to think 'of a more constructive outlet ... than simply shooting at targets of opportunity, a la Benjamin Smith or Buford Furrow'. He would even suggest that

> there are even more useful things for an angry patriot to do than building a truck bomb and blowing up the nearest Federal office building. At this particular moment in the breakdown of our society, these occasional, random acts of violence are not especially helpful. They are not part of a sound strategy.[32]

The argument has continued since the 1990s. In 2000 *Resistance* published an article by Eric Hollyoak. 'The Fallacy of Leaderless Resistance' argued that nothing better defined the 'incompetence of the radical racist resistance' than the idea of leaderless resistance. It was little more than anarchy and, as recent examples demonstrated, quickly degenerated into banditry. It had never worked in history. The American Revolution had been centrally directed. The Order had started as a small cell but its apparent belief that its actions would inspire others had led to failure. Yet if they had studied Guevara, they would have realized that a small band of guerillas cannot bring about a mass revolt. The Order had robbed banks and armoured cars and it had 'shared the loot with phone booth emperors who were vying for the same mailing list'. They had also killed 'a particularly obnoxious Jew', blown up a synagogue and murdered one of their own recruits. But they had not succeeded in generating significant support for 'their crime spree'.

For an exemplary example of individual leaderless resistance, Hollyoak suggested, Eric Rudolph deserved attention. 'Personally', he remarked, 'my reaction to the bombing of abortion clinics and fag bars is, "Where's the crime?"' He had developed ever more sophisticated devices, and enjoyed some support. But he worked alone in 'his holy mission', and was unable to extend it. A 'properly constituted resistance organization' would separate out such tasks as financing and targeting. It should be directed by a policy-making body which would delegate the execution of plans to others in the chain of command. Starting with armed cells first inevitably led to a search for recruits that would allow in government informants. Anyone who advocated this approach should 'stay home with the women'. Serious resistance needed a separation of responsibilities and the 'rigid authoritarianism' of a centralized organization.[33]

The response was furious. Alex Curtis argued that the Order should have used smaller cells and been more selective in its recruitment. If Rudolph had belonged to an organization, government infiltration would have made it impossible for him to kill Jewish abortionists, while Guevara's failure in Bolivia had to be set against the Cuban Revolution's initiation by a small group. Leaderless resistance, if carried out by activists who did not allow themselves to be traced through involvement in open organizations, was the way forward. Hollyoak's article was better understood if it was read as a parody. It described a 'silly fantasy command structure', and Tim McVeigh, Eric Rudolph or Joseph Paul Franklin should not have to wait for its orders before carrying out actions.[34]

A Canadian-based racist women's magazine, *Sigrdrifa*, published responses from members of the Order. Gary Lee Yarborough, who was serving fifteen years for weapons offences and sixty years for racketeering, described Hollyoak's article as 'journalistic racial treason'. The Order had not been criminal or an example of leaderless resistance. It had been directed by a small group, with Mathews as the most important, and among the 'phone booth emperors' who had received its 'loot' was Pierce himself. In the absence of real leaders, leaderless resistance was preferable to the organizations that existed. One day, the time for 'large scale, organized resistance' would hopefully come.[35]

In another statement for the same publication, Randy Duey, who had been sentenced to 100 years for racketeering, conspiracy and robbery, argued that if the members of the Order had spent time studying guerilla warfare, they probably would have done nothing. He still was not sure if they had done as well as they could, but while they had wanted to be a spark, there had been no agreement on what would follow. Neither leaderless resistance or any other theory was the only way forward. There was 'room for variety', but his inclination was to do without leaders. 'The last thing we need is another government to oppress us', while if a thousand Eric Rudolphs or twenty-five Orders arose, the system would be really in danger.[36]

The next issue of *Resistance* returned to the issue, with a letter from Richard Scutari, who was serving forty years for racketeering and conspiracy and twenty years for robbery. He was unaware, he wrote, if Hollyoak was deliberately spreading disinformation or was simply ignorant. He had great respect for Pierce and it was understandable he could not be keeping an eye on everything that was published in *Resistance*. But Hollyoak's article had denigrated the Order. Most racist leaders, Scutari declared, had been involved in its support structure and received money from the Order. It was either deceit or naivety to believe that only an aboveground organization could 'run an effective revolution'. They were always infiltrated, and while their role in propaganda was vital, what was needed was for leaderless resistance cells to emerge, unite with others and then put the movement as a whole under their command.[37]

Writing in the National Alliance bulletin in March 2000, Pierce attacked Metzger and Curtis, declaring that leaderless resistance was 'simply an excuse for losers, cowards, and shirkers to do nothing except talk to each other'. It had been a mistake, however, for the *Resistance* article to treat the Order as an example of leaderless resistance when in fact it had been centralized with a strong leader. Continuing the argument in the July *Bulletin*, he attacked leaderless resistance yet again. It was a 'copout' for shirkers and cowards because there were not 'enough Earl Turners or Oscar Yeagers' to do more than cause the government some irritation. Nor was it true that leaderless resistance was secure from infiltration. Federal informants could approach activists with talk of violence and get them jailed. When the time came to 'deal with traitors, we will deal with them collectively and finally, not by picking off one or two of them now with harebrained "leaderless resistance" schemes'.[38]

Pierce's criticism of Hollyoak's *Resistance* article did not persuade its author. George Michael identifies Hollyoak as Steven Barry, a former Special Forces sergeant. Pierce had sought to correct his account of the Order, Barry subsequently noted, and he did not know if the books and articles he had drawn on for his article had been accurate or not. But it was not up to him 'to mend fences with those who persist in their error'. WAR, the Order and others were engaging in 'a campaign of backbiting and mudslinging', but none of the responses to his article could cite one example in history of leaderless resistance.[39]

Beam's *Essays of a Klansman* had been among the books Order members were encouraged to read, and some of what he had said in it exerted an influence on other militants. Thus White Patriot Party leader Glenn Miller's declaration of war had proclaimed that party members should 'pick up the sword'. Yahweh would fill their hearts with courage, and Aryan warriors should receive one point for every black they killed, ten for every Jew and fifty for every judge.[40] But it was Beam's defence of leaderless resistance that would be particularly influential. In its video, 'The Aryan Republican Army Presents: The Armed Struggle', the ARA described itself as part of a broader struggle and complained that it was 'tired of funding all these other phantom cells'. Imprisoned Order veteran David Lane also authored an article in which he called for the creation of what he called Wotan, the Will Of The Aryan Nation. Lane proposed a division between a political arm and an armed party. The political wing should remain completely distinct from the armed wing, and focus its energies on the dissemination of propaganda. The armed party would be made up of 'small autonomous cells, one man cells if possible'. They would use 'fire, bombs, guns, terror, disruption, and destruction', and those who performed 'valuable service for the system' would be the targets. 'Judges, lawyers, bankers, real estate agents, judeo-Christian preachers, federal agents, and other assorted treacherous swine take note, Wotan is coming. Your wealth, your homes, your women, and your lives are at risk when you commit treason.'[41]

The National Socialist Movement also became involved. 'Revolution for Beginners', an article on its website, declared that 'young idealists' had been imprisoned for 'actions that didn't harm the System in the least. The government couldn't care less if you kill a non-white.' What was needed, however, was the creation of cells which could attack the proper targets. Some would rob banks or armoured cars or dope dealers. Some would assassinate key officials, from federal judges and media bosses to 'anti-white' politicians and Anti-Defamation League leaders. Others could disrupt the economy, while others could win popular support by eliminating those who raped or murdered whites.[42]

But the debate over leaderless resistance had not ended with the responses to Barry's article. The National Alliance remained opposed to the idea, although during the period it was cooperating with the Church of the Creator, one of the Alliance's then leading activists, David Pringle, wrote two leaflets for the church. In one, he cited leaderless resistance as one of the failings of the movement. In the other, he declared that it had 'its time and place'. But now was the time to 'recruit the mass of White men and women we will need to win. ... I implore any white man who is now considering a shooting spree or a bombing, not to do it. There will be a time to attack the enemy with direct action.'[43]

Nor was he the only activist who had gained their political experience in the Alliance to think along these lines. In 2003, White Revolution's Billy

Roper argued that there was no 'great divide' between open activity and the lone wolf or single cell theory.

> We need a two-tiered approach. We need people who are willing to be exposed and public ... and it is my hope that in the future we will need completely anonymous, unknown racial loyalists who will be able to express themselves in a manner which our enemies will find equally unambiguous, in a less public manner.

The day had not yet come, he went on, when race traitors were afraid to show their faces in public. 'I can't yet open the newspaper and read every day about the brave exploits of anonymous lone wolves, and until I can, my job isn't done.'[44]

If David Pringle or White Revolution saw a role for leaderless resistance, Aryan Nations has been even more sympathetic, with August Kreis declaring that a membership organization would not suit everyone. Dedicated and trained individuals could strike strong blows against Zionism. 'If you have any plans to operate as a lone wolf individual then NEVER become affiliated with a known organization.'[45] But while leaderless resistance has attracted some on the extreme right, it has alienated others. Nor has it been the only argument extreme rightists have had over political violence. Another, for instance, has divided Identity believers.

In 1990 Richard Kelly Hoskins published *Vigilantes of Christendom*. In the Old Testament, he observed, an Israelite was described as having sought to take 'a Midianitish woman' as his wife. A man named Phineas had taken 'a javelin in his hand ... and thrust both of them through ... and the Lord spake ... saying Phineas ... hath turned my wrath away from the children of Israel'. God had forbidden racial intermarriage, and Phineas had enforced his law, and the Bible had gone on to say that there would be 'an everlasting priesthood'. Robin Hood had been a Phineas priest, as had King Arthur and Jesse James. In Denver, the Order had killed Alan Berg. In the Midwest, a sniper had killed inter-racial couples. As the Japanese had the Kamikaze and Islam had militant Shi'ites, so Christendom had the Phineas priesthood.[46]

Hoskins' book influenced the Aryan Republican Army.[47] But it has also been criticized within the extreme right. In 'Can There Be Vigilantes in Christendom?', one Identity figure, Dan Gayman, argued that no Christians 'in good conscience' should take it upon themselves to 'execute vengeance out of the barrel of a gun'. In 'Is There Such a Thing as Christian Justifiable Homicide?', the Identity preacher Jack Mohr reported that many men had asked questions 'regarding the scriptural right of a Christian to take the Law into their own hands'. Did Phineas' action mean that modern-day Israelites could kill a white man for consorting with a black woman or execute a Jewish abortionist? No individual, he believed, had the right to 'execute vengeance' on murderers or adulterers. Violence in self-defence was justified, but to stop such evils as abortion Christians should not resort to force. Nor would it be wise to do so. As the Oklahoma City bombing demonstrated, Christian Patriots did not benefit from violence. The New World Order did.[48]

Yet another Identity figure, Ted Weiland, also opposed Hoskins' view. One writer, he noted, had stated that he had often been asked how he had become a Phineas priest. The answer was that after Phineas had taken action, Yahweh had established a perpetual priesthood. To be one of his priests today was to act on personal initiative to carry out Yahweh's judgement. But the Biblical passage that such writers cited was not compatible with such claims. Numbers 25 specifically said that an 'everlasting priesthood' would be the legacy of Phineas' 'seed'. But it was impossible for any Identity believer to trace back his lineage to Phineas, and to believe that you were acting on Yahweh's behalf would merely lead a self-styled priest to lawlessness.[49]

In turn, the Aryan Nations journal has published a reply to Gayman. He had argued that as a priest, Phineas had been authorized to exact judgement. But did this mean that 'present-day vigilantes' were not authorized to defend Christ's Kingdom? On the contrary, Christ had established the Priesthood of Believers whereby Christians could reign and sit in judgement with him. The 'Christian vigilante of today' would have to be 'spiritually prepared and called to action' but if so, he was 'no less authorized than Phineas of old'.[50]

Indeed, different fragments of Aryan Nations have claimed to incarnate the Phineas priesthood. The Kreis faction has declared that the priesthood 'is alive and well' while the Church of the Sons of Yahweh has also claimed to be continuing the priesthood tradition.[51] Yet if the argument about the Phineas priesthood has affected and divided Identity believers, other arguments have reached further. Al-Qaeda's attacks on the World Trade Center and the Pentagon led to a global war on terror. As we discuss in Chapter 8, this is a development which the extreme right has discussed extensively. But the extreme right had much to say too about the attacks themselves. In part, it concerned who had launched the attacks. For some, it was far from believable that Islamist terrorists were responsible. Perhaps, *American Free Press* speculated, the attackers had really been controlled by Israeli intelligence or, taking up a theory circulating in the Patriot movement, perhaps the aircraft had not been hijacked but had been remotely controlled. For others on the extreme right, however, the attacks were indeed carried out by al-Qaeda hijackers.[52]

But for those extreme rightists who believed that 9/11 was the work of Islamists, there was still a question. Was it to be condemned? *Aryan Loyalist*, a Florida-based newsletter, carried the headline 'Blitzkrieg!!! Jew York and Washington D.C. Attacked, Otto Skorzeny Style!!!' The chairman of another small grouping, the American Nazi Party, declared that it was 'a DISGRACE that in a population of at least 150 MILLION White/Aryan

Americans, we provide so FEW that are willing to do the same'. Tom Metzger, writing on the WAR website, commented that 'This operation took some long-term planning, and, throughout the entire time, these soldiers were aware that their lives would be sacrificed for their cause. If an Aryan wants an example of "Victory or Valhalla", look no further.' Finally, the National Alliance's Billy Roper declared that 'anyone who is willing to drive a plane into a building to kill jews is alright to me'.[53]

Others, however, were opposed to the attacks. William Pierce, for instance, denounced them for killing 'thousands of young White women' who were working as receptionists, secretaries and file clerks in the World Trade Center and the Pentagon, while on the Stormfront site, one respondent declared that while he opposed Jewish schemes 'as much as anyone. . . . No one who flies airplanes full of ARYANS into buildings full of ARYANS is a friend of the ARYANS.'[54]

This dispute has escalated with the decision of some extreme rightists to support Islamist terrorism as a crucial way forward for the fight against Zionism. The Kreis faction of Aryan Nations has published an array of material supporting Islamist terrorism. One suggested that for those who were 'serious about NATIONAL SOCIALIST HOLY WAR', anything that disrupted the System was positive. Hamas, Hezbollah and al-Qaeda were all to be seen in this light. On one page, it was suggested that national socialists should join with or aid the Muslims who had taken up arms against Zionism and its lackeys. Another proposed that while a 'Turner Diaries scenario' might yet occur, this was up to Yahweh, and for now it was Muslims who were 'conduits for his wrath'.[55] In an interview, Kreis declared his admiration of al-Qaeda. He considered the group to be freedom fighters and he wanted Bin Laden to know, 'the cells are out here and they are already in place. They might not be cells of Islamic people, but they are here and they are ready to fight.'[56]

Even more strikingly, two years before the al-Qaeda attacks, Alex Curtis' Racist Readers Forum had published a posting observing that Bin Laden had weapons of mass destruction and would be aware of the White House, the Pentagon, Capitol House and the New York Stock Exchange. 'Lock and Load', it continued, 'to perdition with white race murdering financier billionaire jews, gentiles, and their paid-for murderers of the White race: politicians, judges, media, law enforcement, and militaries'.[57]

The subsequent support for the 9/11 attacks by some on the extreme right did not represent all of them, and as we saw in Chapter 5, there was fierce argument over whether extreme rightists should support Muslims. In 2002, however, the Aryan Nations website carried a warning that unless the US stopped aiding Israel and working against Saddam Hussein, suicide bombers would emerge on American soil. 'Will the sons and daughters of YHVH God be joining with the zealous soldiers of Mohammed, rising up in righteous indignation? Will the Phineas Priests and Phineas Priestesses begin awaking all over this country . . . ?'. Another document by the same author praised a 'glorious suicide bombing' in 'Jewish Occupied Palestine'. The Hamas member had lost his life, but he had 'done a great service to his people and to his God'.[58]

These were not the only such documents to appear on the Aryan Nations site. George Michael's discussion of the links between the extreme right and radical Islam include an extended extract of a fictional account which appeared on the site depicting a Hamas suicide bomber killing a Jewish white slave trafficker. In 2005, Aryan Nations published part 1 of a National Socialist 'Guide to Understanding Islam'. Devoted to what it described as 'martyrdom operations', it explained that killing oneself in pursuit of a higher aim derived from the Islamic belief that life on Earth was only a stage. Those that died while carrying out an attack would be judged by Allah as would any non-combatant killed during the incident. Another essay, 'Are Martyrdom Operations Lawful?', concluded that they were in accord with Muslim teaching. Bin Laden, it noted, had character-ized such attacks as inflicting great harm on the United States and Israel, and the aims of those who carried them out were pure. The article, it was revealed, had been written by the British extreme rightist David Myatt, and had also been placed on the Hamas website.[59]

Nor have suicide bombings been the only form of terrorism to attract some extreme rightists as the Middle East conflict rages on. They have also fantasised about assassinating government officials responsible for Amer-ican intervention abroad. In 2004, Vanguard News Network published an imaginary account of a white Iraq war veteran's radicalization. He returns home, devastated at the death of a fellow Marine who would have lived if there had not been a chronic shortage of body armour. Then he comes upon the Vanguard News Network site, and learns how the man he mourns had died in 'a war started by jews to benefit jews', and that the reason why there was not enough body armour was because 'the jews stole the money. ... It took all his self-control not to run out and slaughter the first jew he saw, and continue slaughtering jews, until either he was killed, or he ran out of jews to slaughter.' Instead he lies in wait outside a synagogue, inside which is the Jewish Assistant Secretary of Defense, and as the story comes to an end, the veteran fires a silenced carbine into the man's brain.[60]

Two years later, the National Alliance published a fictional account of 'the launch of the Second American Revolution'. American troops have retreated from Iraq, and almost 2,000 soldiers are killed by suicide bombers in Lebanon. The White Liberation Movement decides to provoke the gov-ernment to move against the white population. Teams of assassins are sent to eliminate government officials. The subsequent publication of the names of those they had killed, the author observed, 'would have alerted even the most dimwitted American to the reality that Jews now occupied almost all the senior posts in the government'.[61]

In these two responses to the Iraq War, extreme rightists are once again expressing the anti-Semitism that has defined much of their response to everything which they deplore. But if many of them agree on the need for political violence, they have not resolved the argument on how that violence can prevail. The clash between leaderless resistance and a centralized guerrilla strategy goes on, and as we saw with Aryan Nations' pronouncements on suicide bombings, the idea of a Phineas priesthood is also still in circulation. The result is a divided extreme right, but one in which dreams of violence are disturbingly powerful.

8 Race and the right

The 1950s were a key moment for the American extreme right. The *Brown* decision was crucial to the revival of the Ku Klux Klan, while subsequently first the Liberty Lobby, then the National States Rights Party, then the American Nazi Party, emerged as key organizations. But if the decade was key for the extreme right, it was central too for two other strands of the right. In part, the rise of these other strands would give the extreme right real opportunities. But it would also present it with great obstacles.

While conservatism had existed before the 1950s, the emergence in 1955 of a new magazine, *National Review*, represented its rebirth in a modern form. The new publication insisted that the right should focus its attentions on the threat of communism. For some, America was threatened by the decline of traditional authority. For others, it was endangered by the erosion of liberty. Communism could be seen as antagonistic to both tradition and liberty, and one effect of focusing on its defeat was to bring different strands of the right closer together. Conservatives were fiercely hostile to liberalism, which they saw as soft on communism and responsible for the creation of a massively bloated government. This latter aspect would be important for many of the battles that conservatives would fight in the future. But it was the global war against communism that was central to the rise of modern conservatism. It was crucial too to the growth of the modern radical right.[1]

In its most common usage, the latter described an array of militant anti-communist groupings that became highly visible in the early 1960s.[2] But it is best retained for those who are motivated by the conviction that America has long been under attack by a conspiracy, and fear that the conspiracy has been winning. The crucial group in this regard is the John Birch Society. Named after an American intelligence operative killed by Chinese communists following the end of the Second World War, the Society emerged in 1958. It was soon discovered, however, that a book authored by its founder, Robert Welch, took anti-communism further than many on the right were willing to go. At the beginning of the decade, Senator McCarthy had claimed that the American government had been infiltrated by communists. *The Politician*, however, speculated that President Eisenhower was himself an agent of the communist conspiracy. This was not the only way in which the Society differed from its McCarthyist forebears. Initially, it still believed the danger came from communism. By the mid-1960s, however, it had adopted the theory that would become crucial for the later radical right. Communists, it came to believe, were not the main enemy. Instead, a more ancient conspiracy had created communism.[3]

Conservatives and radical rightists shared a great deal. But they differed as to why America was in danger, and attempts to forge an alliance between them proved to be far from easy. In 1964 they worked together in an ultimately unsuccessful attempt to elect Republican senator Barry Goldwater as president. The following year, however, *National Review* declared that the Society's claims that a communist conspiracy controlled the American government made it not a valuable part of the American right, but an obstacle to its advance.[4]

But conservatives were not the only section of the right to denounce the Society. Just as conservatives were initially welcoming to the Society, it in turn had initially been willing to include extreme rightists among its numbers. In 1963, however, Welch published a pamphlet, *The Neutralizers*, accusing anti-Semites of distracting attention away from the real nature of America's enemies and how to fight them. Nor, he suggested, was this by chance. The *Protocols*, he speculated, could well have been forged by Lenin himself as part of a long-range plan to neutralize those who would oppose communism. In 1965, the issue became more heated still following a much-publicized speech by a leading Society member, Revilo Oliver. Arguing that any conspiracy theory was in danger of over-simplifying, he had declared that even if, 'by some miracle all the Bolsheviks or all of the Illuminati or all the Jews were vaporized at dawn tomorrow', America would still be in danger. The subsequent furore resulted in Oliver's resignation from the Society. Later in the decade, he was to come to see the National Youth Alliance as the way forward.[5]

He was not the only extreme rightist to break with the Society, and in 1970, the *Thunderbolt* printed statements by former members attacking Welch's leadership. Oliver was quoted as having engaged in an extended investigation that culminated in his discovering that Welch was the 'cunning' agent of a 'sinister and alien force'. Another defector claimed that not only were Society members not being told 'the whole truth about the Conspiracy' but that the Society was serving the conspirators by misdirecting the efforts of its members. Prominently displayed in the article was a letter to Welch from former Society member (and future founder of the Church of the Creator) Ben Klassen. 'You know as well as anybody', he had written, 'that we are not threatened by a "Communist" conspiracy, but in the clutches of a Jewish conspiracy'. Yet Society literature gave no hint of this, because Welch himself was an agent of the Jews.[6]

The Society had, of course, generated its own alternative theory of who was behind communism, but it was one that infuriated extreme rightists.

The *Thunderbolt* attacked the appearance of Gary Allen's *None Dare Call It Conspiracy*. The Jews, it declared, had Americans 'under firm mind control', but they knew there was a chance that this would fail. In anticipation of this eventuality, they were trying to place the blame for their plotting elsewhere, and Allen's work was an example of just this ploy. Allen demonstrated that the banks and the media were controlled by Jews. But he argued that some of the conspirators were Gentiles, and he explicitly rejected the idea that the conspiracy itself was Jewish. The hour was late, but the Society was still leading 'White Christians' astray.[7]

The extreme right has continued to attack the Society. In 1996, for instance, William Pierce recalled that over thirty years earlier he had briefly been a member of the Society. He had proposed that it should emphasize the link between 'the Jewish founders of Communism and today's Jewish media bosses', and had been given a pamphlet to read. It was Robert Welch's *The Neutralizers*, and in response he had written to the author arguing that 'the real enemy of our people was the Jew. ... Welch was not impressed by my evidence or my arguments, and the John Birch Society and I parted company.'[8]

As we have already seen, the extreme right has continued its conflict with the radical right within the Patriot movement. But if those who believe the enemy is racial continue to see the radical right as an enemy, their attitude to conservatism is more complex. If we look at the extreme right's doctrinal statements, what is initially most evident is the gap between the two belief systems. One article in an ANP journal, for instance, is entitled 'National Socialists *Are Not* "Conservatives"'. Where national socialists supported free enterprise, it declared, they opposed capitalism. It exploited workers for the benefit of Zionism, and while conservatives were reactionary, only national socialism could smash communism in America. An article published slightly later in the National Youth Alliance's periodical, 'Why Conservatives Can't Win', argued that faced with a danger from the revolutionary left, those who opposed it could not be satisfied with such goals as getting a conservative on the Supreme Court or electing a Republican to the White House. Fifty years earlier, conservatives had defended eugenics and laws against miscegenation. Now they had lost sight of what they once defended. An 'outstanding anti-communist leader' (the article did not name him as Hitler) had once called for 'a fanatical belief' in 'the victory of a revolutionary new order'. It was this that was needed, and young Americans who were uninspired by conservatism would rally to the call for Western man to destroy the enemies of their race.[9]

But these two pronouncements were by particularly intransigent sections of the extreme right. Furthermore, they were particularly aimed at arguing why those who were already rightists should choose to join an extreme right organization. Liberty Lobby, however, took a very different view of how the extreme right should relate to conservatism. Furthermore, conservatism in its early years seemed to offer particular opportunities to those who did see race as all important. We can see this if we examine how conservatives responded to the *Brown* decision and the rise of the Civil Rights Movement. As a recent history of the magazine by its long-time senior editor laments, at the beginning of the 1960s *National Review* had argued that 'In the Deep South, the Negroes are, by comparison with the Whites, retarded' and that it was irresponsible to 'hand over ... the raw political power' by which blacks could change the South. (Indeed, three years earlier the magazine had contended that 'the White community in the South is entitled to take such measures as are necessary to prevail'. It was 'the advanced race', and 'the claims of civilization' superseded those of universal suffrage.)[10] Most importantly, regardless of what they thought about its potential for the rise of a racial consciousness, extreme rightists had to respond to conservatism's advance during the period. It was becoming a strong force in America, and they needed to try to seek to grow in that context.

In 1964, the Republicans decided to nominate Senator Barry Goldwater for the presidential election. Goldwater was both a leading anti-communist and an opponent of the 1964 Civil Rights Act. But he was also Jewish.

The ANP was particularly hostile to Goldwater. The senator, it complained, was really an advocate of integration, and during the 1950s, instead of offering Senator McCarthy unstinting support, he had criticized him. Now the people were becoming increasingly aware of what needed to be done, and the Jews were manoeuvring to stop them. Communism was led by Jews, and it was vital that its opponents not look to a Jew to lead the fight against it.[11]

The *Thunderbolt* too challenged Goldwater's stance on race. In the 1950s, it complained, the senator had told a conference of the NAACP that Eisenhower was seeking to eliminate 'every vestige of segregation and discrimination in American life'. But it took issue too with his claim that he had never known of a Jew who was not a patriot. On the contrary, it declared, 'WE DON'T KNOW OF ANY JEW WHO WAS A PATRIOT!'[12]

The United Klans, however, supported Goldwater. Liberty Lobby too argued for his support. It described Goldwater's nomination as releasing 'one of the greatest bursts of energy ever seen in the American people'. What was needed, however, was for the Republican party to adopt policies that would attract white workers and give blacks the opportunity to return to Africa. Most surprisingly, in contrast to the ANP, the dissident national socialists of the *Free American* declared that they endorsed Goldwater. He was only partly a Jew, and the key task was to defeat the Democratic candidate, and elect a right-winger.[13]

Whether as critics or supporters, the extreme right played little part in the 1964 presidential campaign. Four years later, however, the right's division over two candidates gave the extreme right greater opportunities. George Wallace had been the Democrat governor of Alabama, and in 1964 he had been unsuccessful in seeking the party's presidential nomination. In 1968, he became the candidate for the recently formed American Independent Party.

The Republican candidate was Richard Nixon. For most conservatives, Wallace was unacceptable because he favoured greater government spending than they could support. But in other ways he was highly compatible. He defended the Vietnam War and denounced Washington bureaucrats.[14] But he was most associated with race. The outbreak of riots in the North had led to accusations that the civil rights agitation was a threat to law and order, while some accused it of links with communism. As we saw in previous chapters, these arguments were used by the extreme right. But they were also made by the John Birch Society, for instance, and made it all the easier for extreme right and radical right to stand together behind the Wallace candidacy.[15]

Extreme right support for Wallace was particularly evident among its southern contingents. His speeches were written by former Klan organizer Asa Carter, while in early 1968, the United Klans of America declared that 'Communist anti-Christ Zionist Jews' and 'Negro guerillas' had come together in an attempt to destroy white Christian America. George Wallace's campaign for the presidency offered a ray of hope, and the Klan had launched a voter registration drive.[16]

But Wallace's support was not restricted to extreme rightists in the South. In its comments on the need for Republicans to reach beyond the Goldwater constituency, Liberty Lobby had observed that Wallace's vote in Democratic primaries in the North had shown his strength. In a subsequent pamphlet, it presented Wallace as an opponent of desegregation who pursued a responsible use of government spending in his own state and who appealed to whites outside the South. As we have seen, Carto was instrumental in the launch of the National Youth Alliance in 1968. But he had been central too in the creation of its predecessor, Youth for Wallace. Liberty Lobby had been involved in preparation for Wallace's presidential bid from early on, and its pamphlet was distributed by the governor's own campaign.[17]

Once again, however, the extreme right did not speak with one voice. Commenting on the candidates in the election, the NSWPP leader, Matt Koehl, observed that Wallace 'stands relatively closer to the National Socialist position'. But whether he was an opportunist or naive, he had not taken a clear stand in support of the white race. Only when the situation in America greatly worsened would whites demand 'radical National Socialist surgery'. Until then the party would not play silly games at the ballot box but build the organization that would one day wrest power in America.[18]

Nor did the party change its mind after the election. Wallace was an opportunist, *White Power* claimed, who had been brought into the race because 'the System' had feared 'that the voters might catch onto the rotten Jewish-democratic fraud'. Some of his supporters had defended their stance by arguing that it was 'better to have something than nothing'. But this was wrong. 'Our job as National Socialists and revolutionaries is to demand the whole loaf.'[19]

Symptomatic of the times, Wallace gained nearly 10 million votes and over 13 per cent of the vote. But if the extreme right was hopeful that Wallace's election might have advanced its cause, it had no such hopes for Nixon. His election met with a bitter response. His criticism of the courts' calls for rapid integration was attacked by the NSWPP as merely a sop to Southern voters, and the *Thunderbolt* even called for his impeachment. Seeking election, it declared, he had promised voters that he would 'ease up' on integration. In office, however, he was continuing to try to bring 'race-mixing' about.[20]

Wallace's candidacy had appealed to racial fears, and Dan Carter has argued that in doing so, he left a lasting legacy for a conservatism which saw in white backlash a chance for power.[21] But while Nixon was seeking to win back voters who had chosen Wallace over him, in the long term a conservative appeal was being forged which did not prioritize racial resentment. Conservatives condemned inner-city riots and were highly critical of affirmative action. Furthermore, some of the issues they raised had racial elements, whether it was denouncing welfare spending or attacking liberals as soft on crime. But conservatives were taking up a wide range of issues, and some of the most important other issues appealed to very different discontents. During the 1970s, as we noted in Chapter 5, an anti-abortion movement had sprung up. Towards the end of the decade, the liberalization of abortion, the rise of a gay movement and attempts at regulation of religious institutions brought another movement onto the political stage. The Christian Right saw itself as defending faith and family against the attacks of a secular state, and it looked to the Republican Party to defend its interests. Furthermore, still another form of conservatism entered into the mix. During the 1970s, a group of veteran liberals had argued that it was vital to win the Cold War. Dubbed neoconservatives by their opponents, they were subsequently to become a key force within the conservative movement. During the 1980 presidential election campaign, conservatives emphasized the fight against both communism and liberalism. The Cold War could be won, they argued, while at home not only an over-mighty state but sexual permissiveness needed to be confronted. Their victorious candidate was Ronald Reagan.

For some on the extreme right, Reagan deserved support. As Reagan prepared to launch his campaign, Invisible Empire leader Bill Wilkinson declared that 'the Republican platform reads as if it were written by a Klansman'. (He subsequently claimed that 'the ideals of the Klan' had risen so far that 'the GOP platform parallels our views almost one-hundred percent'.)[22] The NSRP expressed its concern that Reagan might select George Bush as his vice-presidential candidate. It noted, however, that he was opposed by black organizations and had come out against abortion, affirmative action and busing. 'While we shall remain constructive, critics of Reagan will work hard to influence him for the right and pray that he will reverse his pro-Israeli stand after he is elected.'[23]

Others, however, were less willing to see a virtue in Reagan. While Tom Metzger complained that Klansmen were being called upon to register voters for the Republican candidate, leading Identity preacher Sheldon Emry accused Reagan of mouthing 'patriotic platitudes' while really supporting communism.[24] Of the different groupings, the National Alliance was particularly critical. Commenting at the end of 1980 on 'The Reagan Victory', it declared that as bad as the 25 million who had voted for Carter were the 42 million who had voted for Reagan. Some would have done so because they could see no other alternative to the Democrat. 'But the fact remains that a solid majority of America's White voters really believe that *their* man will be entering the White House. It would be funny, were it not so tragic.' Reagan would not even try to deal with the country's problems. What he might do was undermine environmental legislation, letting 'the chainsaw capitalists loose on our redwoods, the strip-mine capitalists loose on our mountainsides'. He might repay 'election debt' to evangelicals by stopping free abortion to women on welfare and undermining the teaching of evolution. But he would not try to wrest control of the media from those who controlled it. Nor would he stop 'the thousands of non-White aliens' who were pouring across the border every day.[25]

By the 1984 re-election campaign, little extreme right support persisted. Wilkinson once again called on Klansmen to work for Reagan's election. More symptomatic was the *Thunderbolt*'s declaration that it regretted ever supporting Reagan. He had proved to be a supporter of affirmative action, and he had approved government efforts to infiltrate 'right-wing Patriotic groups, undermine them, disrupt and neutralize our activity'. Now it would be right to support 'anyone EXCEPT Reagan'.[26] Elsewhere on the extreme right, others were seeking to organize against the president. The *Spotlight* had initially been sympathetic to Reagan, but it was soon arguing that the administration was under the influence of the Trilateral Commission. It also accused Reagan of having established 'concentration camps' to intern opponents.[27] It was in this context that a new political party began to emerge.

The Populist Party was important for several reasons. One was its ability to win over experienced activists, ranging from former organizers in the Klan and the National States Rights Party to leading Christian Patriots Defense League figure Jack Mohr.[28] Another was the role it played in the political aspirations of one of the leading figures on the extreme right, David Duke. A third was the promulgation of Carto's idea that what America needed was not conservatism, but populism.

America, he declared, was dominated by monopoly finance capitalism. But this was alien to the country's populist heritage. Populists had long been concerned with defending rural dwellers. But, above all, they stood for opposition to the threat that 'modern, industrial society' posed to family, nation and race. Not only liberals but conservatives advocated a new world order in which nations would give way to a global government. Populism would fight for nationalism.[29]

In its 1984 platform, the Populist Party combined denunciation of the Federal Reserve with calls for the protection of the American farmer and the American economy. It attacked busing and immigration, defended gun ownership and denounced homosexuality. Foreign policy, it proclaimed, should seek to avoid intervention abroad unless America was directly endangered. Reflecting Liberty Lobby's debt to Yockey, it argued that no racial minority should divide a country 'through control of the media, culture distortion or revolutionary political activity'.[30]

Populists saw themselves as opposed to the direction in which Reagan was taking America. But this did not mean that they insisted that only their party's candidates could be supported. In 1988, David Duke ran as its presidential candidate. The following year, however, he ran as a Republican for a seat in the Louisiana state legislature. He was victorious, and when he attended the 1989 Populist Party convention shortly after, he declared 'My victory in Louisiana was a victory for the white majority movement in this country.' As the Populist presidential candidate, he had declared that whites were being denied equal rights, and it was this approach that was crucial to his subsequent election as a Republican state legislator. (As he later wrote, in his campaign he had addressed issues from the 'racial discrimination against whites called affirmative action' and 'the educational disaster of forced integration' to the use of 'incentives to lower the high illegitimate welfare birthrate'.) But as the Populist presidential candidate, he had also accused George Bush of being under the control of Zionism.[31]

His ability to take racial concerns and make them central to electoral victory was crucial to the hopes that many on the extreme right placed in him. But in the long term, opposition to the foreign policy of conservative presidents would be crucial not only for him but for the extreme right as a whole. If Reagan's popularity owed much to his opposition to big government, it also owed much to his anti-communism. Reagan's successor would not be so fortunate. The early stages of the George Bush administration coincided with the collapse of the Soviet Union, and conservatism no longer had the all-important priority of defeating 'the evil empire'. Bush's unwillingness to champion the issues of the Christian Right lost him crucial support, and his willingness to raise taxes lost yet more. His launching of a war against Iraq in response to Saddam Hussein's invasion of Kuwait accentuated divisions on the right, and brought to prominence two very different foreign policy preferences. For neoconservatives, America's new role should be to use its power to create a democratic world order. For a number of other conservatives, however, particularly Reagan's former director of communications, Pat Buchanan, it was the Gulf War that had been the mistake, and only Israel and its American supporters had wanted such a war.[32]

Bush would be defeated by Bill Clinton, and for the remainder of the 1990s anger about abortion and, increasingly, gay marriage would be crucial for his conservative opponents. The election of George W. Bush in 2000 owed much to evangelical votes, and the years that followed would be marked by the continuing prominence of issues concerned with faith and family. But it would be al-Qaeda's attacks on 9/11 and the administration's response that would most define the conservatism of the early twenty-first century. It would bring neoconservatism to the centre of disputes about the future of the American right. It would shed new light too on the American extreme right's relationship to conservatism.

If anti-Semitism was central to the extreme right's breach with radical rightists, disputes over neoconservatism have been even more racially charged. At the beginning of the 1970s, a Liberty Lobby-linked publication had claimed that the American Jewish Committee had ordered the editor of the hitherto liberal magazine, *Commentary*, to 'make like a Conservative'. It was a theme that would recur. Shortly after Reagan's inauguration, the National Alliance noted that the editor of *Commentary* now called for resisting the decline of American power. Jews were strengthening their influence over conservatism and guiding it in directions favourable to their interests.[33] Neoconservatism's extreme right opponents insisted that its support for Israel was vitally linked with the ethnic background of key neoconservatives. In the beginning of 2001, for instance, the *Jubilee* drew attention to the presence of Richard Perle, Paul Wolfowitz and others on the list of Bush's foreign policy advisers published by the *New York Times*. 'Someone has assembled a most arrogant and ruthless tribe of anti-Arab, pro-Israel, anti-Christian warmakers to advise (if not to dictate) the foreign policy for Baby Bush.'[34] It was an argument that would come to the fore later in the year.

On 11 September, al-Qaeda attacked the World Trade Center and the Pentagon. In response, President Bush announced the launching of a War on Terror. First Afghanistan, then Iraq, was invaded, and *Commentary* and other neoconservative publications called for the overthrow of the governments of Syria, Iran and other Middle Eastern states. The World Church of the Creator declared that the 'Jewish-dominated government' was using white Americans as '"human shields"' when the righteous wrath of the Arab people' turned to violence. David Duke accused powerful Jews of bringing war about, and the successor to the *Spotlight*, the *American Free Press*, published a book-length attack on the new turn in Bush's foreign policy. Neoconservatives, it declared, had forged close ties between the American government and right-wing Zionists in Israel. But they had done far more than this. They believed in an American global hegemony, an empire, in which America itself would be the pawn of a hidden elite.[35]

The book did not only attack neoconservatism. It also attacked the Christian Right for its support for Israel. The extreme right had long felt antipathy to evangelical conservatives. In the 1980s, for instance, James Warner's Christian Defense League had attacked it and, as we have seen, so too did the National Alliance. But while the Christian Right's support for Israel was not the only factor in the extreme right's hostility, it was already crucial. In the mid-1980s, for instance, the *Thunderbolt* published an attack on Moral Majority leader Jerry Falwell. He had declared on his TV programme, *The*

Old Time Gospel Hour, that he was a Zionist who had long worked to get evangelicals to take a stand beside the Jewish people. A Judas goat was an animal used by meat packing companies to lead other animals to their deaths. This was the right description for a man who was trying to lead Christians to support 'the most anti-Christ race of people on earth'.[36]

But if the extreme right had long been hostile to the Christian Right, it was a mere shadow of its hatred for neoconservatism. A politics which supported Israel and argued for widespread intervention shaped the Bush administration, and was seen as the result of decades of neoconservative plotting. The extreme right's hostility to neoconservatives was strikingly demonstrated in the years that followed Bush's election. Michael Collins Piper of the *American Free Press*, for instance, was invited to Abu Dhabi to attack the government's foreign policy, while David Duke visited Syria to express his support for its 'people and their just stances'. The intensity of extreme right opposition to neoconservatism was even more evident if we turn to the National Alliance. In the previous chapter, we noted its publication of an assassination fantasy aimed at the architects of the Iraq War. If we compare it with a list of 'Jews in the first Bush administration who drove the war in Iraq' which appeared in an earlier issue of *National Vanguard*, we see how close various real names and positions in the administration are to those given to the different figures slain by the fictional hit squads of the white revolution.[37]

But if the extreme right is hostile to those conservatives who support Israel and favour the overthrow of Middle Eastern regimes, so too is a strand within conservatism. As we noted earlier, the Gulf War had been opposed by Pat Buchanan. He subsequently entered primaries for the Republican presidential nomination in 1992 and 1996. In 2000, he ran as a candidate for a third party. He argued against the liberalization of abortion and denounced the effects of free trade on the American economy. Immigration, he urged, should be restricted while American foreign policy should avoid unnecessary entanglements abroad. In arguing for these policies, Buchanan was representative of paleoconservatism, a strand that had emerged in reaction to neoconservatism.[38]

How the extreme right saw paleoconservatism is illuminated by how it reacted to his efforts to win the presidency. Already in the early 1990s, extreme rightists had expressed hope in Buchanan. The *Populist Observer* had declared that his 'message' was 'virtually identical' to the Populist Party, while the *Truth At Last*'s Edward Fields had described him as potentially the figure 'who eventually leads the struggle to save America from Zionist domination'. Extreme right support for Buchanan was noticeably evident as his 1996 bid for the presidency approached. In 1995, for instance, the *Populist Observer* published an evaluation of Buchanan's effort to gain the Republican nomination. He was well liked by many party supporters, it declared. He described himself as a populist and opposed the North American Free Trade Agreement. But he had a long record as a

Republican insider, continued to praise the so-called Reagan revolution and worried some by focusing on abortion at the expense of more important issues. Populists would be wise to 'watch him carefully', perhaps gaining 'some practical experience in his campaign' and 'hope, for the sake of America, that he is the real thing'.[39]

The *Spotlight*, for its part, described Buchanan as an opponent of the plutocrats it detested. It supported his candidacy. But what he needed to do, it declared, was break with the 'corrupt political organization' for whose nomination he was bidding, and turn instead to build a new party that would 'quickly enlist the support of the populist, pro-American, hard working and God-fearing people' in both the Democrats and Republicans.[40]

Other groupings also expressed sympathy for Buchanan's candidacy. The *Truth At Last* described him as the only candidate to demand a moratorium on immigration and the repeal of free trade treaties. He was 'the only true conservative in the race', and had dared to challenge the liberal establishment's plans for 'the economic impoverishment of our people under a New World Order U.N. government'. A national socialist publication, the *New Order*, also supported Buchanan, noting that he wanted a moratorium on immigration, called for the repeal of NAFTA, opposed affirmative action and abortion and had been accused by Jews of racism. His victory would be a huge gain for white people and allow national socialists to continue their struggle under changed conditions. Buchanan was only a 'moderate pro-White' candidate, but national socialists should support him, and when whites saw what Jews would do to stop him, they would enlist in their millions in the armies of the white revolution.[41]

The National Alliance, however, published two different reactions to Buchanan's 1996 candidacy. The first, by Pierce, argued that mainstream Republicans feared that Buchanan might gain mass support for his proposals to stem illegal immigration and stop the export of American jobs. But their real anger was that Buchanan refused to kowtow to Jewish demands. When Reagan had laid a wreath in a German military cemetery where SS men were buried, he had supported it. When a Ukrainian-American had been charged with war crimes, he had defended the man's rights. When George Bush had launched the Gulf War, he had declared that it was not America's war, but Israel's. Buchanan was not a revolutionary. He was only a conservative. But when he was attacked as an extremist, Buchanan supporters could 'understand who their real enemy is … I hope that they will'.[42]

A subsequent article by another writer, however, took a different view. Conservatives, it argued, were divided into two groups. Neoconservatives agreed with liberalism except in economics. Paleoconservatives were less concerned with economics than with cultural issues, and the differences between the two camps were most evident around race. Neoconservatives were multiracialists who had no objection to black men marrying white women. In contrast, some paleoconservatives were forthright on matters of race. But those paleoconservatives who criticized non-whites would never take a clear position on 'the Jewish question'. Indeed, it had recently been revealed in a paleoconservative publication that Buchanan had Jewish advisors. He was 'not a racial patriot' and in supporting him, Jews were seeking to stop a real nationalism from emerging.[43]

By the time of the next presidential campaign, Buchanan had changed parties, and where before he had unsuccessfully sought the Republicans' nomination, he was now the candidate for a grouping that rejected both the major parties, the Reform Party. But how this would affect the extreme right was harder to interpret. A report by an anti-fascist group, the Center for New Community, appeared during the campaign. Liberty Lobby, it reported, had set up the Americans for Buchanan Committee, describing him as the candidate who could turn America's 'plutocrat-controlled' party system upside down. The American Nationalist Union was also sympathetic to Buchanan's campaign while another group, the American Friends of the British National Party, had called on its supporters to volunteer for the Buchanan campaign. Many of them had already done so, it had reported.[44]

The report focused on those extreme rightists who supported Buchanan's Reform Party campaign. It had briefly noted that Liberty Lobby had initially taken the view that Buchanan no longer deserved its support. After he had abandoned the Republican party, that view had changed. It did not, however, discuss those racialists whose critique of Buchanan did not abate. (WAR, for instance, argued that Buchanan had never 'really addressed the hard issues of White survival'. He had made 'token' remarks on Israel's influence on Congress but supported Israel itself, and the large numbers of racists who had come out in support of him had failed to defend white interests.)[45] Subsequently to the report's appearance, yet more racists became estranged from the Buchanan campaign. The candidate's choice of a black running-mate, Ezola Foster, was particularly unwelcome to racists. The *Nationalist Times*, for instance, broke with Buchanan, although it took the unusual stance that while some were angry at her selection 'simply because she is black, that is not the real issue'. She was an articulate conservative, it contended, but she was unqualified to be vice president. The changing demography of America was the key issue, but the selection of Foster had sent the wrong signal and supporters who 'exhibited any racial consciousness' were reportedly being purged from national campaign headquarters. It was now all too clear that Buchanan had refused 'to take on the system' and chosen the wrong side 'on the issue of race and white survival'.[46]

If extreme rightists were divided on Buchanan, this was not its only divide on paleoconservatism. Where Buchanan had antagonized them by how he conducted his election campaign, they often felt more in common with another paleoconservative, Sam Francis. In 1994, for instance, the *Populist Observer* published an article by Francis. The white race, he declared, was under attack. As Lothrop Stoddard had written in the early twentieth century, there was a 'Rising Tide of Color', and its modern form could be seen in Martin Luther King's declaration of American blacks' solidarity with

Africa or in the appearance of his widow beside Nelson Mandela at his inauguration. Not only were liberals and radicals undermining the white race, but conservatives were too, and the only answer was to articulate a racial consciousness. Whites had created American civilization, and now they should assert their identity.[47]

But if the American Nationalist Union felt kinship with Francis, other extreme rightists were less persuaded. For Alex Linder and others involved in Vanguard News Network, for instance, what was key was that Francis refused to 'name the Jew', and rather than representing an authentic white national-ism, he served as a diversion from it. His argument appeared on a website that ought to appeal to different sections of 'the outcast right'. Some on the site, however, agreed neither with Francis nor Linder. What was crucial about Francis, it was suggested, was that he had 'a national voice', and some who read his words would then be ready for a more uncompromising argument.[48]

In arguing that paleoconservatives should not only consciously position themselves as defenders of a racial group but openly embrace anti-Semitism, extreme rightists were not making a new argument. Among the early responses to the *Brown* decision had been a pamphlet by a Mississippi judge, Tom Brady. The Supreme Court, he declared, had made a 'socialistic decision' on segregation. God had seen fit to create different races, and while the white man established the arts and sciences and sailed the oceans, his 'negroid brother' was 'impervious to the Divine ... yearning for advance-ment'. He was 'only one half-step from the primordial brute', and had only been eventually 'saved from savagery' by being brought to America.[49]

Brady's pamphlet had called for the creation of 'law abiding' resistance organizations that would be distinct from 'the nefarious Ku Klux Klans', and in the months that followed such groups emerged. In July the first Citizens' Council was organized in Mississippi, while groups elsewhere took such names as the States' Rights Council and the Committee for Individual Rights. In 1956, however, many of the different organizations came together to form the Citizens' Councils of America. Its secretary was the founder of the first Council, Robert Patterson.[50]

Shortly after the creation of the organization, Patterson had sent out a circular in which he provided a recommended reading list for opponents of integration. The list included material produced by Gerald L. K. Smith, Gerald Winrod and other veteran extreme rightists. Patterson denied being anti-Semitic, however, and the Mississippi Councils published a pamphlet urging Jews to oppose integration. In the early 1960s, the Citizens' Councils of Alabama denounced one Council for circulating anti-Semitic literature. (One of its leaflets claimed that while the greatest lie was that Jews were white, the next biggest was 'the propaganda fraud that Adolph Hitler killed six million Jews'.) In turn, the leader of the Southern Knights of the Ku Klux Klan claimed that Patterson was 'dominated by the Jews'.[51]

But if the Citizens' Councils were in dispute with the Klan, this did not mean that it was opposed to the extreme right as a whole. Crucially, it was linked with Liberty Lobby. Tom Brady was among the members of the Lobby's advisory board. Furthermore, both groups were involved in an effort to oppose the *Brown* ruling by drawing on the findings of academics who rejected racial equality. In 1959, a number of them had been brought together in the International Association for the Advancement of Ethnology and Eugenics. Its literature was sold by Citizens' Councils and in 1962 leading members of the Association testified at an attempt by white parents in Georgia to stop the desegregation of local schools. Among its directors were two prominent members of Liberty Lobby, Alfred Avins and Robert Kuttner.[52]

The Citizens' Councils did not succeed in its fight to defend segregation. In 1985, however, its Midwest organizer, Gordon Lee Baum, was instrumental in the launch of a new group, the Council of Conservative Citizens. Its paper, the *Citizens' Informer*, carried a regular column by the original secretary of the first Citizens' Council, Robert Patterson. Opposed both to affirmative action and immigration, the paper defended Southern states' continued flying of the Confederate flag and accused Republican leaders of failing to oppose 'FORCED INTEGRATION'.[53] The Council did not portray America as threatened by a Jewish conspiracy, and *American Free Press* writer Michael Collins Piper has even accused one of its leading figures, Jared Taylor, of being a possible 'asset of the CIA' and accused him and the Council of promoting a supposed racism which in reality was concerned to 'defame the Arab and Muslim peoples' on behalf of Zionism.[54] As with paleoconservatism, extreme rightists had no simple answer on how they should see the Council of Conservative Citizens. (In contrast to the Carto network, for instance, the American Nationalist Union was distinctly favourable, arguing that it and the Council were 'mainstream' alternatives to more radical nationalist groupings.) It was appropriate, then, that in the final years of his life (he died in early 2005), Francis became the *Citizens Informer*'s editor.[55]

The extreme right has faced ongoing problems over how it should relate to paleoconservatism and the Council of Conservative Citizens. A greater issue, however, was how it should react to the George W. Bush administration.

As the 2004 election approached, a National Alliance broadcast reviewed how the extreme right was reacting to the election. Bush only claimed to care for Americans. He was working hand in hand with the enemies of white Americans, and patriots were divided over what to do. 'The estimable publisher' of the *Truth at Last*, Edward Fields, had endorsed Ralph Nader because of his anti-Zionism. David Duke called for 'anybody but Bush', arguing that to vote for Kerry would send a message that 'traitors to America like Bush' deserved to be punished by being removed from office. But National Alliance Chairman Erich Glebe, it was suggested, was most persuasive. When anyone attacked 'President Bush and his lies', he had observed, 'even the most seasoned racialist' might become distracted. But the Alliance was 'not overly concerned about who wins this election or any other'. Kerry could sound good compared with Bush, but neither deserved support. Instead, all efforts had to be devoted to building the Alliance.[56]

But George W. Bush's second term did not only involve foreign policy. It has also concerned immigration policy, a subject which, as we have seen, has long concerned racists. (National Vanguard, for instance, has recently accused Democrats and Republicans of turning America into 'a flop house where anyone can slither across the border'. But it was Bush, it declared, who was guilty of 'allowing the largest invasion in American history'.)[57] Here, too, the extreme right faces the problem of how to deal with other sections of the right. As critics have noted, opposition to immigration has long attracted some conservatives. On occasion, this has resulted in cooperation with extreme rightists. It has also led to the appearance of favourable reference to conservative anti-immigration groups in extreme right publications. (In the early 1990s, for instance, one Identity group had the conservative American Foundation to Control Immigration cited describing 'open immigration and multiracialism' as 'a mortal threat to American civilization'.)[58] During George W. Bush's presidency, it became a crucial issue, and his unwillingness to take up demands to seal the Mexican border met with bitter criticism. One symptom of this discontent was the rise of the Minuteman Project and other anti-immigration groupings. Faced with this new burst of activity, extreme rightists attempted to join in. Stormfront supporters, for instance, were photographed carrying a banner on a demonstration organized by a California group, Save Our State. Other extreme rightists became involved with the Minuteman Project. The Project, however, denounced attempts to portray it as racist, and in early 2006 one Minuteman demonstration was joined by three uniformed members of the National Socialist Movement, who declared that they were there to make it clear that, unlike those who had organized the event, they recognized that immigration was a racial issue.[59]

The relationships between different sections of the American right have been complex. Rivalry between the radical right and the extreme right has, as we have seen in Chapter 4, been a central feature of the Patriot movement. It was anticipated by the fierce response of the extreme right to the John Birch Society's argument that there was no Jewish conspiracy, and that anti-Semitism indeed was a deliberate device intended to distract patriots from those who really threatened America. Its relationship to conservatism, however, has been more complex. In part, this has been due to the existence of strands within conservatism with which the extreme right feels affinity. But it is also due to the very importance of American conservatism. The extreme right sees the dominant forms of the American right as a crucial barrier to its advance, but believes that many of those attracted to conservative arguments should instead support a racist politics. But the strength of conservatism has not been the only obstacle to the extreme right's advance, and in the next (and final) chapter, we will consider some of the other obstacles it has faced in its long struggle to remake America.

9 Out of the 1950s

When the Supreme Court issued its 1954 decision on the desegregation of schools, the American extreme right had long existed. But *Brown* was crucial for the revival of its oldest strand, the Ku Klux Klan. It encouraged the emergence of new groupings. Most importantly, it prompted racialists to prioritize the fight against the legal attack on desegregation and the subsequent rise of the Civil Rights Movement.

This did not mean that the considerable proportion of extreme rightists who believed that the ultimate enemy was a Jewish conspiracy abandoned this belief. Much of their energies were now focused on fighting against black equality. But, as one *Truth Seeker* writer had already demonstrated two years before *Brown*, the fight against desegregation could be seen through an anti-Semitic lens. 'Equalitarians', he declared, had 'prostituted' the sciences and were close to taking over anthropology, and a key role in this was being played by communists and 'Jewish propagandists'. When the Supreme Court subsequently drew on anti-racist scholars in its ruling against the segregation of schools, extreme rightists were already poised to bring their antagonism to Jews and their rage at integration into a single argument.[1] That many Southerners were determined to retain segregation soon became all too clear. But if anti-Semites' views were easily adaptable to the new situation, the extreme right faced massive problems in seeking to win over those whom *Brown* had outraged. As we have seen, anti-Semitism had indigenous roots. But during the Second World War, extreme rightists had been accused of conspiring with the Nazis. American soldiers had died fighting the Third Reich, and subsequent revelations about its campaign of genocide erected even greater barriers in the way of an American extreme right. One reaction was to argue that Nazism was a foreign doctrine, and that American racialists were different. Another, however, was to insist that Americans had been wrong to fight Hitler. He had been right, and even before *Brown* some were claiming that national socialism had been falsely accused of mass murder.

In part, those who sought to create an American national socialism hoped to benefit from anti-communism. Since the Second World War, the Soviet Union had become America's great enemy, and Hitler could be presented as someone who had attempted to defeat communism when liberal America had been unwilling to do so. But the American extreme right already opposed both communism and integration. Why, then, should it embrace a doctrine that had arisen in another land? For Rockwell, national socialism was right because it was the most intransigent enemy of both Reds and blacks. But he also believed that by using attention-grabbing methods his party could grab the political initiative in a way that other forms of the extreme right had failed.

Two recent biographies have seen Rockwell as a crucial figure in the development of the extreme right. Schmaltz has suggested that one of his lasting contributions was the way in which he used 'comic-book' methods in the ANP's propaganda, producing, for instance, a 'Boat Ticket to Africa' as a way of making his demand that blacks leave America easily accessible to an audience. Both Schmaltz and Simonelli see Rockwell as crucial to the spread of Holocaust revisionism (most importantly, he had espoused it in an interview with *Playboy* magazine). They also emphasize that he decisively broke with both Protestant nativism and the historic national socialist assumption that Nordics were superior. In coining the slogan 'White Power', in arguing that it was crucial to bring all white Americans together, regardless of where in Europe their family had originally hailed from, he was bequeathing a vital legacy to the extreme right that would come after him.[2]

Each of the points that Rockwell's biographers have raised is important. The discussion of his deliberate simplification of propaganda is evocative of William Pierce's use of fiction and music. The reference to Holocaust revisionism, while underestimating how far it had already spread among racists, is undoubtedly right to emphasize his ability to make such views better known. (*Playboy*, remarkably, had a circulation of 3.6 million.)[3] But it is the point about exactly who the extreme right sought to champion that is the most interesting. As we have seen, the belief that Nordics were superior was not simply a view held by Hitler or by a faction in the ANP, but had arisen in the United States in the early twentieth century. Rockwell was challenging not only national socialist orthodoxy or Protestant nativism, he was challenging a racial categorization that had not only emerged on American soil, but was still championed by non-Nazi extreme rightists. (If we look, for instance, at the Southern-based group of the mid-1960s, the American States Rights Party, we can find a defence of the Nordic against other European-Americans.)[4]

As we have seen, it was not those who sought to continue Rockwell's movement but two figures who drew on national socialism without overtly arguing it who would prove to be particularly important following the NSWPP leader's assassination. William Pierce envisaged building a cadre organization which would eventually take up arms and lead a racial revolution. Willis Carto believed instead that a periodical that appealed across the right would play a central role in making Frances Parker Yockey's ideas central to a white America.

If Pierce and Carto advocated two alternative strategies, the Ku Klux Klan represented another form of the extreme right. It often embraced the anti-Semitism central to Northern groupings, while its ally, the National States Rights Party, argued a politics that combined a veneration for the defeated Confederacy (and the original Klan) with an enthusiasm for *Der Stürmer* and the Waffen SS. After the defeat of the battle against desegregation, the most important Klan grouping, David Duke's Knights of the Ku Klux Klan, combined a politics rooted in Southern history with Duke's earlier training in the National Socialist White People's Party. This should remind us that our earlier division of extreme rightists into national socialist, Southern-rooted and Patriot groupings, is far from perfect. We not only need to be careful in tracing the complicated lineage of groupings which sought to blend support for the Confederacy with support for Nazi Germany. We must also not overstate the Southern character of such groups as the Klan or the National States Rights Party. The Klan had a massive membership outside the South in the 1920s, and, as we have noted, both it and the NSRP subsequently had members in a range of states. Furthermore, during its early period, Liberty Lobby saw itself as seeking to 'bring Northern and Southern groups together'. At this point, Carto argued that he was creating a 'coalition' of conservative forces, and we have already noted his links with Citizens' Councils.[5] But we have also noted *Right*'s sympathy with both the ANP and the National States Rights Party. Yet again, we can register where a grouping emerged and what historical reference point it most often referred to, without assuming it cannot emerge in other parts of the country or amalgamate different historical referents.

There are other problems with an over-simplified tripartite division of the American extreme right. We have already seen this, for instance, when we discussed how national socialists can differ on the role of women. But we have seen it too when we noted how groupings from different strands can pursue some of the same approaches, and these can be precisely ones that we might not expect extreme rightists to take. Again, the chapter on women is crucial, but we should also consider questions which did not receive chapter-length treatment.

One is the recurrent efforts of white nationalists to form links with black nationalists. In the 1920s this was true of the Ku Klux Klan, in the 1930s the Christian Front. In the post-war period, as we have seen, this tradition was continued by the National Renaissance Party and Willis Carto's *Right* in the 1950s and by the American Nazi Party and White Aryan Resistance subsequently. Nor have they been the only groups to favour such an alliance. In the late 1980s, for instance, David Duke was photographed with black nationalists while running as a Populist Party presidential candidate. The following decade, Florida members of the Invisible Empire, Knights of the Ku Klux Klan organized demonstrations with black nationalists. This was not welcomed by the group's membership as a whole, but the *Klansman* was supportive, publishing an article entitled 'Unlikely Alliance: Black Activists and Klan Unite Against the System'.[6]

Another important development has also transcended some of the divisions on the extreme right. American racists have long sought to forge links with enemies of Israel in the Middle East. As the National Renaissance Party had demonstrated in the late 1950s, this could well be with secular nationalists, and in the 1990s the White Order of Thule argued that Saddam Hussein was

> the ally of all true Aryan Revolutionaries. … As our vile Federal Government sees Saddam and his 'weapons of mass destruction' as a threat to their system, the very system that is responsible for the slavery and murder of the White Race, then we can only view him as an ally.[7]

In recent years, however, it has been Islamism that American extreme rightists have felt drawn to. As George Michael has argued, a potential exists for cooperation between American extreme rightists and Islamic extremists. But while Aryan Nations, for instance, has been particularly enthusiastic, William Pierce was more cautious, expressing admiration for Bin Laden two years before the 9/11 attacks but subsequently explicitly ruling out 'building alliances' with those in the Middle East 'whose goals or interests are essentially different from ours'. As Michael notes, despite extreme right sympathies, there are serious obstacles to an alliance with Islamists. In part, this is affected by the extreme right's racism and in part, it revolves around its failure to build an effective terrorist infrastructure. But it also concerns the one-sided nature of the relationship. Some extreme rightists would like to cooperate with or emulate Bin Laden. But al-Qaeda is unlikely to reach any such arrangement. (Indeed, a recent discussion on David Pringle's website castigated any hopes of an alliance. For one correspondent, if Islamic radicals joined with White Nationalists, what they would find was 'meetings with no purpose' and 'talk, talk and more talk'. Another agreed; the movement was engaged in a 'childish drama', and the danger was that jihadists might not only burst into laughter but burst their vital blood vessels.)[8]

If extreme rightists of different strands have sought both to ally with black nationalists and Middle Eastern radicals, they have also tried to forge links with leftists. We saw this with Metzger. But it is true too for Carto. In 1971, the anti-Pierce wing of the National Youth Alliance changed its name to Youth Action. Leftists, it declared, had been much taken with holding war crimes trials of those they blamed for the Vietnam War. But they were not going after the real criminals. America's ruling class was an oligarchy of the rich, and in order to expose this group Youth Action had indicted fifteen members of the Council on Foreign Relations. The trial would be held the following year, and 'anyone of ANY political persuasion who is against American involvement in foreign wars' was invited to participate.[9]

The following year, a report of the trial appeared in another publication. Described as a People's Tribunal, it brought together both right and left-wing groups. The accused were found guilty, and the trial had been opened, it was noted, by 'a New Left author' who 'detailed the huge profits' made in the war, and by Willis Carto, 'who discussed the Natural Coalition of left and right'.[10]

Carto's attempt to link with leftists has continued in more recent years. In the late 1990s, for instance, the *Spotlight* observed that while some so-called conservatives supported free trade, 'a growing number of "leftists" are now seeing the light'. They were 'marching in lockstep with patriots on the right against the international plutocrats', and what needed to be done was to convince them that the answer was 'national sovereignty and protectionism'.[11]

Nor are he and Tom Metzger the only extreme rightists who have sought to forge an alliance with leftists. At the end of the 1990s, demonstrators against free trade had been involved in a violent confrontation in Seattle. They had gone up against 'Police State goons', one writer declared, and in the future there would be many more such battles. 'New alliances' would form between those who had seen themselves as right-wingers and those who had defined themselves as leftists. These distinctions would no longer matter; the only concern would be resistance to the thugs of the New World Order. The author of the article was Louis Beam.[12]

This article should remind us of a crucial feature of the extreme right's approach to alliances. If white nationalists have tried to work with black nationalists, Middle Eastern nationalists, Islamists and leftists, they have also tried to forge links with non-racist Patriots and with conservatives. These efforts are importantly different, but they have a vital feature in common. They rely on extreme rightists not emphasizing what makes them extreme rightists. In most cases, anti-black racism becomes eclipsed by anti-Semitism, but it is now argued in terms of anti-Zionism. This is most evident with Carto but in 2001, for instance, even the National Alliance experimented in the use of another language and published a series of demands in 'the name of the people of the United States of America and all peace-loving people throughout the world'. The demands were made to the Israeli government, and included calls to end the use of assassination and torture as 'state policy', recognize a Palestinian state with Jerusalem as its capital, obey the United Nations resolutions concerning the occupation of the Golan Heights and the right of Palestinians to return to their homes, and the dispatch of 'an international peace-keeping force' to Gaza and the West Bank to protect 'innocent Palestinians against acts of Israeli state-sponsored terrorism'.[13]

If in one variant, the conspiracy that extreme rightists attack is described as Zionist, in another it is portrayed in the way that Patriots find most amenable. We noted earlier, for instance, Carto's reference to the new world order in his 1982 book on populism. While he decried the 'destructive' effects of 'modern, industrial society' on 'nation, race and culture', his overall focus was on its economic impact. This could still show traces of his Yock-eyist preoccupations. Thus when he declared that populism stood against exploitation by 'alien forces promoting culture distortion', he was using a language unfamiliar to Patriots.[14] But overall, he was raising an argument while only emphasizing the portion of it most attractive to his audience, and he is not unique in this. Another writer with a considerable Patriot audience is Eustace Mullins. In Chapter 1, we referred to material which appeared in the extreme right press of the 1950s. One was an article that appeared in *Women's Voice* opposing the Korean War. Another was the 'Appreciation of Adolf Hitler' which appeared in the *National Renaissance Bulletin*. Both were written by Mullins. He also wrote for *Common Sense*, and when it published the 'Rabbi's Speech' on the supposed plan to bring about world war and the disappearance of the white race, it was accompanied by a statement by Mullins that it was he who had first gained access to the document in America. His involvement with the extreme right has continued since the 1950s. In the early 1970s, for instance, the *Thunderbolt* published a report of his 'five-year study' of 'losses suffered by white Americans because of black crime and aggression'. Every native-born white citizen over the age of twenty-one, it declared, should receive an 'initial reparations payment of $10,000'. In the early 1990s Aryan Nations reprinted an article on the Gulf War which Mullins had published elsewhere. In it he had attacked 'the Israel First contingent in Washington' which had, he remarked, been described by some as America's Zionist Occupation Government.[15] But it is not this material which has won Mullins an audience outside the extreme right. Since the 1950s, he has written extensively in condemnation of the Federal Reserve and the international bankers, and the Anti-Defamation League has described him as 'a frequent speaker on the militia and anti-government circuit'. But as Chip Berlet and Matthew Lyons have noted, 'Mullins writes in two styles, one ostensibly focusing on banking practices, the other expressing open and vicious anti-semitism.' They go on to suggest that one of his books brings these themes together.[16] But what is crucial about his building a following among racists and non-racists is that he can argue his opposition to bankers in different ways.

Indeed, Berlet has written on Mullins' ability not only to speak to Patriots but to leftists. In the early 1990s, Political Research Associates published Berlet's extended discussion of the disturbing propensity of some on the left to draw on right-wing arguments. A left-wing group, he noted, was selling a videotape of a speech by Mullins, while a New World study group which had been set up in California had both discussed the writings of the left-wing writer Noam Chomsky and shown a videotape of Mullins speaking on international bankers.[17]

As Martin Lee has noted, Mullins was an advisory board member of a group associated with Carto, the Populist Action Committee, and has been described by the *Spotlight* as 'the dean of America's populist authors'. More recently, in his book on 'Zionist Power in America', *American Free Press* author Michael Collins Piper described him as 'the American intellectual whose studies introduced me to the intrigues few would ever write about'.[18] But to observe that some Patriots (or some on the left) give a hearing to Mullins is not to prove that they thereby are anti-Semites. Indeed, the ability to write in more than one style even concerns one of the best-known of extreme right writings, Louis Beam's essay *Leaderless Resistance*. As we have seen, in the aftermath of the Weaver shooting Pete Peters had called a meeting of 'Christian men'. In the subsequent publication of its deliberations, Beam's essay was reprinted, 'slightly edited' by the gathering's Sacred Warfare Action Tactics Committee. The following year, as we have also noted, the essay was also published by the extreme right paper, the *WAR Eagle*. But the two versions were vitally different. The one published by Peters was addressed to 'those who love our people, culture, and heritage'. It discussed the fight against 'state tyranny' and the need to avoid infiltration and destruction by adopting Colonel Amoss' conception of myriad cells without centralized leadership. The version published by the *WAR Eagle* had the same focus, but this time described its audience as 'those who love our Race, culture, and heritage', and recurrently used the term ZOG in characterizing the enemy. Other sections that appeared in the *WAR Eagle* were also absent from the Peters version, including a denunciation of 'the Jews media' and the suggestion that 'the more committed groups' should camouflage themselves by blending with 'mainstream "kosher" groups'.[19]

As we have seen earlier, the extreme right has sought to benefit from the Southern fight against segregation in the 1950s, the Wallace campaign in the 1960s and the radicalization of farmers in the 1980s. It has even tried to intervene in the anti-war movement of the early twenty-first century. Extreme rightists have declared their support of Cindy Sheehan, who following the death of her son, Casey, in Iraq, began a vigil outside President Bush's ranch. She had brought out the truth, National Vanguard declared, that her son had died for Israel. Along with Stormfront supporters, National Vanguard members had joined Sheehan 'to show our solidarity'. Linking their stance on the war with their opposition to immigration, one of their signs declared 'GUARD THE RIO GRANDE NOT THE EUPHRATES'. Another read, 'NEOCONS LIE BRAVE TROOPS DIE'.[20]

In seeking to extend their support, extreme rightists have demonstrated a remarkable agility in both how they speak and who they speak to. Nor is this the only area in which they can surprise us. Even their fight for a white republic is more complex than it may seem. We have already commented on the decision of some on the extreme right to abandon the idea of a white America and to create an Aryan state in the Northwest. This is only true of sections of the extreme right, however, and others envisage a white America or even, as in the case of the National Alliance, envisage a single government ruling over several continents. Indeed, a noticeable development of recent years is the growth of a racialist politics which does not valorize the nation but looks instead to a trans-national racial identity. Thus Volksfront, for instance, has described itself as 'part of an international network of like-minded Aryan organizations' whose 'ideology transcends national barriers'.[21]

But however American extreme rightists envisage the new order of the future, one notable commitment among many of them is to international cooperation with extreme rightists elsewhere. We have already noted Rockwell's launch of the World Union of National Socialists. We have referred too to the American Friends of the British National Party, whose organizer, Mark Cotterill, had argued it could 'only help to bring some much needed unity to a fragmented and therefore not nationally effective movement within the USA'. But there has also been considerable transatlantic traffic between American and European extreme rightists. In the early 1980s, for instance, German extreme rightist Manfred Roeder visited Aryan Nations, while in 1999 Stephen Cartwright of the British National Party spoke both to the American Friends of the BNP and the National Alliance. Travelling in the opposite direction, in 1961, for instance, the National States Rights Party sent a delegation to a 'Nord-Europa encampment' in Britain and in 1989 the Imperial Wizard of the Invisible Empire, Knights of the Ku Klux Klan visited British members, while in 1998, William Pierce attended a 'National Resistance' rally organized by the German National Democratic Party.[22]

Unlike the 1930s, there is no extreme right government in power to provide aid to racialists in other countries. Furthermore, just as the extreme right in America has frequently suffered from splits, the same is true elsewhere, and there is a constant danger to any international links as to which side in any national dispute extreme rightists elsewhere might decide to take. In addition, those who take a national socialist stance, for instance, may well be profoundly unhappy at linking with groupings elsewhere who reject such an identification. But international links remain important to a movement which sees the white race as under attack, and one link is particularly illuminating. If the extreme right is still seeking power in Europe, there is one movement which has been a particular inspiration to sections of the American extreme right, and who it is gives us important insights into the American movement. In the early 1990s, for instance, the *Truth at Last* reported that France's Front National had gained nearly 14 per cent in the recent national elections. Its leader, Jean-Marie Le Pen, had called for a ban on new immigration, the deportation of illegal immigrants and job preference for French people. A recent poll, the report noted, had shown over a third of the French supported his views. 'With over 100,000 members Le Pen and his National Front may well be on their way to political power!'[23]

Fields' paper was not the only one to support the Front National. In 1997, the *Spotlight* greeted plans for the Front's annual convention. Fearful of its electoral advance, the article declared, 'the plutocrats' were seeking to infiltrate agents provocateurs into the organization 'to sabotage it from the inside'. Two years later the *Spotlight* contrasted Le Pen with Pat Buchanan. In the previous presidential election, Buchanan had capitulated to the Republican leadership. Le Pen, however, was an 'international role model', who led 'the largest populist party in the world', and like Liberty Lobby, he had come under attack from enemies within who were really serving the interests of the Anti-Defamation League.[24]

For Carto's paper, Le Pen and Liberty Lobby were suffering the attentions of the same conspiracy. For Fields, the issues the Front raised and its enviable success offered hope of a similar breakthrough in America. For others on the American extreme right, of course, it was the party which had become the largest single party in Germany decades earlier which offered the way forward. But unlike either of these foreign referents, the American extreme right has failed to achieve a mass following.

Duke won election as a Republican, and no other extreme right candidate has been elected either as a major party candidate or running for a third party. Writing in 1999, Leonard Zeskind argued that a new white nationalist movement drew on elements of 'the Klan, Posse Comitatus and neo-nazis' and that Buchanan's candidacy showed its potential to move 'From compounds to Congress'.[25] But those who have come from the paramilitary wing of the Patriot movement, or national socialist groupings, or the Southern-based groupings we discussed in Chapter 3, have not met with electoral success, and despite Thom Robb's hopes, neither have Klansmen. Buchanan too was unsuccessful, but it is certainly true that significant parts of his appeal are associated with his pronouncements on the position of whites. But just as the term white nationalism is problematized by the rise of ideas of pan-Aryan unity, it has difficulties too if it is to be understood as locating Buchanan and Duke, Sam Francis and Louis Beam, in the same movement.

One attempt to distinguish within the right draws a distinction between what it calls the extreme or insurgent right and another broad grouping which includes Patriots and 'White Ethnic Nationalists'.[26] Whichever vocabulary we finally adopt, we should see Buchanan as crucially different from extreme rightists. This is not to deny the very real overlap which we have already discussed.

During the 1990s, for instance, the *Truth at Last* published an article in support of an attempt by Duke to gain election to the Senate. The paper accompanied it with a reproduction of an article recently published in a Jewish paper. It quoted a professor long involved in opposing Duke's electoral aspirations. Buchanan, he declared, was bringing together potentially powerful 'themes of economic and cultural nationalism', and Duke could take advantage of 'the feelings Buchanan has touched on'.[27]

But a different relationship may well be more likely. As one account of Duke's career has noted, in 1989 Buchanan had written a column on Duke's electoral victory. He had not won, Buchanan wrote, because he was a former leader of the Ku Klux Klan. He had won despite it, and he had won because he had opposed taxes, 'made an issue of urban crime' and opposed 'discrimination against white folks'. But this was not an endorsement of Duke. It was a claim that he succeeded because the Republican party had been intimidated by 'moderates and progressives' into avoiding certain issues, and when he returned to the topic two years later, it was to argue that the party should explore why white voters supported Duke, and then 'devise a strategic plan to win them back'.[28] As we discussed in the previous chapter, extreme rightists can see Buchanan as a bridge to greater support. But we should also pay attention to those who see him as a barrier to their advance.

If the extreme right has been electorally unsuccessful, nor has it been successful in achieving a significant membership. As we might expect, estimates have varied as to its total membership. In part, this is related to problems of definition as to which groupings should or should not included in the total. It relates too to the possibility of double-counting, in which, for instance, adding together the members of organizations and the congregations of Identity churches could mean inflating a total which is unable to detect those who belong to both. It relates too to organizations' unwillingness to reveal their membership figures, and conversely a tendency to exaggerate how many members a group has recruited.

Nonetheless, we have some useful figures. In 1981, for instance, an Identity writer, lamenting the rise of the rival conservative movement, gave an estimate of the balance of forces between the two sections of the right. While millions, he declared, were involved in what he described as 'kosher' conservatism, the section of the right 'who know about the Jews' had 'around 50,000 "hard core" people and another 300,000 on the fringe'.[29]

In her 1990 article on the American extreme right, Elinor Langer noted that three groups that monitored the movement estimated that they had around 10,000 to 20,000 members. There was a larger number of up to 200,000 sympathisers, which included the 100,000 or so subscribers to the *Spotlight* and the 44,000 voters who had voted for David Duke when he ran as the Populist candidate for president. There were also 30,000 followers of Christian Identity, who might need to be added to the total number.[30]

We can see in this figure the danger of double-counting. We should be wary too of counting *Spotlight* readers as extreme rightists, when a key factor in its comparatively high circulation is that it does not use language that is obviously anti-black or anti-Semitic. (We might also note that Langer's figure is a lower circulation than the one we gave in Chapter 2. In the early 1980s, it had sold far more.)

The extreme right's weakness can be attributed to a variety of factors. Some relate to the very strength of the political and social system that it abhors. Where they vote, voters look overwhelmingly towards the Democrats and the Republicans, and while the primary system gives some opportunity to maverick candidates to run on a major party ticket, the leadership of the two major parties are far from willing to allow another Duke to emerge. The issues that the extreme right champions can be espoused by one or other of these parties. The extreme right's opposition to immigration or affirmative action can be championed by Republicans, while its opposition to the war in Iraq or the downsizing of manufacturing can be argued by Democrats. Segregationism has been resoundingly defeated and the importance of historic claims to equality and to rights severely limit the chances of building a white nationalist movement. Even if there was a severe economic downturn, in which extreme rightists could attempt to win over beleaguered farmers or newly unemployed workers, the opportunities for a racialist politics to gain a mass following would be highly constrained. Furthermore, regardless of the economic climate, while there are possibilities in the internet and, to a lesser degree, in white power music, the press, television and the popular music industry are all hostile to the beliefs the extreme right holds dear. But there are problems too with the movement itself.

We suggested earlier that it has long sought to build alliances with other movements. But while we have noted how extreme rightists have sought to link up with leftists or other radicals, this has met with little success. In part, this is because where some black nationalists or Middle Eastern radicals might feel a degree of fellow-feeling for sections of the extreme right, for others, and this is even more true of the left, the predominant sentiment is mutual hostility. This has been particularly the case because of the profoundly hostile and sometimes literally murderous sentiments expressed by many on the extreme right. We have seen the former in the views of black people expressed by the ANP, the NSRP and others. We have seen the latter in the white power music lyrics cited in Chapter 2, and other examples are rife. Dobratz and Shanks-Meile, for instance, illustrate their discussion of the movement with WAR cartoons of blacks. In one, a malign-looking black is shown looting a store, while in another a defenceless white is portrayed being brutally attacked by a large black man. Daniels' book on gender and the extreme right reproduces, for instance, a cartoon from the Church of the Creator's paper, in which a black man tells a female she needs to get out of bed: 'WE GOT WHITE FOLKS TA ROB, AND DRUGS TA BUY.'[31] We should recall too the bitter hostility expressed towards black men who are seen as a threat to white women. Thus one article by the NSWPP's Matt Koehl was entitled 'Of Rapes and Apes' while in an issue of the ANP's magazine, the *Stormtrooper*, Rockwell had declared that lynching was an institution which deserved to be restored.[32]

One could supply other examples to illustrate extreme right views of Middle Easterners. The point is clear, though, that while some white nationalists can temporarily suppress their racialism in order to advance that very cause, it is extremely difficult for the movement as a whole. But the difficulties of sustaining any alliances are not the only problem. The extreme right is not only divided on religion, for instance, but potentially murderously so. Aryan Nations has declared that 'Satanic, heathen beliefs' would be 'outlawed' in a future Aryan state, while commenting on plans for migration to the Northwest, Ron McVan of Wotansvolk has noted that 'when people come up here and meet the Identity people, they're turned off. ... People either follow their religion or die.' An attack on Christian

Identity on the Vanguard News Network website included an article from the Christian Separatist Church Society, 'Pagans At War With The Government of God'. The Word of God, it declared, made 'no allowances for non-Christians, no matter how racially conscious these people may claim to be'. Another Identity text, the posting continued, declared that those that blasphemed the name of the Lord should be put to death. Nor it should be added, is the hostility solely one-sided. In the late 1980s, WAR published a cartoon showing Vikings killing monks and burning a church.[33]

But more important than the disputes between different religious belief systems are the ferocious antagonisms between (and within) different organizations. We have already referred, for instance, to the breakaways from the National Alliance and accusations made against WAR's leader Tom Metzger. There are myriad other examples. The NSRP split in the 1960s was precipitated by dissidents' allegations that Fields was putting more effort into the *Thunderbolt* than the party. But they made claims too about his personal life.[34] William Pierce has attacked Willis Carto as a confidence trickster, adept at taking money from his supporters, while Harold Covington has made allegations against the Church of the Creator founder Ben Klassen, bitterly clashed with the National Alliance, and had to deny himself that he was secretly a Jew and was being paid by a government agency to 'destroy the White Resistance'. Indeed, a history of 'White Nationalism' published by National Socialist Vanguard is filled with allegations against its leading figures. One, it is claimed, had been involved in a homosexual relationship at the end of the 1950s, another is described as 'immoral sexually' and 'a con-artist' and a third is described as a transvestite and bisexual.[35]

If there are frequent conflicts and splits, none of the different extreme right groupings have achieved a significant membership. Remarkably, despite the level of publicity it generated, Rockwell's party seems to have only had 200 members at the time of Rockwell's death, while when opponents were discussing the National Alliance's growth at the beginning of the twenty-first century, they were discussing a figure of 1,500.[36] As the estimates for the beginning of the 1980s and 1990s show, the movement as a whole has drawn many more. But none of its constituent organizations has made a decisive breakthrough, and this failure has only fed the ill feelings that contribute to this very failure. To explain it, as we have seen with allegations against Covington or Metzger, some activists believe that the problem is deliberate sabotage by government agents or by the Anti-Defamation League, the Southern Poverty Law Center or other opposition groups. As National Socialist Vanguard's history of the movement or the reference in Chapter 7 to 'phone booth emperors' should remind us, some blame the egos or the appetites of different leaders. And, as Covington's complaint about the people drawn to national socialism or Pierce's last National Alliance convention speech should remind us, some blame the members different organizations so frequently attract. Put together with the barriers of the American political and social system, and the ability of conservatives and others to voice the issues white nationalists seek to use, the problems of the movement are immense, its potential for significant growth imperilled.

But imperilled is not the same as impossible. Today the different Klan groups probably total only a couple of thousand. In the late 1960s, the Klan had 55,000 members. In the 1920s estimates of its peak membership range from one and a half million to over five million.[37] And to take a different perspective, while extreme right organizations may be numerically weak, even small numbers can have a devastating effect if they resort to violence.

This study has been insistent in some areas, tentative in others. One area where, despite appearances, it is ultimately tentative is how the groupings we have discussed can best be described. What is implied by describing them as the extreme right? First, it is to argue that they are part of a larger category, the right. This can be defined negatively, as those which oppose the left and the ideal that is so crucial to it, equality. Whether it can be defined positively, as standing for property or nation, for tradition or liberty, is far more arguable.[38] Not all on the right favour any single one of these, and it may be that a negative definition will have to suffice. If we still find the term right useful, then we need to distinguish within it, and one way of defining what is extreme and what is not, is by distinguishing supporters of dictatorship from democrats. Another way is to separate those who defend terrorism from those who advocate pursuing electoral support. Here, however, we have separated those who believe in a long-term conspiracy from those who believe that liberals are simply wrong, and then to separate racist conspiracy theorists from non-racist ones. None of these distinctions are perfect, and one problem, for instance, is how we should categorize *National Review* or the John Birch Society in their early anti-civil rights incarnations. It may be that we need to make distinctions within both conservatism and the radical right to take account of groupings that do not prioritize racial issues but take them up at particular times. But if we decide to reserve 'extreme right' for those groups that are centrally concerned with race, there are still problems. One is how to deal with those groups which have sought to blend with the conservative or Patriot movements, or both, by using terms such as Zionism instead of Jews, or taking up such questions as affirmative action and immigration without appearing to argue racial superiority. We have suggested that Liberty Lobby and the American Nationalist Union are part of the extreme right, but that a number of anti-immigration groupings are not. The more important case concerns the former, which can be seen as emerging from within the extreme right but seeking to reach beyond it. But this needs to be carefully argued. Another problem is clarifying within the Patriot movement. Some of its segments are clearly on the extreme right, others on the radical right. But what are we, for instance, to make of the *Free American* which sometimes raises extreme right conspiracy theories and sometimes defends different ones?

If defining certain groupings as extreme right has problems, so have other terms. White nationalism, as we have seen, is misleading when we consider the existence of groups that do not fight for race and nation, but believe race is more important than nation. Readers will also have noticed that we have rarely used the term fascism. This is not because we find it wholly inappropriate. In describing the NSDAP as seeking national resurrection, we were consciously drawing on Roger Griffin's definition of fascism, and, as I have suggested elsewhere, applying the term to the National Alliance, for instance, would be consistent with his approach. But in his argument, while other groupings may promote illiberal nationalism, fascism's pursuit of a new order makes it a revolutionary force.[39] In our discussion of the extreme right, we have included the non-revolutionary Klan of the 1950s (and the 1920s) and groups that seek to speak to a conservative audience. We have referred earlier to groups that seek to restore America, which given how extreme rightists argue, may or may not be revolutionary, and may or may not be fascist.

Finally, how useful has been the idea of white rage in exploring the movement? We have already seen how William Pierce has used the notion of rage. He saw it in the audience for white power music. He saw it too in himself, as he reminisced of living in Washington DC and fending off the desire to kill large numbers of those he believed were destroying America. Another quote gives us the title of this book. Interviewed by one author, Tom Metzger discussed the role of his group in recruiting skinheads. 'White rage', he declared, 'is the key'.[40]

Not every extreme rightist has such a positive view of the role of rage. Schmaltz, for instance, has quoted Matt Koehl lambasting skinheads as expressing 'the crude rage of the disenfranchised'.[41] It is important too to recognize that extreme rightists are not only motivated by white rage. In Chapter 6, we referred to the importance of male rage, both at men of other races and white women. But as we suggested in Chapter 1, bitterness and anger can be combined with other sentiments. Extreme rightists talk of a new order, and when they do they are describing a regime they believe will be better than that which presently exists. The World Church of the Creator's Matt Hale, for instance, pictures 'a truly Racial Socialist order' in which whites will never again worry about feeding their family or about jobs being lost overseas. 'Picture a world in which the water is clean, the air is clean, and the earth is clean. ... Picture the day when you need not lock your home at night.'[42] The World Church of the Creator, like many other extreme right groupings, has recruited from the angry and the violent. But just as it tries to appeal for support beyond those it will actually allow within its ranks, so it can appeal to elevated sentiments as well as base ones. We would be mistaken to underestimate its ability to mobilize not only hates, but dreams. It has failed to gain a mass membership, but it is a movement that has persisted in American society for many years. It will not only continue to exist, but to seek to find opportunities to work against the society it loathes, and bring about the new racial order it desperately desires.

Notes

1 Before *Brown*

1 W. C. Wade, *The Fiery Cross. The Ku Klux Klan in America*, Touchstone, New York, 1987, pp. 31–40, 49–79, 90–93, 102–4, 109, 113.
2 W. P. Randel, *The Ku Klux Klan. A Century of Infamy*, Chilton Books, Philadelphia PA, 1965, p. 15.
3 C. Berlet and M. N. Lyons, *Right-Wing Populism in America. Too Close For Comfort*, Guilford Press, New York, 2000, pp. 47, 50; D. H. Bennett, *The Party of Fear. From Nativist Movements to the New Right in American History*, Vintage Books, New York, 1990, pp. 86, 161–64, 171, 174.
4 Bennett, p. 178; S. M. Lipset and E. Raab, *The Politics of Unreason. Right-Wing Extremism in America, 1790–1970*, Heinemann, London, 1971, p. 95; M. N. Dobowski, 'Populist Antisemitism in U.S. Literature', *Patterns of Prejudice* 10, 3, May-June 1976, pp. 22–27.
5 J. Higham, *Strangers in the Land. Patterns of American Nativism 1860–1925*, Atheneum, New York, 1963, pp. 54–55, 150–57, 271–73.
6 Bennett, pp. 183–96.
7 M. W. Cooper, *'Behold A Pale Horse'*, Light Technology Publishing, Sedona AZ, 1991, pp. 275, 278–79, 284.
8 Anon., *Jewish Influences in American Life. Volume III of The International Jew. The World's Foremost Problem*, Dearborn Publishing Company, Dearborn MI, 1921, pp. 65, 102–3, 218–19.
9 Wade, pp. 128–31, 142–44, 150; N. MacLean, *Behind the Mask of Chivalry. The Making of the Second Ku Klux Klan*, Oxford University Press, New York, 1994, p. 137.
10 Wade, pp. 172, 179–80; MacLean, p. 113; Martin, T (1976) *Race First*, Greenwood Press, Westport CT., pp. 345–46.
11 Wade, pp. 160, 176, 186–92, 196, 215–18, 234–35, 239–45, 253, 257–58, 262–63; D. M. Chalmers, *Hooded Americanism. The First Century of the Ku Klux Klan 1865–1965*, Doubleday, New York, 1965, pp. 126, 193, 261.
12 *Liberation* V, 25, 10 February 1934.
13 *Liberation* IV, 16, 5 August 1933; W. D. Pelley, *No More Hunger. The Compact Plan of the Christian Commonwealth*, Pelley Publishers, Asheville NC, 1936, pp. 54, 57, 98–100, 177, 186.
14 G. S. Smith, *To Save a Nation. American 'Extremism', the New Deal, and the Coming of World War II*, Ivan R. Dee, Chicago, 1992, pp. 85–86.
15 G. B. Winrod, *Adam Weishaupt. A Human Devil*, n.p., n.d., pp. 43, 45, 47.
16 C. J. Tull, *Father Coughlin and the New Deal*, Syracuse University Press, Syracuse NY, 1965, pp. 61–63, 77.

17 G. Jeansonne, *Gerald L. K. Smith. Minister of Hate*, Louisiana State University Press, Baton Rouge LA, 1988, pp. 35, 48–51, 60; Tull, p. 147.

18 Tull, pp. 189–97, 206; Smith, p. 133.

19 J. R. Carlson, *Under Cover*, World Publishing Co., Cleveland OH, 1943, pp. 140, 401, 488; Anon., 'DEAR CHRISTIAN', leaflet, Christian Mobilizers, *c.*1939; *Christian Mobilizer* 1, 1, 23 September 1939.

20 M. Schonbach, *Native American Fascism during the 1930s and 1940s. A Study of Its Roots, Its Growth and Its Decline*, Garland Publishing, New York, 1985, pp. 218–19.

21 P. Jenkins, *Hoods and Shirts. The Extreme Right in Pennsylvania, 1925–1950*, University of North Carolina Press, Chapel Hill NC, 1997, pp. 25, 90; J. Kaplan and L. Weinberg, *The Emergence of a Euro-American Radical Right*, Rutgers University Press, New Brunswick NJ, 1998, pp. 25–26; S. A. Diamond, *The Nazi Movement in the United States 1924–1941*, Cornell University Press, Ithaca NY, 1974, pp. 92, 113, 217, 236, 239; L. V. Bell, *In Hitler's Shadow. The Anatomy of American Nazism*, Kennikat Press, Port Washington NY, 1973, p. 49; Wade, pp. 270–71.

22 Smith, p. 135; Jenkins, pp. 205–206; Schonbach, pp. 170, 309; R. Rollins, *I Find Treason. The Story of an American Anti-Nazi Agent*, George Harrap, London, 1941, p. 193; M. Sayers and A. E. Kahn, *Sabotage! The Secret War Against America*, Harper and Brothers, New York, 1942, pp. 147–48; Carlson, p. 30.

23 Sayers and Kahn, p. 207; Smith, pp. 172–74, 178–79.

24 Sayers and Kahn, p. 49; G. Jeansonne, *Women of the Far Right. The Mothers' Movement and World War II*, University of Chicago Press, Chicago, 1996, pp. 51, 87, 91, 101, 104, 172; *Women's Voice* 2, 3, 28 October 1943.

25 L. P. Ribuffo, *The Old Christian Right. The Protestant Far Right from the Great Depression to the Cold War*, Temple University Press, Philadelphia PA, 1983, pp. 188–212, 336; M. St-George and L. Dennis, *A Trial on Trial. The Great Sedition Trial of 1944*, National Civil Rights Committee, Washington DC, 1946, pp. 71–73, 114–21, 272–76; L. Dennis, *The Coming American Fascism*, Harper & Brothers, New York, 1936, pp. 209, 295.

26 Smith, p. 181; Wade, pp. 272, 275; E. A. Piller, *Time Bomb*, Arco Publishing, New York, 1945, p. 60.

27 Jeansonne, *Smith*, pp. 82, 155–56.

28 Jeansonne, *Smith*, p. 144; R. L. Roy, *Apostles of Bigotry. A Study of Organized Bigotry and Disruption on the Fringes of Protestantism*, Beacon Press, Boston MA, 1953, pp. 65, 67.

29 M. F. Greene, *The Temple Bombing*, Jonathan Cape, London, 1996, pp. 33–36, 145.

30 Anon., *Activities of Ku Klux Klan Organizations in the United States Part 5. Hearings Before the Committee on Un-American Activities*, US Government Printing Office, Washington DC, 1966, pp. 3809, 3820; *Women's Voice* 11, 9, 30 April; 12, 1, 27 August 1953.

31 Chalmers, p. 339.

32 Wade, pp. 276, 279, 285–86, 289, 295; G. Feldman, 'Soft Opposition: Elite Acquiescence and Klan-Sponsored Terrorism in Alabama, 1946–1950', *Historical Journal* 40, 3, 1997, p. 764.

33 W. Goring, 'The National Renaissance Party. History and Analysis of an American Neo-Nazi Political Party', *National Information Center Newsletter*, December 1969–January 1970, p. 6; A. Forster and B. R. Epstein, *Cross-Currents*, Doubleday, Garden City NY, 1956, p. 219; Anon., *Preliminary Report on Neo-fascist and Hate Groups*, Committee on Un-American Activities, Washington DC, 1954, pp. 8, 21–22.

34 *National Renaissance Bulletin*, October 1951; October 1952; May 1953.

35 Roy, pp. 129, 131–33.

36 Anon., *Preliminary Report on Neo-fascist Groups*, p. 11; *Common Sense* VI, 167, 1 August 1952; Forster and Epstein, *Cross-Currents*, pp. 30, 38; *Women's Voice* 10, 5, 25 December 1952; *National Renaissance Bulletin*, January 1952; Jeansonne, *Smith*, pp. 89, 237.
37 Bennett, pp. 286–94, 300–301; *National Renaissance Bulletin* October 1951; January 1952; J. Rorty, 'What Price McCarthy Now?', *Commentary* January 1955, pp. 32–34; Jeansonne, *Smith*, pp. 119–20.
38 Forster and Epstein, *Cross-Currents*, pp. 30, 34, 56, 58–60.
39 *Women's Voice* 10, 5, 27 December 1951; Anon., *Preliminary Report on Neo-fascist Groups*, p. 12; *Common Sense* VI, 167, 1 August 1952.
40 Forster and Epstein, pp. 319–20, 329.
41 Berlet and Lyons, p. 100.
42 Pelley, p. 106; D. S. Strong, *Organized Anti-semitism in America. The Rise of Group Prejudice during the Decade 1930–40*, Greenwood Press, Westport CT, pp. 136–37; Tull, p. 152.

2 American Reich

1 *White Power* 95, n.d., 1980.
2 N. Goodrick-Clarke, *Black Sun. Aryan Cults, Esoteric Nazism and the Politics of Identity*, New York University Press, New York, 2003, pp. 78–79; K. Coogan, *Dreamer of the Day. Francis Parker Yockey and the Postwar Fascist International*, Autonomedia, New York, 1999, p. 460.
3 *National Renaissance Bulletin*, June 1953; Coogan, pp. 264–67.
4 Coogan, pp. 15, 20–24, 85–103, 152–56, 192, 208–9.
5 F. P Yockey, *Imperium. The Philosophy of History and Politics*, Truth Seeker, New York, 1962, pp. 390, 404, 557–58, 574–75, 594–95.
6 Coogan, p. 265.
7 Coogan, pp. 459–60.
8 F. J. Simonelli, *American Fuehrer. George Lincoln Rockwell and the American Nazi Party*, University of Illinois Press, Urbana IL, 1999, pp. 26–31, 81; G. L. Rockwell, *This Time The World*, 7th edn, Liberty Bell Publications, York SC, 2004, pp. 217–18.
9 J. Kaplan (ed.) *Encyclopedia of White Power. A Sourcebook on the Radical Racist Right*, Altamira Press, Walnut Creek CA, 2000, p. 449.
10 *Stormtrooper*, spring 1966; Kaplan, *Encyclopedia of White Power*, pp. 439, 443–44.
11 W. H. Schmaltz, *Hate. George Lincoln Rockwell and the American Nazi Party*, Brassey's, Washington DC, 1999, pp. 115–17, 181, 215.
12 *Stormtrooper* 3, 2, March-August 1964; February 1965; spring 1966.
13 Schmaltz, pp. 119–20; Simonelli, p. 50.
14 Simonelli, pp. 74, 110–13; Rockwell, *This Time the World*, pp. 245, 260, 374; *Stormtrooper*, summer 1965.
15 *Rockwell Report* 6, 3 January 1962.
16 *Rockwell Report* 2, 7, 1 February 1963; II, 17, 15 June 1963; 3, 18, 15 July 1964.
17 Kaplan, *Encyclopedia of White Power*, pp. 154, 327–28; *Free American* 1, n.d. (1964); 3, December YF 75 (1964).
18 Simonelli, pp. 100, 104; Schmaltz, pp. 248, 254, 258, 264; *Truth Seeker*, February 1968.
19 Simonelli, pp. 131, 137, 183; Schmaltz, pp. 129, 168, 173–74, 317; *Thunderbolt* 40, March 1962.
20 Kaplan, *Encyclopedia of White Power*, pp. 558–63.
21 *White Power* 18, July 1971; 20, September 1971; 75, May-June 1977.
22 *White Power* 67, November 1975; 69, January 1976; 71, May-June 1976; 73, January-February 1977; *NS Bulletin* 69, 1 September 1970.

23 *White Power* 62, April 1975; 66, October 1975.
24 www.alphalink.com.au/~radnat/usanazis/barrett.html
25 Anon., *Siege. The Collected Writings of James Mason*, Black Sun Publications, Bozeman MT, 2003, pp. 379–80, 386–90; Kaplan, *Encyclopedia of White Power*, p. 301.
26 *Rockwell Report* 17, 15 June 1962; G. Grau, *Hidden Holocaust?*, Cassell, London, 1995, pp. 165–66, 193–94; Kaplan, *Encyclopedia of White Power*, p. 316; *Dixon Line-Reason* 12, 4, May-June 1975.
27 Schmaltz, pp. 262–63; Kaplan, *Encyclopedia of White Power*, pp. 60–62, 82; J. George and L. Wilcox, *Nazis, Communists, Klansmen, and Others on the Fringe*, Prometheus Books, Buffalo NY, 1992, pp. 358–62; www.alphalink.com.au/~radnat/usanazis/chapter3.html.
28 *White Power* 103, n.d., 1982.
29 J. Kaplan, *Radical Religion in America. Millenarian Movements from the Far Right to the Children of Noah*, Syracuse University Press, Syracuse NY, 1997, p. 63; Schmaltz, pp. 210–11, 337; Kaplan, *Radical Religion*, pp. 32–33, 188.
30 Kaplan, *Encyclopedia of White Power*, pp. 82, 86–87.
31 E. Jensen, 'International Nazi Cooperation', in T. Björgo and R. Witte (eds) *Racist Violence in Europe*, St Martin's Press, New York, 1993, pp. 85–87.
32 George and Wilcox, pp. 367–68; *Michigan Briefing* II, 4, n.d., c.1982; Kaplan, *Encyclopedia of White Power*, pp. 65–66.
33 *Right* 1, October 1955.
34 *Right* 2, November 1955; 4, January 1956; 20, May 1957; 22, July 1957; 23, August 1957; 27, December 1957; 31, April 1958; 46, July 1959; F. P. Mintz, *The Liberty Lobby and the American Right. Race, Conspiracy, and Culture*, Greenwood Press, Westport CT, 1985, pp. 73–74, 77–78.
35 Coogan, p. 36; *Right* 58, July 1960; 60, September 1960.
36 Yockey, pp. xxi, 281–82.
37 Mintz, pp. 87–88; *White Power* 63, May 1975.
38 Mintz, pp. 104, 217; McLemee, 'Spotlight on Liberty Lobby', p. 30.
39 W. W. Turner, *Power on the Right*, Ramparts Press, Berkeley CA, 1971, pp. 68, 78, 153–54, 158, 163; Mintz, pp. 89–90; S. Diamond, *Roads to Dominion. Right-Wing Movements and Political Power in the United States*, Guilford Press, New York, 1995, pp. 153–55; *Spotlight* 18 September 1995.
40 G. Michael, *From Out of the Shadows: Willis Carto and the American Far Right*, forthcoming.
41 *Searchlight* 315, September 2001.
42 *American Mercury*, spring 1969.
43 C. H. Simonds, 'The Strange Story of Willis Carto', *National Review*, 10 September 1971, p. 986.
44 Coogan, p. 519; *Dixon Line-Reason*, October 1972; *Statecraft* 4, 1, January 1972.
45 R. S. Griffin, *The Fame of a Dead Man's Deeds. An Up-Close Portrait of White Nationalist William Pierce*, 1st Books, 2001, pp. 38, 112–13; *White Power* 7, 8, June-July 1969; www.alphalink.com.au/radnat/usanazis/barrett.html
46 P. W. Valentine, 'Rightist Youth Organization Opens Office in Georgetown', *Washington Post*, 23 December 1970, pp. B1, B5; *Action* 17, April 1971.
47 *Attack!* 12, June 1972; 17, January 1973; 23, September 1973.
48 *Attack!* 10, March 1972; 13, July 1972; 15, October 1972; 25, February 1974; 32, January 1975; *National Vanguard* 101, August 1984.
49 *National Vanguard* 68, n.d., 1979; 72, October 1979.
50 *National Vanguard* 67, March 1979; 69, May 1979; 101, August 1984.
51 *National Vanguard* 85, January 1982; 67, March 1979.
52 *National Vanguard* 110, March-April 1989; 113, March-April 1994.
53 Anon., *Membership Handbook for Members of the National Alliance*, National Vanguard Books, Hillsboro WV, 1993, pp. 120–22.

54 Simonelli, pp. 111–13; D. E. Lipstadt, *Denying the Holocaust*, Penguin, London, 1994, pp. 49–156.
55 *National Vanguard* 69, May 1979; 84, November 1981.
56 *Plexus* 14, February 1994; *WAR*, March 2002.
57 Anon., *Membership Handbook*, pp. 108–11.
58 Anon., *Membership Handbook*, pp. 28–31.
59 Anon., *Who Rules America?*, National Vanguard Books, Hillsboro WV, 1993, pp. 2–3, 6; Anon., *Membership Handbook*, pp. 17, 19.
60 www.natvan.com/pub/2002/032302.txt
61 www.overthrow.com/lsn/news.asp?articleID=5082
62 See e.g. Schmaltz, pp. 227–29; *White American*, June 1966.
63 B. A. Dobratz and S. L. Shanks-Meile, *The White Separatist Movement in the United States. 'White Power, White Pride!'*, Johns Hopkins University Press, Baltimore MD, 2000, p. 50; *Monitor* 1, 3, June 1986; 10, January 1988; *WAR '85* 4, 5, n.d., 1985; *WAR* 7, 5, n.d., *c.*1988; 8, 2, n.d., 1989.
64 J. Ridgeway, *Blood in the Face. The Ku Klux Klan, Aryan Nations, Nazi Skinheads, and the Rise of a New White Culture*, Thunder's Mouth Press, New York, 1990, pp. 169–70; P. D. Stachura, *Gregor Strasser and the Rise of Nazism*, Allen and Unwin, London, 1983; *WAR* 8, 1, n.d., 1989; 8, 2, n.d., 1989.
65 *WAR* 8, 3, n.d., 1989.
66 J. Coplon, 'Skinhead Nation', *Rolling Stone* 540, 1 December 1988, pp. 56, 58, 62; D. Burghart (ed.) *Soundtracks to the White Revolution. White Supremacist Assaults on Youth Music Subcultures*, Center for New Community, Chicago, 1999, pp. 32–33; *Resistance* 5, fall 1995; 6, spring 1996; Kaplan, *Encyclopedia of White Power*, pp. 123–29; *Washington Post*, 12 January 2000.
67 *Free Speech* VI, 1, January 2000.
68 *Resistance* 9, fall 1999; www.panzerfaust.com/lyrics/40020.shtml.
69 *New Statesman*, 14 November 2005; L. Theroux, *The Call of the Weird. Travels in American Subcultures*, Macmillan, Basingstoke, UK, 2005, pp. 270, 273–74.
70 www.aryan-nations.org/headlinenews/rock_against_israeli.htm; *Intelligence Report* 107, fall 2002.
71 *Intelligence Report* 108, winter 2002; *National Alliance Bulletin*, March 2000.
72 www.vanguardnewsnetwork.com/2004b/52104lindertopekarally.htm; www.adl.org/learn/extremism_in_america_updates/groups/white_revolution/white+revolution_update_0501.htm
73 www.vanguardnewsnetwork.com/2004b/52104lindertopekarally.htm; www.panzerfaust.com/forum/showthread.php?t=842; www.adl.org/learn/extremism_in_america_update/sa/white_rev/white_rev_update_0501.htm
74 www.whiterevolution.com/archives/20050904/wr-announces-cartridges-for-katrina-program; www.whiterevolution.com/wrra/jan0112005.shtml
75 *Intelligence Report* III, fall 2003.
76 *Intelligence Report* 118, summer 2005; www.nationalvanguard.org/story.php?id=5517
77 www.overthrow.com/lsn/news.asp?articleID=8998; www.vnnforum.com/showthread.php?p=400659; www.natvan.com/adv/2006/07-08-06.html; www.adl.org/learn/extremism_in-the/White_Supremecy/strom4.07.htm.
78 www.natall.com/pdf/2005/04-30-05.pdf
79 M. Dees and S. Fiffer, *Hate on Trial. The Case Against America's Most Dangerous Neo-Nazi*, Villard Books, New York, 1993, pp. 3–7, 20–21, 168–69, 272; Kaplan, *Encyclopedia of White Power*, pp. 337–38.
80 *Calling Our Nation* 73, *c.*1994; Anon., '1996 Aryan Youth Congress', leaflet, 1996.
81 *Intelligence Report* 121, spring 2006; www.adl.org/learn/extremism_in_america_updates/groups/white_revolution/white+revolution_update_0501.htm

3 Out of the Southland

1 Chalmers, pp. 343, 368, 370; Wade, pp. 304, 315–16, 333.
2 Wade, pp. 310–11, 324–25.
3 P. Sims, *The Klan*, Scarborough, New York, 1982, pp. 245–48.
4 Wade, pp. 344–45, 349–54; Sims, p. 291.
5 Anon., *The Principle of the United Klans of America Knights of the Ku Klux Klan*, leaflet, n.d.; National Knights of the Ku Klux Klan, Inc., *Its Problems, Its Programs, Its Purposes*, leaflet, n.d., 1964.
6 Wade, pp. 437–38.
7 Anon., *Principle of the United Klans*; National Knights, *Its Problems*; Anon., *Activities of Ku Klux Klan organizations Part 3*; p. 2747.
8 *Fiery Cross* 8, 3, 1973.
9 Anon., *Activities of Ku Klux Klan Organizations in the United States Part 4. Hearings before the Committee on Un-American Activities*, US Government Printing Office, Washington DC, 1966, pp. 2916–17; Anon., *Activities of Ku Klux Klan Organizations in the United States Part 5*, p. 3619.
10 *Fiery Cross*, 20 May 1964; Wade, pp. 343, 437.
11 Wade, pp. 320, 335, 434.
12 T. B. Edsall with M. D. Edsall, *Chain Reaction. The Impact of Race, Rights, and Taxes on American Politics*, W. W. Norton, New York, 1992, pp. 35, 48.
13 G. Michael, *Confronting Right-wing Extremism and Terrorism*, Routledge, London, 2003, p. 156; D. Cunningham, *There's Something Happening Here. The New Left, the Klan, and FBI Counterintelligence*, University of California Press, Berkeley CA, 2004, pp. xi, 27, 87–89, 130–31, 161–62, 248, 273–76.
14 J. Nelson, *Terror in the Night. The Klan's Campaign Against the Jews*, Simon and Schuster, New York, 1993, pp. 17, 64, 117, 164–66, 173–87; Sims, pp. 261, 319, 324.
15 T. Bridges, *The Rise of David Duke*, University Press of Mississippi, Jackson MS, 1994, pp. 35, 40–41.
16 *Crusader* 47, n.d., 1980.
17 Bridges, pp. 19–35.
18 Wade, pp. 185, 409–29; D. Lowe, *Ku Klux Klan: The Invisible Empire*, W. W. Norton, New York, 1967, pp. 105–6; Anon., *Activities of Ku Klux Klan Organizations Part 4*, p. 3087; Sims, pp. 101, 118.
19 Sims, p. 200; Wade, p. 368; Bridges, pp. 45–49, 51, 55–56, 67; *Crusader* 41, n.d., c.1979.
20 *Crusader* 47, n.d., 1980; Wade, pp. 373–75, 389–90; Bridges, pp. 87–88.
21 *Klansman* 54, June 1980 mini-edition (n.d.); Wade, pp. 375, 394, 396.
22 Dobratz and Shanks-Meile, pp. 51–52; B. Stanton, *Klanwatch. Bringing the Ku Klux Klan to Justice*, Mentor, New York, 1992, pp. 200–2, 243, 258–60; Wade, pp. 372–73.
23 *White Patriot*, special introductory issue, n.d.; *Monitor* 1, 4, September 1986; Anon., *The American Farmer and the Extremists*, Anti-Defamation League of B'nai Brith, New York, 1986, p. 8.
24 www.kkk.bz/women8.htm; Lee, p. 490.
25 *Klan Krusader*, March-April 1989; R. Crawford, S. L. Gardner, J. Mazzochi and R. L. Taylor, *The Northwest Imperative*, Coalition for Human Dignity, Portland OR, 1994, p. 1.23.
26 *Klan Krusader*, March-April 1989; *White Beret* 1–92, Dec-Feb (1991–92).
27 Wade, pp. 373, 385, 392–93; Bridges, pp. 76–79; Ridgeway, pp. 87–88.
28 Stanton, pp. 92–97, 113; *Hammer* 9, spring 1985.
29 www.simson.net/ref/leaderless/1983.inter_klan_newsletter.pdf; http://kelticklan.com/Klan_Newsletter_Survival_Alert_1983_5.htm; L. R. Beam Jr, *Essays of a Klansman*, A.K.I.A. Publications, Hayden Lake ID, 1983, pp. ii–v, 3–8.

30 R. S. Ezekiel, *The Racist Mind*, Penguin Books, Harmondsworth, UK, 1995, pp. 92, 98–99; Dobratz and Shanks-Meile, p. 52

31 E.Wheaton, *Codename GREENKIL. The 1979 Greensboro Killings*, University of Georgia Press, Athens GA, 1987, pp. 99, 118; www.pbs.org/wgbh/pages/frontline/transcripts/102.html; Wade, pp. 378, 382, 388–89.

32 H. L. Bushart, J. R. Craig and M. Barnes, *Soldiers of God: White Supremacists and their Holy War for America*, Pinnacle, New York, 1998, pp. 112, 142–43, 222–23, 228, 233.

33 *Spokesman Review*, 3 October 2004.

34 *Intelligence Report* 93, winter 1999.

35 *Klanwatch Intelligence Report* 39, August 1988; www.stormfront.org/forum/showthread.php?t=18464.

36 *Monitor* 16, October 1989; 18, March 1990.

37 www.stormfront.org/forum/showthread.php?t=18464; www.stormfront.org/forum/showthread.php?t=21779; www.k-k-k.com/news.html; *Intelligence Report* 103, fall 2001; 121, spring 2006.

38 *Klanwatch Intelligence Report* 39, August 1988; www.stormfront.org/forum/showthread.php?t=21779.

39 Dobratz and Shanks-Meile, p. 50.

40 Anon., *The Ku Klux Klan: A History*, p. 44; *Monitor* 1, 2, March 1986.

41 *Confederate Leader*, special introductory edition, n.d., 1986; Anon., *The Ku Klux Klan: A History*, pp. 44–45.

42 E. Langer, 'The American Neo-Nazi Movement Today', *Nation*, 16–23 July 1990, p. 95; Bridges, pp. 87–88, 266.

43 *NAAWP News* 26, n.d.; C. M. Swain and R. Nieli (eds) *Contemporary Voices of White Nationalism in America*, Cambridge University Press, Cambridge, 2003, pp. 167–68; www.adl.org/learn/extremism_in_america_updates/individuals/david_duke/duke; www.adl.org/learn/extremism_in_america_updates/individuals/david_duke/duke_update_021218.htm; *Intelligence Report* 114, summer 2004.

44 Lee, p. 357; Swain and Nieli, pp. 154–55.

45 www.overthrow.com/lsn/news.asp?articleID=9170; www.overthrow.com/lsn/news.asp?articleID=9176

46 www.k-k-k.com/news.html; www.overthrow.com/messageboards/index.asp?messageID=25384; Langer, p. 83.

47 *Fiery Cross* 7, 10, 1972; *Attack!* 6, summer 1971.

48 *Crusader* 47, *c.*1980.

49 *Women's Voice* 13, 3, October 1954.

50 Greene, pp. 156, 161–62.

51 *Thunderbolt* 73, January 1966.

52 *Thunderbolt* 50, April 1963; 67, May 1965.

53 Wade, pp. 324–26, 503.

54 D. T. Carter, *The Politics of Rage. George Wallace, the Origins of the New Conservatism, and the Transformation of American Politics*, Louisiana State University Press, Baton Rouge LA, 1995, p. 165; J. G. Cook, *The Segregationists*, Appleton-Century Crofts, New York, 1962, p. 170; *Thunderbolt* 38, January 1962; 48, January 1963; 51, May 1963; 54, November 1963; 65, March 1965; 67, May 1965.

55 *Thunderbolt* 94, October 1967; 218, June 1977.

56 *Thunderbolt* 51, May 1963; 95, November 1965; T. Linehan, *British Fascism 1918–39. Parties, Ideologies and Culture*, Manchester University Press, Manchester, UK, 2000, pp. 71, 78.

57 *Thunderbolt* 304, n.d., *c.*1985.

58 *Thunderbolt* 28, April 1961; Cook, pp. 170–71.

59 Schmaltz, pp. 153–54.

60 Cook, pp. 137–38; *Women's Voice* 13, 3, October 1954.

61 *Thunderbolt* 67, May 1965; Dobratz and Shanks-Meile, pp. 4–5, 295–96; *Truth At Last* 352, n.d., 1991; 385, *c.*1995.

62 Greene, pp. 1, 283–87, 402–13; Anon., 'A Party not a Publication', American States Rights Party, Birmingham AL, n.d., *c.*1965; *Hammer* 6, spring 1984; www.adl.org/learn/ext_us/Fields.asp

63 Ezekiel, p. 115.

64 Dobratz and Shanks-Meile, p. 83; www.nationalvanguard.org/story.php?id=668; www.nationalvanguard.org/story.php?id=6794

4 Not all Patriots

1 *Patriot Report*, July 1996; M. C. Campbell Jr, *Kingdoms at War. The Second North American Revolution*, revised edn, pp. 14, 47–48.

2 *Freeman Letter* 10, 4, April 1992; Anon., *Operation Vampire Killer 2000. American Police Action Plan for Stopping World Government Rule*, PATNWO, Phoenix AZ, 1992, p. 42; *Taking Aim* 4, 3, June 1997; *Patriot Report*, April 1994.

3 M. J. 'Red' Beckman, *Born Again Republic*, Freedom Church, Billings MT, 1981, pp. 16–17; J. W. Wardner, *The Planned Destruction of America*, Longwood Communications, DeBary FL, 1994, pp. 19–21.

4 Beckman, p. 97.

5 Wardner, pp. 53, 66, 78.

6 Anon., *Operation Vampire Killer*, pp. 10, 16.

7 Anon., *Operation Vampire Killer*, pp. 9–10.

8 Wardner, pp. 66–68; M. W. Jefferson, *America Under Siege. 'A Lesson in Treason, Treachery and Conspiracy'*, Freedom and Liberty Foundation, Knoxville TN, 1994, pp. 13–15, 22.

9 Jefferson, pp. 35–55.

10 Gurudas, *Treason. The New World Order*, Cassandra Press, San Rafael CA, 1996, pp. 12–13; K. Stern, *A Force Upon the Plain. The American Militia and the Politics of Hate*, Simon and Schuster, New York, 1996, p. 145; *Patriot Report*, August 1995.

11 D. Levitas, *The Terrorist Next Door. The Militia Movement and the Radical Right*, Thomas Dunne Books, New York, 2002, pp. 108–9.

12 Levitas, pp. 1–2, 61–62, 127–29, 178, 184, 223–24; *Calling Our Nation* 43, n.d., *c.*1984; *P. N. Report*, January 1984.

13 J. Ridgeway, *Blood in the Face. The Ku Klux Klan, Aryan Nations, Nazi Skinheads, and the Rise of a New White Culture*, Thunder's Mouth Press, New York, 1990, pp. 120–24; Levitas, pp. 217–20.

14 L. T. Sargent (ed.) *Extremism in America. A Reader*, New York University Press, New York, 1995, pp. 285, 292; Levitas, p. 287.

15 Seymour, pp. 284, 287–88.

16 Seymour, pp. 267–68, 272–73, 314, 347–50.

17 Anon., *Hate Groups in America*, Anti-Defamation League of B'nai Brith, New York, 1982, p. 47; *National Educator*, May 1979.

18 M. Barkun, *Religion and the Racist Right. The Origins of the Christian Identity Movement*, University of North Carolina Press, Chapel Hill NC, 1994, p. 215; H. L. Church, 'John R. Harrell Lays It on the Line in Speech at McKendree College', newspaper article reproduced by CPDL, *c.*1983.

19 J. Mohr, 'Why a Citizens Emergency Defense System?', Christian-Patriots Defense League and Citizens Emergency Defense System, Flora IL, February 1984; S. Emry, 'Subject: Citizens Emergency Defense System (CEDS)', America's Promise, Phoenix AZ, 1979; Sargent, pp. 327–28, 330.

20 *Newsletter*, August-September 1984.

21 Anon., *Hate Groups in America*, 1982, p. 51; J. A. Aho, *The Politics of Righteousness. Idaho Christian Patriotism*, University of Washington Press, Seattle WA, 1990, p. 231; J. E. Stern, 'The Covenant, the Sword, and the Arm of the Lord (1985)', in J. B. Tucker (ed.) *Toxic Terror. Assessing Terrorist Use of Chemical and Biological Weapons*, MIT Press, Cambridge MA, 2000, pp. 148–152.

22 Levitas, pp. 7, 108–9, 111, 260; D. Burghart and R. Crawford, *Guns and Gavels. Common Law Courts, Militias and White Supremacy*, Coalition for Human Dignity, Portland OR, 1996, pp. 22, 43–45.

23 J. E. Rosenfeld, 'The Justus Freemen Standoff', in C. Wessinger (ed.) *Millennialism, Persecution, and Violence*, Syracuse University Press, Syracuse NY, 2000, pp. 324–25, 338–39; *Taking Aim* II, 11, January 1995.

24 R. Crawford, S. L. Gardner, J. Mazzochi and R. L. Taylor, *The Northwest Imperative*, Coalition for Human Dignity, Portland OR, 1994, pp. 228–29; *American's Bulletin*, May 1992.

25 See e.g. *American's Bulletin* 15, 6, June 1996; 16, 12, December 1997.

26 *Patriot Report*, special edn, n.d., 1993; September 1995; February 1996; November 1996; February 1998.

27 *Free American*, March 1997, October 2001.

28 *Spotlight*, 17 September 1975; S. Emry, *Billions for the Bankers Debts for the People*, Spotlight Reprint, 3 February 1986; Jefferson, p. 102; Durham, 'American Far Right and 9/11', pp. 108, 111.

29 Stern, *A Force Upon the Plain*, pp. 172, 192.

30 D. Mulloy, *Homegrown Revolutionaries. An American Militia Reader*, Arthur Miller Centre for American Studies, University of East Anglia, Norwich, UK, 1999, p. 27; Anon., *The Declaration of the Third Continental Congress*, n.d., *c.*1968; Anon., *Clarification of the New and Unusual Position of the Original and Official Constitution Parties of the United States*, n.d., *c.*1970.

31 Anon., *Hate Groups in America*, 1982, pp. 49–50; Anon., *Hate Groups in America*, Anti-Defamation League of B'nai Brith, New York, 1988, p. 49; Seymour, pp. 20, 26.

32 Stern, *A Force Upon the Plain*, pp. 21, 23–25, 40.

33 Anon., *Special Report on the Meeting of Christian Men Held in Estes Park, Colorado, October 23, 24, 25, 1992*, Scriptures for America Ministries, LaPorte CO, n.d., pp. 2–4, 7–8, 12, 16, n.p.; *Jubilee* 5, 3, November-December 1992.

34 Stern, *A Force Upon the Plain*, pp. 58–64, 71, 109.

35 M. Dees with J. Corcoran, *Gathering Storm. America's Militia Threat*, HarperCollins, New York, 1996, pp. 88–89; Levitas, p. 304.

36 Anon., *M.O.M's 1997 Preparedness Catalog*, Militia of Montana, Noxon MT, 1997, pp. 4–7, 17, 19; Mulloy, pp. 327–30.

37 *Spotlight*, 9 January 1995.

38 Stern, *A Force Upon the Plain*, pp. 83, 223; M. Mariani, 'The Michigan Militia: Political Engagement or Political Alienation?', *Terrorism and Political Violence* 10, 4, 1998, pp. 133–34.

39 Stern, *A Force Upon the Plain*, pp. 246–47; Dees with Corcoran, pp. 49–69.

40 Levitas, pp. 9–10, 301–2, 327; L. Crothers, *Rage on the Right. The American Militia Movement from Ruby Ridge to Homeland Security*, Rowman and Littlefield, Lanham MD, 2003, pp. 5, 94–95, 173.

41 N. Cohn, *Warrant for Genocide. The Myth of the Jewish World Conspiracy and the Protocols of the Elders of Zion*, Serif, London, 1996, pp. 30–36; N. H. Webster, *Secret Societies and Subversive Movements*, Christian Book Club of America, n.d., pp. 238, 245, 384–87; Mintz, pp. 59–61.

42 R. Welch, *The New Americanism and Other Speeches and Essays*, Western Islands Publishers, Belmont MA, 1966, p. 135; Mintz, p. 147; Aho, p. 255.

43 Wardner, pp. 198–200; Gurudas, pp. 14, 15, 19, 218–19; Anon., *M.O.M.'s Preparedness Catalog*, p. 20.

44 L. Michel and D. Herbeck, *American Terrorist. Tim McVeigh and the Oklahoma City Bombing*, Regan Books, New York, 2001, pp. 59–60, 119–20, 130–31, 166, 205–06, 224–28, 233, 365, 369.

45 *Taking Aim* 4, 4, July 1997; *Patriot Report*, August 1997; www.vex.net/nizkor/ftp.cgi/orgs/american/militias/alabama/alabama-declaration

46 *Southern Ranger*, July-August 1997.

47 Racial Readers Forum 011200.html at http://web.archive.org/web/20001018194253/http://www.whiteracist.com/

48 *WAR*, March 2003.

49 *Free Speech* 2, 1, January 1996; www.natvan.com/american-dissident-voices/adv061293.html

50 *Resistance!* 47, February 1995.

51 Kaplan, *Encyclopedia of White Power*, p. 224; *NSV Report* 12, 3, July-September 1994; 13, 2, April-June 1995.

52 *NSV Report* 6, 3, July-September 1988.

53 Emry, *Billions for the Bankers*; *Americanism Bulletin* 51, July 1954; Kaplan, *Encyclopedia of White Power*, pp. 120–21; www.scripturesforamerica.org/html2/jm0030.htm

54 *NSV Report* 6, 3, July-September 1988; www.scripturesforamerica.org/html2/jm0084a.htm; *Christian Crusade for Truth Intelligence Newsletter*, July 1987.

55 K. Lane (ed.) *Deceived, Damned and Defiant. The Revolutionary Writings of David Lane*, 14 Word Press, St Maries ID, 1999, pp. 147, 149; www.stormfront.org/archive/t-87429.

56 *Spotlight*, 13 September 1993.

57 M. Durham, 'A Global Master Plan? The American Far Right and *The Protocols of the Learned Elders of Zion*', in J. H. Brinks, S. Rock and E. Timms (eds) *Nationalist Myths and Modern Media. Contested Identities in the Age of Globalization*, Tauris, London, 2006, pp. 32, 35–36.

5 Race and religion

1 Barkun, *Religion and the Racist Right*, pp. 9–11; J. H. Allen, *Judah's Sceptre and Joseph's Birthright. An Analysis of the Prophecies of Scripture in Regard to the Royal Family of Judah and the Many Nations of Israel*, Destiny Publishers, Merrimac MA, n.d., pp. 296–97.

2 Barkun, *Religion and the Racist Right*, pp. 8–11.

3 Allen, pp. 263–64, 276–81.

4 Barkun, *Religion and the Racist Right*, pp. 47–71, 122–26; *Identity* 7, 6, February 1975.

5 Levitas, pp. 23, 25, 405, 438.

6 Levitas, pp. 26, 41, 94, 110, 413; Kaplan, *Encyclopedia of White Power*, p. 472.

7 *Imperial Nighthawk* LXVIII, 1, n.d.; Ezekiel, pp. 127–28, 132; *Thunderbolt* 50, April 1963; Seymour, pp. 67–68.

8 *Thunderbolt* 98, February 1968.

9 *Rockwell Report* 7, 15 January 1962; 16, 1 June 1962; 3, 8, 1 February 1964; March 1966; Simonelli, pp. 117, 120–21, 175.

10 Kaplan, *Encyclopedia of White Power*, p. 330; Levitas, p. 66; *Christian Vanguard* 37, December 1974; 77, May 1978.

11 Sims, p. 175; Barkun, *Religion and the Racist Right*, p. 210; Michael, *Confronting Right-Wing Extremism*, p. 63; Kaplan, *Encyclopedia of White Power*, p. 165.

12 *Calling Our Nation*, Foundation Edition, 1979.

13 *Calling Our Nation* 50, c.1985.

14 Barkun, pp. 233–38; M. Gardell, *Gods of the Blood. The Pagan Revival and White Separatism*, Duke University Press, Durham NC, 2003, pp. 112–13.

15 K. Flynn and G. Gerhardt, *The Silent Brotherhood. Inside America's Racist Underground*, Signet, New York, 1990, pp. 88–91; *From the Mountain*, July-August 1984.

16 Flynn and Gerhardt, pp. 93, 116–17.

17 Kaplan, *Encyclopedia of White Power*, pp. 75, 213; *From the Mountain*, March-April 1988.

18 Levitas, pp. 325–26; Kaplan, *Encyclopedia of White Power*, p. 76.

19 Michael, *Confronting Right-Wing Extremism*, p. 177.

20 *Intelligence Report* 101, spring 2001; 107, fall 2002.

21 www.adl.org/Learn/ext_us/Aryan_nations_break_up.asp; www.adl.org/learn/extrem ism_in_america_updates/groups/aryan_nations/aryan+nations_update.0502.htm

22 J. Kaplan, 'The Context of American Millenarian Revolutionary Theology: The Case of the "Identity Christian" Church of Israel', *Terrorism and Political Violence* 5, 1, 1993, pp. 30–82; Barkun, p. 232; Crawford *et al.*, pp. 3.11–15, 3.27–32.

23 Crawford *et al.*, pp. 3.19–20; www.scripturesforamerica.org/html2/aspecia_mohr. htm; Aryan Nations Newsletter 83, n.d.

24 Barkun, *Religion and the Racist Right*, pp. 181–84.

25 C. L. Mange, *The Two Seeds of Genesis 3:15*, n.p., n.d., 1998, pp. 7–8, 10–11, 15, 30, 33–34, 37, 39, 41–42, 44.

26 S. E. Jones, *The Babylonian Connection Between Ancient and Modern Religions*, America's Promise, Phoenix AZ, 1978, p. 42; T. R. Weiland, *Eve. Did She or Didn't She? The Seedline Hypothesis under Scrutiny*, Mission to Israel, Scottsbluff NE, 2000, pp. 9–11, 64–65, 94–103, 105–6, 133.

27 Anon., *The 'Apple' Story. Genesis 3:15. The War between the Children of Light and the Children of Darkness*, American Institute of Theology, Harrison AR, 2001, pp. 1, 35–37.

28 Anon., *The 'Apple' Story*, pp. 34, 43, 54, 68–69.

29 Anon., *The 'Apple' Story*, p. 36; C. A. Weisman, *Who Is Esau-Edom?*, Weisman Publications, Burnsville MN, 1996, pp. 5–6, 118–19.

30 Kaplan, *Radical Religion in America,* pp. 15, 185; Gardell, p. 167; *Right* 50, November 1959.

31 *Free American* 1, n.d. (1964).

32 G. Thayer, *The Farther Shores of Politics. The American Political Fringe Today*, Allen Lane the Penguin Press, London, 1968, pp. 68–70; Gardell, p. 167.

33 Kaplan, *Encyclopedia of White Power*, p. 46; Gardell, pp. 165–77; Kaplan, *Radical Religion*, pp. 18–19, 87–89, 92–94.

34 Gardell, pp. 191–99, 204–5; Flynn and Gerhardt, pp. 248, 466; Lane, pp. 81–82.

35 R. McVan, *Creed of Iron. Wotansvolk Wisdom*, 14 Word Press, St Maries ID, 1997, pp. 10–11, 16–17.

36 Goodrick-Clarke, *Black Sun*, pp. 79–81; Coogan, p. 291; *National Renaissance Bulletin* 23, 1–2, January-February 1972.

37 *National Renaissance Bulletin* 26, 7–8; July-August 1975; 26, 9–10, September-October 1975; 27, 1–2, January-February 1976; 27, 3–4, March-April 1976.

38 J. Kaplan and L. Weinberg, *The Emergence of an Euro-American Radical Right*, Rutgers University Press, New Brunswick NJ, 1999, pp. 115–16.

39 *Crossing the Abyss* 3, autumnal equinox 1997.

40 *Abyss* 1, summer 1996; *Crossing the Abyss* 3, autumnal equinox 1997.

41 http://overthrow88.blogspot.com/2006_07_17_overthrow88_archive.html; www.nazi sozi.com; nazi.org/community/forum/YaBB.pl?num=1152548493/24; http://over throw.com/lsn/news.asp?articleID=9622; www.overthrow.com/lsn/news.asp?articleID =9684; www.americannaziparty.com/news/index.php?report_date=2006-03-07.

42 *White Power* 7, 6, n.d., 1968; Gardell, pp. 315–17; Griffin, p. 184; www.stormfront. org/archive/t-30206.

43 Griffin, pp. 186–87, 197–201, 203.

44 *National Renaissance Bulletin* 22, 7–8, July-August 1972.
45 *National Renaissance Bulletin* 24, 1–2, January-February 1973.
46 www.creator.org/holybooks/wmb/credo57.html; B. Klassen, *Nature's Eternal Religion*, second printing, Milwaukee Church of the Creator, Milwaukee WI, 1992, pp. 134–35, 372, 376, 378.
47 Goodrick-Clark, p. 254.
48 G. Michael, 'RAHOWA! A History of the World Church of the Creator', *Terrorism and Political Violence*, 18, 4, p. 566; www.adl.org/learn/news/sup-GroupsJoin.asp; J. Kaplan, 'Religiosity and the Radical Right: Toward the Creation of a New Ethnic Identity', in J. Kaplan and T. Bjorgo (eds) *Nation and Race. The Developing Euro-American Racist Subculture*, Northeastern University Press, Boston MA, 1998, p. 120.
49 Anon., *The Creator Membership Manual (Fourth Edition)*, World Church of the Creator, East Peoria IL, XXIX AC (2002), p. VI; *Intelligence Report* 114, summer 2004; www.adl.org/learn/extremism_in_america_updates/groups/creativity_movement/Creativity_Update_3_14_05.htm
50 J. P. Jackson, *Science for Segregation. Race, Law, and the Case against Brown v. Board of Education*, New York University Press, New York, 2005, pp. 55–63, 220–21; Coogan, p. 486; *Right* 17, February 1957; Anon., *Pax Americana. The Elite Whiteman's Guidebook*, Institute for Biopolitics, Chicago, n.d.
51 Barkun, *Religion and the Racist Right*, p. 118; *From the Mountain*, November-December 1982; May-June 1983; March-April 1985; January-February 1987.
52 www.americannaziparty.com/rockwell.html
53 *National Socialist* 4, spring 1982.
54 Gardell, p. 206; Barkun, *Religion and the Racist Right*, p. 209; *WAR*, November 2000.
55 Ridgeway, p. 175; *WAR* 8, 2, *c.*1989; July 1999; October 2000; Gardell, p. 178.
56 *NSV Report* 7, 4, October-December 1989; www.stormfront.org/forum/forumdisplay.php?f=80
57 www.christianseparatist.org/aw/aw980202.html
58 Gardell, p. 223.
59 Gardell, p. 221; www.kelticklankirk.com/plot_thickens_turns_nasty_and_foul.htm
60 www.agentofchaos.invisionzone.com/index.php?showtopic=499; www.agentofchaos.invisionzone.com/index.php?showtopic=446; www.agentsofchaos.invisionzone.com/index.php?showtopic=1492
61 *Calling Our Nation* 68, April 20th-Year 103 (1992).
62 *Fenris Wolf* 6, summer solstice 1999.
63 McVan, p. 24.
64 www.geocities.com/booknet01/rvtr-10.html
65 *Racial Loyalty* 69, April 1991.
66 *Struggle* LXXII, June XXVIII AC (2001).
67 *White Power* 109, n.d., 1984.
68 *WAR*, September 2000; November 2000; Anon., *Membership Handbook*, pp. 48–50.
69 www.vnnforum.com/showthread.php?t=471
70 www.natall.com/pub/2003/061403.txt; www.nationalvanguard.org/story.php?id=6678

6 Fighting for women

1 M. Durham, *Women and Fascism*, Routledge, London, 1998, pp. 22–24.
2 Durham, *Women and Fascism*, pp. 17–18, 23.
3 Chalmers, pp. 20–21; MacLean, pp. 115–16, 142, 148.
4 Anon., *Preliminary Report*, pp. 21–22.
5 *National Socialist World* 2, fall 1966; *White Power*, 94, November-December 1979.
6 *New Order* 45, November-December 1981; *Stormer* 2, 7, April 1981.

7 *National Vanguard* 86, May 1982; Anon., *Membership Handbook*, pp. 30–31.

8 *Thunderbolt* 105, September 1968; 251, March 1980.

9 *Calling Our Nation*, Foundation Edition, 1979; *Christian Vanguard*, October 1977; J. Stephenson, *Women in Nazi Society*, Croom Helm, London, 1975, p. 41.

10 www.creativityohio.com/wmb/credo28.html

11 *Fiery Cross* 8, 2, 1973; *Thunderbolt* 158, March 1973.

12 M. Durham, *The Christian Right, the Far Right and the Boundaries of American Conservatism*, Manchester University Press, Manchester, UK, 2000, pp. 84–86; *Torch* 8, 1, March 1976; *Jubilee* 7, 3, November-December 1994.

13 *White Nationalist* 1, 4, July-August 1973; *Confederate Leader*, special introductory edition, c.1986; *WAR* 8, 3, n.d., 1989.

14 J. Daniels, *White Lies. Race, Class, Gender, and Sexuality in White Supremacist Discourse*, Routledge, New York, 1997, pp. 67–8; *Thunderbolt* 233, September 1978.

15 *Thunderbolt* 230, June 1978.

16 *National Vanguard* 81, April 1981; *WAR*, November 1995.

17 *Thunderbolt* 203, March 1976; *Racial Loyalty* 72, August 1991; *WAR* 11, 2, n.d., c.1992.

18 Daniels, p. 91; *Thunderbolt* 154, October 1972; *Truth At Last* 369, n.d., c.1993.

19 *National Vanguard* 126, May-June 2005; *Stormtrooper*, spring 1966; *NS Bulletin* 6, June 1967; *White Power* 21, October-November 1971.

20 Griffin, pp. 307, 429; Ridgeway, p. 90.

21 N. Ryan, *Homeland. Into a World of Hate*, Mainstream Publishing, Edinburgh, UK, 2003, pp. 232–33, 241; *Thunderbolt* 201, 15 February 1976.

22 *Thunderbolt* 234, October 1978; Daniels, pp. 123–24.

23 www.whiterevolution.com/wrra/dec142003text.shtml; McDonald, *Turner Diaries*, pp. 160–61.

24 Durham, *Women and Fascism,* pp. 18, 21–22; MacLean, pp. 114–15, 264.

25 G. L. Rockwell, *White Power*, 2nd edn, 1977, pp. 450–51.

26 M. Stibbe, *Women in the Third Reich*, Arnold, London, 2003, p. 17; Anon., 'Program of the World Union of National Socialists', ANP leaflet, n.d.; *White Power* 20, September 1971.

27 *Calling Our Nation*, Foundation Edition, 1979; N. H. Baynes (ed.) *The Speeches of Adolf Hitler April 1922-August 1939*, Oxford University Press, London, 1942, pp. 528–30; Stephenson, p. 49.

28 *Calling Our Nation* 68, April 20th-Year 103 (1992); 72, n.d., c.1994.

29 *Christian Vanguard*, November 1983; Blee, pp. 143, 235.

30 W. G. Simpson, *Which Way, Western Man?*, Yeoman Press, Cooperstown NY, 1978, pp. 254, 260–62, 264–65, 270.

31 *National Vanguard* 92, January 1983.

32 *National Vanguard* 111, June-July 1990.

33 www.skadi.net/forum/showthread.php?t=3451

34 www.vanguardnewsnetwork.com/index207.htm; www.vanguardnewsnetwork.com/jan03/index637.htm

35 *Aryan Alternative* 3, fall 2005.

36 J. Coates, *Armed and Dangerous. The Rise of the Survivalist Right*, Hill and Wang, New York, 1987, pp. 87, 89; Lane, pp. 91, 210–11, 347.

37 www.solargeneral.com/library/renaissance.html

38 Blee, *Inside Organized Racism*, p. 195.

39 Durham, *Women and Fascism,* pp. 18–21.

40 K. M. Blee, *Women of the Klan. Racism and Gender in the 1920s*, University of California Press, Berkeley CA, 1991, pp. 50–52, 192–93.

41 www.wakeupordie.com/html/lovewa2.html; www.elishastrom.com/Articles/cloud-and-sand.html

42 www.adl.org/special_report/extremism_women_on_web/print.asp

43 www.nationalvanguard.org/story/php?id=4913; www.nationalvanguard.org/story/php?id=6678
44 *WAR* 8, 2, *c.*1989.
45 A. L. Ferber and M. S. Kimmel, '"White Men Are This Nation": Right-wing Militias and the Restoration of Rural American Masculinity', in A. L. Ferber (ed.) *Home-grown Hate. Gender and Organized Racism*, Routledge, London, 2004, pp. 143–44, 158.
46 Kaplan, *Encyclopedia of White Power*, pp. 537, 543–45; *WAR*, June 2000.
47 www.adl.org/special_report/extremism_women_on_web/print.asp; *Aryan Action Line*, fall 1992; www.nsm88.com/articles/sstein4.html
48 *Calling Our Nation* 59, n.d.; *White Power* 105, n.d., *c.*1983; J. George and L. Wilcox, *Nazis, Communists, Klansmen, and Others on the Fringe*, Prometheus Books, Buffalo NY, 1992, p. 358.
49 www.vanguardnewsnetwork.com/index217.htm
50 www.stormfront.org/archive/t-91464
51 www.vnnforum.com/showthread.php?t=819; www.vnnforum.com/showthread.php?t=1877
52 www.stormfront.org/forum/threadid53684.php
53 www.stormfront.org/threads/topic/46981.html
54 *Today's Aryan Woman* 3, 17, April-June 1991; *Valkyrie Voice* 1, n.d.; IV, n.d.; *Rational Feminist* XI, 1, spring 1997.
55 K. M. Blee, *Inside Organized Racism*, p. 221; Anon., 'Attention White Woman!', leaflet, Aryan Women's League; Anon., 'What is the Aryan Women's League', leaflet, Aryan Women's League.
56 Blee, *Inside Organized Racism*, pp. 146, 236.
57 *White Sisters* 1, spring 1990; 2, winter 1991; 3, spring-summer 1991; 4, fall 1991; 5, winter 1991.
58 Anon., *World Church of the Creator: One Year Later*, Center for New Community, Chicago, 2000, p. 6; *Intelligence Report* 95, summer 1999; *Sisterhood of the World Church of the Creator*, IV, November 26 AC (1999); *Women's Frontier Newsletter* 15, 1, September 26 AC (1999, e-zine).
59 www.wcotc.com/wcotcwf/declaration.html
60 www.wcotc.com/wcotcwf/views.html
61 *Women's Frontier Newsletter* 1, 14, August 26 AC (1999).
62 www.churchfliers.com/women.html; www.wcotc.com/wcotcwf/hate.html
63 www.adl.org/special_report/extremism_women_on_web/print.asp
64 *Women's Frontier Newsletter*, n.d. (January 26 AC? [1999]).
65 *Intelligence Report* 109, spring 2003; wau.rac-usa.org/missionstatement.html; http://66.101.143.208/messageboards/index.asp?messageID=24722&boardedID=8; www.volksfront-usa-org/vfwomen.html; *Intelligence Report* 114, summer 2004 ARA Research Bulletin Winter-Spring 2002.
66 Kaplan, *Radical Religion in America*, p. 59; *Intelligence Report* 92, fall 1998; Ryan, *Homeland*, pp. 232, 234, 240.
67 *Jubilee*, March-April 2001; May-June 2001; July-August 2001.
68 Blee, *Inside Organized Racism*, pp. 114, 149–51.

7 A call to arms

1 *Hammer* 9, spring 1985; *Monitor* 18, March 1990.
2 Beam, pp. 29–30, 55, 71, n.p.
3 Flynn and Gerhardt, pp. 117, 318–19; Ridgeway, p. 82.
4 P. Finch, *God, Guts, and Guns*, Seaview/Putnam, New York, 1983, pp. 111–12.
5 Anon., *Siege*, pp. 195–99; www.courttv.com/onair/shows/mugshots/indepth/franklin_document1.html; *From the Mountain*, July-August 1984.
6 *Attack!* 7, fall 1971.

7 *Attack!* 6, summer 1971.
8 Macdonald, *Turner Diaries*, pp. iii, 1, 4–5, 38–39, 46–48, 60–61, 69–73.
9 Macdonald, *Turner Diaries*, pp. 89–92, 95–99, 118, 146, 155, 161–62, 190, 201–5, 210–11.
10 Flynn and Gerhardt, pp. 105, 124–26, 347; Kaplan, *Encyclopedia of White Power*, pp. 523–24.
11 Flynn and Gerhardt, pp. 137–38, 165–66, 178–79, 182–88, 193, 196–97, 204–8, 244–50, 279–89.
12 Flynn and Gerhardt, pp. 235, 333–34, 432–47, 466, 469, 473.
13 Flynn and Gerhardt, p. 450; *National Vanguard* 103, January-February 1985.
14 Flynn and Gerhardt, pp. 121–24; Michael, *Confronting Right-Wing Extremism*, p. 101.
15 Griffin, pp. 209–10, 424; *Free Speech* 1, 12, December 1995.
16 M. S. Hamm, *In Bad Company. America's Terrorist Underground*, Northeastern University Press, Boston MA, 2002, pp. 157, 289.
17 M. Fisher and P.M. Combs, 'The Book of Hate', *Washington Post*, 25 April 1995.
18 *WAR*, July 1997.
19 http://groups.yahoo.com/group/christianidentity/message/6448
20 *Hammer* 9, spring 1985; *Seditionist* 12, February 1992.
21 *Richard Cotten's Newsletter* 7, December 1965; *Woman Constitutionalist*, 7 May 1966; Turner, p. 163; Diamond, p. 51.
22 Mohr, 'Why a Citizens Emergency Defense System?'.
23 Dobratz and Shanks-Meile, p. 268; Michael, pp. 106, 119.
24 www.covenantnews.com/newswire/archives/014451.html; www.covenantnews.com/newswire/archives/011417.html
25 www.apfn.net/edomite_jew.htm; www.rightwingnews.com/crackpots/rudolph.php
26 A. Macdonald, *Hunter*, National Vanguard Books, Hillsboro WV, 1989, pp. iii, 1–4, 12, 37–38, 41–42, 57–62.
27 Macdonald, *Hunter*, pp. 65–75, 82–84, 94–116, 133–34, 138–41, 151–53.
28 Macdonald, *Hunter*, pp. 231–32, 242, 249, 259.
29 Michael, *Confronting Right-Wing Extremism*, pp. 117–18.
30 Kaplan, *Encyclopedia of White Power*, pp. 220–21.
31 *WAR Eagle* 1, 2, fall 1993.
32 *Free Speech* V, 9, September 1999.
33 *Resistance* 10, winter 2000.
34 www.whiteracist.com/proresponds.html
35 http://sigrdrifa.net/sigrdrifa/sigsupyarborough.html; Flynn and Gerhardt, p. 473.
36 http://sigrdrifa.net/sigrdrifa/sigsupduey.html; Flynn and Gerhardt, pp. 463–64.
37 *Resistance* 11, spring 2000.
38 *National Alliance Bulletin*, March 2000; July 2000.
39 Michael, *Confronting Right-wing Extremism*, pp. 120–21.
40 Flynn and Gerhardt, p. 120; Dees with Corcoran, pp. 98–99.
41 Hamm, pp. 183–84; *WAR* 12, 3, n.d., *c.*1993.
42 www.nsm88.com/articles/sstein17.html
43 www.churchfliers.com/recruiting.html; www.churchfliers.com/sub-articles/tactics1.html
44 www.whiterevolution.com/march182003text.shtml
45 www.agentofchaos.invisionzone.com/index.php?showtopic=667
46 R. K. Hoskins, *Vigilantes of Christendom. The History of the Phineas Priesthood*, Virginia Publishing, Lynchburg VA, 1997, pp. vii, 24, 26, 61, 381–83.
47 Hamm, pp. 134–36, 185.
48 Kaplan, 'The Context of American Millennarian Theology', pp. 59–60, 82; www.scripturesforamerica.org/htm12/jm0029.htm
49 T. R. Weiland, *The Phinehas Hoods. A Biblical Examination of Unscriptural Vigilantilism*, Mission to Israel Ministries, Scotsbluff NE, n.d.

50 *Calling Our Nation* 68, April 20th-Year 103 (1992).
51 www.adl.org/Learn/ext_us/Aryan_nations_break_up.asp
52 M. Durham, 'The American Far Right and 9/11', *Terrorism and Political Violence* 15, 3, 2003, pp. 106, 108, 111.
53 Durham, 'American Far Right and 9/11', pp. 98, 100–2.
54 Durham, 'American Far Right and 9/11', p. 99. www.stormfront.org/forum/printthread.php?t=186943
55 www.agentofchaos.invisionzone.com/index.php?showtopic=252; www.agentofchaos.invisionzone.com/index.php?showtopic=228; www.agentofchaos.invisionzone.com/index.php?showtopic=446
56 www.cnn.com/2005/US/03/29/schuster.column/index.html
57 Racial Readers Forum 090299.html at http://web.archive.org/web/20001018194253/http://www.whiteracist.com/
58 www.ocweekly.com/printme.php&eid=33895; www.aryan-nations.org/headlinenews/the_valley_of_decision.htm
59 G. Michael, *The Enemy of My Enemy. The Alarming Convergence of Militant Islam and the Extreme Right*, University Press of Kansas, Lawrence KS, 2006, pp. 140–42; www.aryan-nations.org/forum/index.php?showtopic=696; www.agentofchaos.invisionzone.com/index.php?showtopic=236
60 www.vanguardnewsnetwork.com/2004b/White100804SandsofIraq.htm
61 *National Vanguard* 131, March-April 2006.

8 Race and the right

1 Diamond, *Roads to Dominion*, pp. 29–39.
2 D. Bell, 'The Dispossessed', in D. Bell (ed.) *The Radical Right*, Anchor Books, Garden City NY, 1964, pp. 1–5.
3 Diamond, *Roads to Dominion*, pp. 37–38, 53; Mintz, pp. 142–43.
4 J. Hart, *The Making of the American Conservative Mind. National Review and Its Times*, ISI Books, Wilmington DE, 2005, pp. 157–59.
5 R. Welch, *The Neutralizers*, John Birch Society, Belmont MA, 1963, pp. 2–7; R. P. Oliver, *Conspiracy or Degeneracy*, 2nd edn, Liberty Bell Publications, Reedy WV, 1984, pp. 8–9; Turner, p. 163.
6 *Thunderbolt* 125, May 1970.
7 *Thunderbolt* 157, February 1973.
8 *National Vanguard* 116, August-September 1996.
9 *Stormtrooper* spring 1966; *Attack!* 4, March 1971.
10 Hart, pp. xii, 103–4; Diamond, *Roads to Dominion*, pp. 34–35, 318.
11 *Rockwell Report* September 1964.
12 *Thunderbolt* 52, July 1963.
13 Chalmers, pp. 383–84; Mintz, pp. 94–95; *Free American* 2, September YF 75 (1964).
14 Diamond, *Roads to Dominion*, pp. 88–89, 114, 130; Carter, pp. 335, 345.
15 B. R. Epstein and A. Forster, *Report on the John Birch Society 1966*, Vintage Books, New York, 1966, pp. 7–11.
16 *Fiery Cross* III, 4, April 1968.
17 Mintz, pp. 93, 95–96, 129; Carter, pp. 295–97.
18 *White Power* 7, 6, n.d., 1968.
19 *White Power* 7, 7, n.d., 1969.
20 Diamond, *Roads to Dominion*, p. 143; *White Power* 9, August-September 1969; *Thunderbolt* 116, August 1969.
21 Carter, pp. 12, 465–68.
22 Wade, pp. 387–88.
23 *Thunderbolt* 252, April 1980.

24 Finch, p. 142; *WAR '84* 3, 5, n.d., 1984.
25 *National Vanguard* 79, December 1980.
26 *National Anti-Klan Network Newsletter* winter-spring 1984; *Thunderbolt* 296, March 1984.
27 M. Barkun, *A Culture of Conspiracy. Apocalyptic Visions in Contemporary America*, University of California Press, Berkeley CA, 2003, pp. 73–74; S. McLemee, 'Spotlight on the Liberty Lobby', *Covert Action Quarterly* 50, fall 1994, p. 31.
28 *Hammer* 7, summer 1984; *National Anti-Klan Network Newsletter*, fall 1984; *Facts* 30, 2, fall 1985.
29 W. Carto (ed.) *Profiles in Populism*, Flag Press, Old Greenwich CT, 1982, pp. ix–xi.
30 Sargent, pp. 18–23.
31 Bridges, pp. 136–55; E. A. Rickey, 'The Nazi and the Republican: An Insider View of the Response of the Louisiana Republican Party', in D. D. Rose (ed.) *The Emergence of David Duke and the Politics of Race*, University of North Carolina Press, Chapel Hill NC, 1992, pp. 62–63; W. H. McMahon, 'David Duke and the Legislature', in Rose, p. 124.
32 Diamond, *Roads to Dominion*, pp. 284–94.
33 Mintz, p. 134; *National Vanguard* 80, February 1981.
34 *Jubilee*, January-February 2001.
35 Durham, 'American Far Right and 9/11', p. 101; Michael, *Enemy of My Enemy*, p. 238; M. C. Piper, *The High Priests of War*, American Free Press, Washington DC, 2004, pp. 2, 42–45, 97, 103.
36 *CDL Report* 38, September 1981; *Thunderbolt* 304, n.d., *c.*1985.
37 Piper, p. 121; www.memri.org/bin/opener_latest.cgi?ID=SD103505; *National Vanguard* 126, May-June 2005.
38 Berlet and Lyons, pp. 243–44, 279–81, 338–40
39 *Monitor* 22, March 1991; *Populist Observer* 107, May-June 1995.
40 Dobratz and Shanks-Meile, pp. 250–51.
41 *Truth At Last*, 387, n.d., *c.*1996; *New Order* 120, January-February 1996.
42 *Free Speech* II, 3, March 1996.
43 *Free Speech* II, 8, August 1996.
44 www.newcomm.org/party/partyplain.htm
45 *WAR*, July 2000.
46 *Nationalist Times*, September 2000.
47 *Populist Observer* 100, September 1994; www.adl.org/learn/ext_us/CCCitizens.asp
48 www.originaldissent.com/forums/archive/index.php/t-6210.html
49 N. R. McMillen, *The Citizens' Council. Organized Resistance to the Second Reconstruction, 1954–64*, University of Illinois Press, Urbana IL, 1971, pp. 17–18; T. P. Brady, *Black Monday*, Association of Citizens' Councils, Winona MS, 1955, pp. iv, 10–11.
50 McMillen, pp. 18–19, 121.
51 McMillen, pp. 22, 23, 55–56.
52 Winston, pp. 187–91; I. A. Newby, *Challenge To The Court. Social Scientists and the Defense of Segregation, 1954–1966*, Louisiana State University Press, Baton Rouge LA, 1967, pp. 144–45; Turner, pp. 153–54.
53 *Intelligence Report* 93, winter 1999; *Citizens Informer* 24, 2, 1993; 27, fall 1996; 28, summer 1997.
54 Piper, pp. 88–91; *Spotlight* XXV, 11, 15 March 1999.
55 *Nationalist Times*, September 2000; *Intelligence Report* 122, summer 2006;
56 www.natall.com/adv/2004/10-30-04.html
57 www.nationalvanguard.org/story.php?id=7115
58 M. Novick, *White Lies White Power. The Fight Against White Supremacy and Reactionary Violence*, Common Courage Press, Monroe MA, 1995, pp. 172–73, 266; *CDL Report*, February 1992.

59 *Intelligence Report* 121, spring 2006; www.kvoa.com/Global/story.aspS?=3147861
&nav=menu216_7; http://nationalist88.blogspot.com; http://la.indymedia.org/news/
2005/07/133017_comment.php

9 Out of the 1950s

1 Jackson, pp. 58–59.
2 Schmaltz, pp. 342–43; Simonelli, pp. 100–2, 112, 141.
3 Simonelli, pp. 113, 172.
4 *White American*, September 1964.
5 *Right* 24, September 1957.
6 *Klanwatch Intelligence Report* 39, August 1988; Dobratz and Shanks-Meile,
p. 108.
7 Gardell, pp. 311–12.
8 Michael, *The Enemy of My Enemy*, pp. 140–48, 164–67, 280–86, 307; www.white
wire.net/?p=267
9 *Statecraft* 4, 1, January 1972
10 *National Educator*, October 1972.
11 *Spotlight*, XXIII, 16, 21 April 1997.
12 www.louisbeam.com/seattle.htm; *Intelligence Report* 106, summer 2002.
13 Michael, *Enemy of My Enemy*, pp. 164–65; www.natvan.com/demands/
14 Carto, p. ix.
15 *Common Sense* VI, 167, 1 August 1952; *Thunderbolt* 161, June 1973; *Calling Our
Nation* 63, n.d., *c*.1991.
16 Anon., *Vigilante Justice*, p. 28.
17 Berlet and Lyons, pp. 195, 380; C. Berlet, *Right Woos Left*, Political Research
Associates, Somerville MA, 1993, pp. 44–45, 48–49.
18 Lee, p. 359; M. C. Piper, *The New Jerusalem. Zionist Power in America*, American Free Press, Washington DC, 2004, p. 5.
19 Anon., *Special Report*, pp. 8, 19–23; *WAR Eagle* 1, 2, fall 1993.
20 www.nationalvanguard.org/story.php?id=5856; www.stormfront/showthread.php?
t=224966
21 Kaplan and Weinberg, p. 82.
22 *Thunderbolt* 29, May 1961; *Intelligence Report* 103, fall 2001.
23 *Truth at Last*, 359, n.d., *c*.1992.
24 *Spotlight* XXIII, 16, 21 April 1997; XXV, 10, 8 March 1999.
25 L. Zeskind, 'From Compounds to Congress', *Searchlight* 287, May 1999, pp. 20–23.
26 C. Berlet, 'Hard Times on the Hard Right', *Public Eye* XVI, 1, spring 2002, p. 1.
27 *Truth at Last* 390, n.d., *c*.1996.
28 Bridges, pp. 243–44.
29 *CDL Report* 38, September 1981.
30 Langer, p. 85.
31 Dobratz and Shanks-Meile, pp. 118–19; Daniels, p. 85.
32 *White Power*, October 1974; *Stormtrooper*, September-October 1964.
33 Gardell, p. 113; www.vnnforum.com/showthread.php?t=613; *WAR* 8, 2, *c*.1989.
34 Anon., 'A Party Not a Publication', *White American*, March 1965.
35 *National Alliance Bulletin*, March 1994; Kaplan, *Encyclopedia of White Power*,
pp. 84–85, 89, 421, 427.
36 Simonelli, p. 36;
37 ADL, *Hate Groups*, 1982, pp. 86; Berlet and Lyons, p. 97.
38 R. Eatwell, 'The Nature of the Right, 1: Is There an "Essentialist" Philosophical
Core?', in R. Eatwell and N. O'Sullivan (eds) *The Nature of the Right. European
and American Politics and Political Thought since 1789*, Pinter Publishers,
London, 1989, pp. 47–61.

39 R. Griffin, *The Nature of Fascism*, Routledge, London, 1991, pp. 117–18; R. Griffin, *International Fascism. Theories, Causes and the New Consensus*, Arnold, London, 1998, p. 14; M. Durham, 'The Upward Path: Palingenesis, Political Religion and the National Alliance', *Totalitarian Movements and Political Religions* 5, 3, 2004, pp. 464–65.
40 V. Coppola, *Dragons of God. A Journey Through Far-right America*, Longstreet Press, Atlanta GA, 1996, pp. 76–77.
41 Schmaltz, p. 340.
42 www.creator.org/editorials/s-68.html

Bibliography

Books, journal articles and leaflets

Aho, J. A. (1990) *The Politics of Righteousness. Idaho Christian Patriotism*, University of Washington Press, Seattle WA.

Allen, J. H. (n.d.) [1902] *Judah's Sceptre and Joseph's Birthright. An Analysis of the Prophecies of Scripture in Regard to the Royal Family of Judah and the Many Nations of Israel*, Destiny Publishers, Merrimac MA.

——(n.d.) 'Attention White Women', leaflet, Aryan Women's League.

——(n.d.) *Pax Americano*. The Elite Whiteman's Guide book, Institute for Biopolitics, Chicago, IL.

——(n.d.) *The Principle of the United Klans of America Knights of the Ku Klux Klan*, leaflet.

——(n.d.) 'Program of the World Union of National Socialists', leaflet, ANP.

——(n.d.) *Special Report on the Meeting of Christian Men Held in Estes Park, Colorado, October 23, 24, 25, 1992*, Scriptures for America Ministries, LaPorte CO.

——(n.d.) '*What is the Aryan Women's League*', leaflet, Aryan Women's League.

Anon. (n.d., *c.*1965) *A Party not a Publication*, American States Rights Party, Birmingham AL.

——(n.d., *c.*1939) 'DEAR CHRISTIAN', leaflet, Christian Mobilizers.

——(1954) *Preliminary Report on Neo-fascist and Hate Groups*, Committee on Un-American Activities, Washington DC.

——(n.d., *c.*1968) *The Declaration of the Third Continental Congress*.

——(n.d., *c.*1970) *Clarification of the New and Unusual Position of the Original and Official Constitution Parties of the United States*.

——(n.d., *c.*1996) '1996 Aryan Youth Congress', leaflet, Aryan Nations.

——(1921) *Jewish Influences in American Life*, Dearborn Publishing Company, Dearborn MI.

——(1966) *Activities of Ku Klux Klan Organizations in the United States Part 5. Hearings Before the Committee on Un-American Activities*, US Government Printing Office, Washington DC.

——(1966) *Activities of Ku Klux Klan Organizations in the United States Part 4. Hearings Before the Committee on Un-American Activities*, US Government Printing Office, Washington DC.

——(1988) *The Ku Klux Klan: A History of Racism and Violence*, Klanwatch, Montgomery AL.

——(1992) *Operation Vampire Killer 2000. American Police Action Plan for Stopping World Government Rule*, PATNWO, Phoenix AZ.

——(1993) *Membership Handbook for Members of the National Alliance*, National Vanguard Books, Hillsboro WV.

——(1993) *Who Rules America?*, National Vanguard Books, Hillsboro WV.

——(1997) *M.O.M's 1997 Preparedness Catalog*, Militia of Montana, Noxon MT.

——(1997) *Vigilante Justice. Militias and 'Common Law Courts' Wage War Against the Government*, Anti-Defamation League, New York.

——(2000) *World Church of the Creator: One Year Later*, Center for New Community, Chicago IL.

——(2001) *The 'Apple' Story. Genesis 3:15. The War between the Children of Light and the Children of Darkness*, American Institute of Theology, Harrison AR.

——(2003) *Siege. The Collected Writings of James Mason*, Black Sun Publications, Bozeman MT.

Barkun, M. (1994) *Religion and the Racist Right. The Origins of the Christian Identity Movement*, University of North Carolina Press, Chapel Hill NC.

——(2003) *A Culture of Conspiracy. Apocalyptic Visions in Contemporary America*, University of California Press, Berkeley CA.

Baynes, N. H. (ed.) (1942) *The Speeches of Adolf Hitler April 1922–August 1939*, Oxford University Press, London.

Beam, L. R. Jr (1983) *Essays of a Klansman*, A.K.I.A. Publications, Hayden Lake ID.

Beckman, M. J. 'Red' (1981) *Born Again Republic*, Freedom Church, Billings MT.

Bell, D. (1964) 'The Dispossessed' in D. Bell (ed.) *The Radical Right*, Anchor Books, Garden City NY.

Bell, L. V. (1973) *In Hitler's Shadow. The Anatomy of American Nazism*, Kennikat Press, Port Washington NY.

Bennett, D. H. (1990) *The Party of Fear. From Nativist Movements to the New Right in American History*, Vintage Books, New York.

Berlet, C. (1993) *Right Woos Left*, Political Research Associates, Somerville MA.

——(2002) 'Hard Times on the Hard Right', *Public Eye* XVI, 1, pp. 1–22.

Berlet, C. and Lyons, M. N. (2000) *Right-Wing Populism in America. Too Close For Comfort*, Guilford Press, New York.

Blee, K. M. (1991) *Women of the Klan. Racism and Gender in the 1920s*, University of California Press, Berkeley CA.

——(2002) *Inside Organized Racism. Women in the Hate Movement*, University of California Press, Berkeley CA.

Brady, T. P. (1955) *Black Monday*, Association of Citizens' Councils, Winona MS.

Bridges, T. (1994) *The Rise of David Duke*, University Press of Mississippi, Jackson MS.

Burghart, D. (ed.) (1999) *Soundtracks to the White Revolution. White Supremacist Assaults On Youth Music Subcultures*, Center for New Community, Chicago, IL.

Burghart, D. and Crawford, R. (1996) *Guns and Gavels. Common Law Courts, Militias and White Supremacy*, Coalition for Human Dignity, Portland OR.

Campbell, M. C. Jr (1990) *Kingdoms at War. The Second North American Revolution*, revised edn, n.p.

Carlson, J. R. (1943) *Under Cover*, World Publishing Co., Cleveland OH.

Carter, D. T. (1995) *The Politics of Rage. George Wallace, The Origins of the New Conservatism, and the Transformation of American Politics*, Louisiana State University Press, Baton Rouge LA.

Carto, W. A. (ed.) (1982) *Profiles in Populism*, Flag Press, Old Greenwich CT.

Chalmers, D. M. (1965) *Hooded Americanism. The First Century of the Ku Klux Klan 1865–1965*, Doubleday, Garden City NY.

Coates, J. (1987) *Armed and Dangerous. The Rise of the Survivalist Right*, Hill and Wang, New York.

Cohn, N. (1996) *Warrant for Genocide. The Myth of the Jewish World Conspiracy and the Protocols of the Elders of Zion*, Serif, London.

Coogan, K. (1999) *Dreamer of the Day. Francis Parker Yockey and the Postwar Fascist International*, Autonomedia, New York.

Cook, J. G. (1962) *The Segregationists*, Appleton-Century Crofts, New York.

Cooper, M. W. (1991) *'Behold A Pale Horse'*, Light Technology Publishing, Sedona AZ.

Coplon, J. (1988) 'Skinhead Nation', *Rolling Stone* 540, 1 December, pp. 54–58, 62–65, 94.

Coppola, V. (1996) *Dragons of God. A Journey Through Far-Right America*, Longstreet Press, Atlanta GA.

Crawford, R., Gardner, S. L., Mazzochi, J. and Taylor, R. L. (1994) *The Northwest Imperative*, Coalition for Human Dignity, Portland OR.

Crothers, L. (2003) *Rage on the Right. The American Militia Movement from Ruby Ridge to Homeland Security*, Rowland and Littlefield, London M.D.

Cunningham, D. (2004) *There's Something Happening Here. The New Left, the Klan, and FBI Counterintelligence*, University of California Press, Berkeley CA.

Daniels, J. (1997) *White Lies. Race, Class, Gender, and Sexuality in White Supremacist Discourse*, Routledge, New York.

Diamond, S. (1995) *Roads to Dominion. Right-Wing Movements and Political Power in the United States*, Guilford Press, New York.

Diamond, S. A. (1974) *The Nazi Movement in the United States 1924–1941*, Cornell University Press, Ithaca NY.

Dobratz, B. A. and Shanks-Meile, S. L. (2000) *The White Separatist Movement in the United States. 'White Power, White Pride!'*, Johns Hopkins University Press, Baltimore MD.

Dobowski, M. N. (1976) 'Populist Antisemitism in U.S. Literature', *Patterns of Prejudice* 10, 3, May-June, pp. 19–27.

Durham, M. (1998) *Women and Fascism*, Routledge, London.

——(2000) *The Christian Right, the Far Right and the Boundaries of American Conservatism*, Manchester University Press, Manchester.

——(2003) 'The American Far Right and 9/11', *Terrorism and Political Violence* 15, 3, pp. 96–111.

——(2004) 'The Upward Path: Palingenesis, Political Religion and the National Alliance', *Totalitarian Movements and Political Religions* 5, 3, pp. 454–68.

——(2006) 'A Global Master Plan? The American for Right and the Protocols of the Learned Elders of Zion' in J.H. Brinks, S. Rock and E. Timms (eds) Nationalist myths and Modern Media. Contested Identies in the Age of Globalization, Tauris, London.

Dyer, J. (1997) *Harvest of Rage. Why Oklahoma City is Only the Beginning*, Westview Press, Boulder CO.

Eatwell, R. (1989) 'The Nature of the Right, 1: Is There an "Essentialist" Philosophical Core?', in R. Eatwell and N. O'Sullivan (eds) *The Nature of the Right. European and American Politics and Political Thought since 1789*, Pinter Publishers, London.

Edsall, T. B. with Edsall, M. D. (1992) *Chain Reaction. The Impact of Race, Rights, and Taxes on American Politics*, W. W. Norton, New York.

Epstein, B. R. and Forster, A. (1966) *Report on the John Birch Society 1966*, Vintage Books, New York.

Ezekiel, R. S. (1995) *The Racist Mind*, Penguin Books, Harmondsworth.

Feldman, G. (1997) 'Soft Opposition: Elite Acquiescence and Klan-Sponsored Terrorism in Alabama, 1946–1950', *Historical Journal* 40, 3, pp. 753–77.

Ferber, A. and Kimmel, M. S. (2004) '"White Men Are This Nation": Right-Wing Militias and the Restoration of Rural American Masculinity', in A. L. Ferber (ed.) *Home-grown Hate. Gender and Organized Racism*, Routledge, London.

Finch, P. (1983) *God, Guts, and Guns*, Seaview/Putnam, New York.

Fisher, M. and Combs, P. M. (1995) 'The Book of Hate', *Washington Post*, 25 April.

Flynn, K. and Gerhardt, G. (1990) *The Silent Brotherhood. Inside America's Racist Underground*, Signet, New York.

Forster, A. and Epstein, B. T. (1956) *Cross-Currents*, Doubleday, Garden City NY.

Gardell, M. (2003) *Gods of the Blood. The Pagan Revival and White Separatism*, Duke University Press, Durham NC.

George, J. and Wilcox, L. (1992) *Nazis, Communists, Klansmen, and Others on the Fringe*, Prometheus Books, New York.

Goodrick-Clarke, N. (2003) *Black Sun. Aryan Cults, Esoteric Nazism and the Politics of Identity*, New York University Press, New York.

Goring, W. (1969–70) 'The National Renaissance Party. History and Analysis of an American Neo-Nazi Political Party', *National Information Center Newsletter*, December–January.

Greene, M. F. (1996) *The Temple Bombing*, Jonathan Cape, London.

Griffin, R. (1991) *The Nature of Fascism*, Routledge, London.

——(1998) *International Fascism. Theories, Causes and the New Consensus*, Arnold, London.

Griffin, R. S. (2001) *The Fame of a Dead Man's Deeds. An Up-Close Portrait of White Nationalist William Pierce*, 1st Books.

Gurudas (1996) *Treason. The New World Order*, Cassandra Press, San Rafael CA.

Hamm, M. S. (2002) *In Bad Company. America's Terrorist Underground*, Northeastern University Press, Boston MA.

Hart, J. (2005) *The Making of the American Conservative Mind. National Review and its Times*, ISI Books, Wilmington DE.

Higham, J. (1963) *Strangers in the Land. Patterns of American Nativism 1860–1925*, Atheneum, New York.

Jackson, J. P. Jr (2005) *Science for Segregation. Race, Law, and the Case against Brown v. Board of Education*, New York University Press, New York.

Jeansonne, G. (1988) *Gerald L. K. Smith. Minister of Hate*, Louisiana State University Press, Baton Rouge LA.

——(1996) *Women of the Far Right. The Mothers' Movement and World War II*, University of Chicago Press, Chicago, IL.

Jefferson, M.W. (1994) *America Under Siege. 'A Lesson in Treason, Treachery and Conspiracy'*, Freedom and Liberty Foundation, Knoxville TN.

Jenkins, P. (1997) *Hoods and Shirts. The Extreme Right in Pennsylvania, 1925–1950*, University of North Carolina Press, Chapel Hill NC.

Jensen, E. (1993) 'International Nazi Cooperation', in T. Bjorgo and R. Witte (eds) *Racist Violence in Europe*, St Martin's Press, New York.

Jones, S. E. (1978) *The Babylonian Connection Between Ancient and Modern Religions*, America's Promise, Phoenix AZ.

Kaplan, J. (1993) 'The Context of American Millenarian Revolutionary Theology: The Case of the "Identity Christian" Church of Israel', *Terrorism and Political Violence* 5, 1, pp. 30–82.

——(1997) *Radical Religion in America. Millenarian Movements from the Far Right to the Children of Noah*, Syracuse University Press, Syracuse NY.

——(1998) 'Religiosity and the Radical Right: Toward the Creation of a New Ethnic Identity', in Kaplan, J. and Bjorgo, T. (eds) *Nation and Race. The Developing Euro-American Racist Subculture*, Northeastern University Press, Boston MA.

Kaplan, J. (ed.) (2000) *Encyclopedia of White Power. A Sourcebook on the Radical Racist Right*, Altamira Press, Walnut Creek CA.

Kaplan, J. and Weinberg, L. (1998) *The Emergence of a Euro-American Radical Right*, Rutgers University Press, New Brunswick NJ.

Klassen, B. (1992) *Nature's Eternal Religion*, 2nd printing, Milwaukee Church of the Creator, Milwaukee WI.

Lane, K. (ed.) (1999) *Deceived, Damned and Defiant. The Revolutionary Writings of David Lane*, 14 Word Press, St Maries ID.

Langer, E. (1990) 'The American Neo-Nazi Movement Today', *Nation* 16–23, July, pp. 82–105.

Levitas, D. (2002) *The Terrorist Next Door. The Militia Movement and the Radical Right*, Thomas Dunne Books, New York.

Linehan, T. (2000) *British Fascism 1918–39. Parties, Ideologies and Culture*, Manchester University Press, Manchester.

Lipset, S. M. and Raab, E. (1971) *The Politics of Unreason. Right-Wing Extremism in America, 1790–1970*, Heinemann, London.

Lipstadt, D. E. (1994) *Denying the Holocaust*, Penguin, London.

Lowe, D. (1967) *Ku Klux Klan: The Invisible Empire*, W. W. Norton, New York.

Macdonald, A. (1980) *The Turner Diaries*, National Vanguard Books, Hillsboro WV.

——(1989) *Hunter*, National Vanguard Books, Hillsboro WV.

MacLean, N. (1994) *Behind the Mask of Chivalry. The Making of the Second Ku Klux Klan*, Oxford University Press, New York.

Mange, C. L. (1998) *The Two Seeds of Genesis 3:15*, Charles Lee Mange, n.p.

Martin, T. (1976) *Race First*, Greenwood press, Westport, CT.

Mariani, M. (1998) The Michigan Militia: Political Engagement or Political Alienation?, *Terrorism and Political Violence*, 10, 4, pp. 123–48.

McLemee, S. (1994) 'Spotlight on the Liberty Lobby', *Covert Action Quarterly* 50, fall, pp. 23–32.

McMahon, W. H. (1992) 'David Duke and the Legislature', in D. D. Rose (ed.) *The Emergence of David Duke and the Politics of Race*, University of North Carolina Press, Chapel Hill NC.

McMillen, M. R. (1971) *The Citizens' Council. Organized Resistance to the Second Reconstruction, 1954–64*, University of Illinois Press, Urbana IL.

McVan, R. (1997) *Creed of Iron. Wotansvolk Wisdom*, 14 Word Press, St Maries ID.

Michael, G. (2003) *Confronting Right-wing Extremism and Terrorism*, Routledge, London.

——(2006) *The Enemy of my Enemy. The Alarming Convergence of Militant Islam and the Extreme Right*, University Press of Kansas, Lawrence KS.

——(2006) 'RAHOWA! History of the world church of the creator', *Terrorism and Political Violence*, 18, 4, pp. 561–83.

Mintz, F. P. (1985) *The Liberty Lobby and the American Right. Race, Conspiracy, and Culture*, Greenwood Press, Westport CT.

Mulloy, D. (1998) *Homegrown Revolutionaries*. An American Militia Reader, Arthur Miller Center for American Studies, University of East Anglia, Norwich.

National Knights of the Ku Klux Klan, Inc. (n.d.) *Its Problems, Its Programs, Its Purposes*, leaflet.

Nelson, J. (1993) *Terror in the Night. The Klan's Campaign Against the Jews*, Simon and Schuster, New York.

Newby, I. A. (1967) *Challenge to the Court. Social Scientists and the Defense of Segregation, 1954–1966*, Louisiana State University Press, Baton Rouge LA.

Novick, M. (1995) *White Lies White Power. The Fight Against White Supremacy and Reactionary Violence*, Common Courage Press, Monroe MA.

Oliver, R. P. (1984) *Conspiracy or Degeneracy?*, 2nd edn, Liberty Bell Publications, Reedy WV.

Pelley, W. D. (1936) *No More Hunger. The Compact Plan of the Christian Commonwealth*, Pelley Publishers, Asheville NC.

Piller, E. A. (1945) *Time Bomb*, Arco Publishing, New York.

Piper, M. C. (2004) *The High Priests of War*, American Free Press, Washington DC.

——(2004) *The New Jerusalem. Zionist Power in America*, American Free Press, Washington DC.

Randle, W. P. (1965) *The Ku Klux Klan. A Century of Infamy*, Chilton Books, Philadelphia PA.

Ribuffo, L. P. (1983) *The Old Christian Right. The Protestant Far Right from the Great Depression to the Cold War*, Temple University Press, Philadelphia PA.

Rickey, E. A. (1992) 'The Nazi and the Republican: An Insider View of the Response of the Louisiana Republican Party', in D. D. Rose (ed.) *The Emergence of David Duke and the Politics of Race*, University of North Carolina Press, Chapel Hill NC.

Ridgeway, J. (1990) *Blood in the Face. The Ku Klux Klan, Aryan Nations, Nazi Skinheads, and the Rise of a New White Culture*, Thunder's Mouth Press, New York.

Rockwell, G. L. (1977) *White Power*, 2nd edn, Liberty Bell Publication, Reedy WV.

Rorty, J. (1955) 'What Price McCarthy Now?', *Commentary*, January, pp. 30–35.

Rosenfeld, J. E. (2000) 'The Justus Freemen Standoff', in C. Wessinger (ed.) *Millennialism, Persecution, and Violence*, Syracuse University Press, Syracuse NY.

Roy, R. L. (1953) *Apostles of Bigotry. A Study of Organized Bigotry and Disruption on the Fringes of Protestantism*, Beacon Press, Boston MA.

Sargent, L. T. (ed.) (1995) *Extremism in America. A Reader*, New York University Press, New York.

Sayers, M. and Kahn, A. E. (1942) *Sabotage! The Secret War Against America*, Harper and Brothers, New York.

Schmaltz, W. H. (1999) *Hate. George Lincoln Rockwell and the American Nazi Party*, Brassey's, Washington DC.

Schonbach, M. (1985) *Native American Fascism During the 1930s and 1940s. A Study of Its Roots, Its Growth and Its Decline*, Garland Publishing, New York.

Seymour, C. (1991) *Committee of the States. Inside the Radical Right*, Camden Place Communications, Mariposa CA.

Simonds, C. H. (1971) 'The Strange Story of Willis Carto', *National Review* 10 September, pp. 978–89.

Simonelli, F. J. (1999) *American Fuehrer. George Lincoln Rockwell and the American Nazi Party*, University of Illinois Press, Urbana IL.

Simpson, W. G. (1978) *Which Way, Western Man?*, Yeoman Press, Cooperstown NY.

Sims, P. (1982) *The Klan*, Scarborough Books, New York.

Smith, G. S. (1992) *To Save a Nation. American 'Extremism', the New Deal, and the Coming of World War II*, Ivan R. Dee, Chicago, IL.

Stanton, B. (1992) *Klanwatch. Bringing the Ku Klux Klan to Justice*, Mentor, New York.

St-George, M. and Dennis, L. (1946) *A Trial on Trial. The Great Sedition Trial of 1944*, National Civil Rights Committee, Washington DC.

Stephenson, J. (1975) *Women in Nazi Society*, Croom Helm, London.

Stern, J. E. (2000) 'The Covenant, the Sword, and the Arm of the Lord (1985)', in J. B. Tucker (ed.) *Toxic Terror. Assessing Terrorist Use of Chemical and Biological Weapons*, MIT Press, Cambridge MA.

Stern, K. (1996) *A Force Upon the Plain. The American Militia and the Politics of Hate*, Simon and Schuster, New York.

Stibbe, M. (2003) *Women in the Third Reich*, Arnold, London.

Strong, D. S. (1979) *Organized Anti-Semitism in America. The Rise of Group Prejudice During the Decade 1930–40*, Greenwood Press, Westport CT.

Swain, C. M. and Nieli, R. (eds) (2003) *Contemporary Voices of White Nationalism in America*, Cambridge University Press, Cambridge.

Thayer, G. (1968) *The Farther Shores of Politics*, Allen Lane The Penguin Press, London.

Theroux, L. (2005) *The Call of the Weird. Travels in American Subcultures*, Macmillan, Basingstoke.

Tull, C. J. (1965) *Father Coughlin and the New Deal*, Syracuse University Press, Syracuse NY.

Turner, W. W. (1971) *Power on the Right*, Ramparts Press, Berkeley CA.

Valentine, P. W. (1970) 'Rightist Youth Organization Opens Office in Georgetown', *Washington Post*, 23 December, pp. B1, B5.

Wade, W. C. (1987) *The Fiery Cross. The Ku Klux Klan in America*, Touchstone, New York.

Wardner, J. W. (1994) *The Planned Destruction of America*, Longwood Communications, DeBary FL.

Webster, N. H. (n.d.) *Secret Societies and Subversive Movements*, Christian Book Club of America, Hawthorne CA.

Weiland, T. R. (2000) *Eve. Did She Or Didn't She? The Seedline Hypothesis Under Scrutiny*, Mission to Israel Ministries, Scottsbluff NE.

——(n.d.) *The Phinehas Hoods. A Biblical Examination of Unscriptural Vigilantilism*, Mission to Israel Ministries, Scottsbluff NE.

Weisman, C. A. (1996) *Who Is Esau-Edom?*, Weisman Publications, Burnsville MN.

Welch, R. (1963) *The Neutralizers*, John Birch Society, Belmont MA.

——(1966) *The New Americanism and Other Speeches and Essays*, Western Islands Publishers, Boston MA.

Wheaton, E. (1987) *Codename GREENKIL. The 1979 Greensboro Killings*, University of Georgia Press, Athens GA.

Winston, A. S. (1998) 'Science in the Service of the Far Right: Henry E. Garnett, the IAAEE, and the Liberty Lobby', *Journal of Social Issues* 54, 1, pp. 179–210.

Yockey, F. P. (1962) *Imperium. The Philosophy of History and Politics*, Truth Seeker, New York.

Zeskind, L. (1999) 'From Compounds to Congress', *Searchlight* 287, May, pp. 20–23.

Extreme right periodicals

Abyss (Black Order)
Action (National Youth Alliance)
American Free Press (Willis Carto)
American Mercury (Willis Carto)
Aryan Action Line (SS Action Group)
Aryan Alternative (Vanguard News Network) Aryan Nations Newsletter
Attack! (National Youth Alliance)
CDL Report (Christian Defense League)
Calling Our Nation (Aryan Nations)
Christian Crusade for Truth Intelligence Report
Christian Vanguard (New Christian Crusade Church)
Common Sense
Confederate Leader (White Patriot Party)
Crusader (Knights of the Ku Klux Klan)
Crossing the Abyss (White Order of Thule)
Fenris Wolf (White Order of Thule)
Fiery Cross (United Klans of America)
Free American (Dan Burros)
Free Speech (National Alliance)
From the Mountain (Mountain Church of Jesus Christ the Saviour)
Imperial Nighthawk (National Knights of the Ku Klux Klan)
Jubilee
Klan Krusader (Illinois Knights of the Ku Klux Klan)
Klansman (Invisible Empire, Knights of the Ku Klux Klan)
Liberation
Liberty Letter (Liberty Lobby)
Michigan Briefing (SS Action Group)
National Alliance Bulletin (National Alliance)
National Socialist
National Socialist World (World Union of National Socialists)
National Renaissance Bulletin (National Renaissance Party)
National Vanguard (National Alliance)
Nationalist Times (American Nationalist Union)
New Order (National Socialist Party of America/NSDAP-AO)
Newsletter (Covenant, Sword and the Arm of the Lord)
NS Bulletin (National Socialist White People's Party)
Patriot Report (Present Truth)
P. N. Report (Posse Comitatus)
Plexus (National Workers League)
Populist Observer (Populist Party)
Rational Feminist
Racial Loyalty (Church of the Creator)
Resistance (Resistance Records)
Resistance! (National Socialist White People's Party)
Richard Cotton Newsletter
Right (Willis Carto)
Rockwell Report (American Nazi Party)

Seditionist (Louis Beam)
Sisterhood of the World Church of the Creator (World Church of the Creator)
Spotlight (Liberty Lobby)
Statecraft (National Youth Alliance/Youth Action)
Stormer (National Socialist White Workers Party)
Stormtrooper (American Nazi Party)
Struggle (World Church of the Creator)
Today's Aryan Woman
Torch (National People's Committee to Restore God's Laws)
Thunderbolt (National States Rights Party)
Truth at Last (Edward Fields)
Truth Seeker
Valkyrie Voice
WAR (White Aryan Resistance)
WAR Eagle
White American (American States Rights Party/National White Americans Party)
White Beret (White Knights of the Ku Klux Klan)
White Nationalist (American White Nationalist Party)
White Patriot (Knights of the Ku Klux Klan)
White Power (National Socialist White People's Party)
White Sisters (Aryan Women's League)
Women's Frontier Newsletter (World Church of the Creator)
Women's Voice

Other right-wing periodicals

American's Bulletin
Citizens Informer (Council of Conservative Citizens)
Free American
Freeman Letter
Southern Ranger
Taking Aim
Woman Constitutionalist

Opposition periodicals and websites

ARA Research Bulletin
Dixon Line-Reason
Facts
Hammer
Intelligence Report
Monitor
Searchlight
www.adl.org

Extreme right websites

http://kelticklan.com
http://nazi.org/community/forum

http://overthrow88.blogspot.com
http://yahoo.com/group/christianidentity
www.agentofchaos.invisionzone.com
www.aryan-nations.org
www.childrenofyahweh.com
www.churchfliers.com
www.creativityohio.com
www.creator.org
www.elishastrom.com
www.kkk.bz
www.k-k-k.com
www.natall.com
www.natvan.com
www.nationalvanguard.org
www.nazisozi.com
www.nsm88.com
www.overthrow.com
www.panzerfaust.com
www.scripturesforamerica.org
www.sigrdrifa.net
www.stormfront.org
www.vanguardnewsnetwork.com
www.vnnforum.com
www.wakeupordie.com
www.wcotc.com
www.whiteracist.com
www.whiterevolution.com
www.whitewire.net

Index

Ministries 71; and the Order 102; and Weaver shootings 58, 59, 136
Phineas priesthood 110–12
Pierce, W. 27–30, 33; on P. Buchanan 125; on W. Carto 141; and Cosmotheism 75; on gender 89; on John Birch Society 117; on leaderless resistance 106, 108; on R. Mathews 102; and the Order 107; and National Democratic Party 137; on 9/11 112; and the Order 107; on Patriot movement 61; on religion 77, 81; on terrorism 106; and *Turner Diaries* 101; and white power music 31–32; and white rage 143; on women 94; and World Church of the Creator 76
Piper, M. C. 124, 128, 136
Political Research Associates 135
Populist Action Committee 135
Populist Observer 124, 126
Populist Party 26, 121–22, 124, 132
Potito, O. 68
Posse Comitatus 53–54, 56, 57, 70
Pringle, D. 34, 45, 109, 133
Protocols of the Learned Elders of Zion 6; and Christian Identity 71; and Citizens Bar Association 56; and C. Coughlin 10; and W. Cooper 64–65; and German-American Bund 11; and John Birch Society 116; and Knights of the Ku Klux Klan 39, 40; and militias 59; and National Association for the Advancement of White People 45; and G. Winrod 9

Racial Loyalty 71
racism and extreme right 1–2, 4, 7, 14, 21–27. 28, 37, 39, 46–47
Rational Feminist 94
Reagan, R. 24, 26, 120–21, 125
religion and extreme right 16, 66–82
Resistance 106, 108
Resistance Records 31–32, 33, 34
Reynolds, M. 59
Right 25, 72, 76
Robb, T. 40, 41; on abortion 85; and Christian Identity 69; and elections 41, 138; and E. Fields 49; on race 87
Rockwell, G. L. 20–22, 23; as crucial figure in extreme right 131; on homosexuality 23; on lynching 140;

and National States Rights Party 48; National Youth Alliance on 27; and W. Pierce 77; and religion 68; on women 88
Roeder, M. 137
Roper, B. 33, 34, 109–10, 112
Royal Confederate Knights 43
Rudolph, E. 104, 107, 108

Schmaltz, W. H. 131
Scriptures for America 70, 88
Scutari, R. 108
Seditionist 103
Shanks-Meile, S. L. 42, 140
Shelton, R. 36, 38, 39, 49
Sigrdrifa 107
Silver Shirts 8, 16, 19
Simonelli, F. J. 131
Sisterhood 97
Sisterhood, the 94, 95, 97
Smith, B. 104, 106
Smith, C. 76
Smith, G. K. 10; and America First Party 12; and Christian Nationalist Party 15; and Citizens Councils 127; on Holocaust 14; and K. Goff 26; and Middle East 16; and W. Swift 67
Social Justice 10, 11
Soldiers of the Cross 26
Southern Knights of the Ku Klux Klan 13, 127
Southern Poverty Law Center 33, 35, 44, 59, 70
Spotlight on P. Buchanan 125; on Front National 137–38; on militias 57, 59; on E. Mullins 135; on R. Reagan 121; for right-left alliance 134; sales 26, 139; on Waffen SS 64
SS Action Group 24, 92
Stern, K. 59
Stoner, J.B. 13, 46, 48–49, 68, 69
Stormfront on abortion 94; and D. Black 45; and immigration 129; and Iraq 136; and religion 78; and terrorism 104; on women 93
Stormtrooper 140
Strom, E. 91
Strom, K. 34–35, 45, 62, 81, 91
Swift, W. 67–68, 70

Taking Aim 58
Tarrants, T. 38
terrorism and extreme right 99–114

Teutonia Association 10
Teutonic Knights 45
Thunderbolt on abortion 85, 86; on
anti-Semitism 48; on *Brown* 47; on
Christian Right 123–24; on eugenics
85; and E. Fields 49; on B.
Goldwater 118; on Holocaust 48; on
immigration 47; on John Birch
Society 116, 117; and Ku Klux Klan
48; and E. Mullins 135; on race 68,
87, 120; on G. L. Rockwell 48, 121;
on Waffen SS 48
Today's Aryan Woman 94
Tomassi, J. 23
Torch 87
Trochmann, J. 26, 58, 59
Truth at Last 49, 124, 125, 128, 137,
138
Truth Seeker 76, 130
Turner, L. 96–97
Turner Diaries 28, 30, 61, 87, 93, 101,
102, 103, 104, 106, 112

US Klans 43
US Klans, Knights of the Ku Klux
Klan 36
Union Party 10
United White Party 20, 21, 46
United Klans of America (UKA)
36–38; on abortion 85; cross-lighting
ceremonies 39; dissolved 40; and B.
Goldwater 118; and R. Miles 100;
and G. Wallace 119

Valkyrie Voice 94
Vanderboegh, M. 61
Vanguard News Network on Christian
Identity 141; on S. Francis 127; on
Iraq 113; and National Alliance 34;
on women 89, 93
Venable, J. 38, 48
Vinlanders Social Club 43
Virginia Citizen's Militia 61
Volksfront 97, 136–37

Walker, S. 34
Wallace, G. 118–20
WAR 78, 81, 86, 92
WAR Eagle 104, 136
Warner, J. 22, 23, 38, 68, 72
Weaver, R. 58, 59
Webster, N. 60
Weiland, T. 71, 111
Welch, R. 115–17

Weisman, C. 71–72
Weiss, F. C. 13, 21, 22
We the Mothers Mobilize for America
12
White American Political Association
44
White American Resistance 44
White Aryan Resistance (WAR) 30–31,
44; on abortion 86; and Aryan
Women's League 94–95; on P.
Buchanan 126; and lawsuit 34–35; on
leaderless resistance 105, 108; on
masculinity 91–92; on militias 61;
on 9/11 112; on race 140; and
women 92, 93; and Women's
Frontier 96
White, B. 74
White Camelia Knights 43, 44
White Circle League 14
White Order of Thule 74, 79, 133
White Party 22
White Patriot 40
White Patriot Party 44, 86, 109
White Power 22, 23, 27, 80, 92, 119
White Student Alliance 23, 39
White Knights of the Ku Klux Klan
36, 37, 38, 41
White Revolution 33–34 on leaderless
resistance 109–10; and National
Socialist Movement 35; and race 87;
on terrorism 104
White Sentinel 14
White Sisters 94, 95
Wickstrom, J. 53–54, 70
Wilkinson, B. 40, 120, 121
Williams Intelligence Survey 14, 15
Williams, R. 14, 16
Winrod, G. 9, 12, 15; and anti-Semitic
conspiracism 60; and Citizens
Councils 127; and W. D. Pelley 16
women and the extreme right 39,
83–98
Women for Aryan Unity 97
Women's Frontier 94–97
Women's Voice 12, 14, 15, 135
Worden, C. 61
World Church of the Creator 76; and
Middle East 123; and National
Alliance 76, 109; and Racial
Socialism 143; and terrorism 104;
and women 94–97
World Union of National Socialists 20,
84
Wotansvolk 73, 140